"WHY WE CAN'T WAIT"

"WHY WE CAN'T WAIT"

Racism and the Church

Catherine Punsalan-Manlimos
Tracy Sayuki Tiemeier
Elisabeth T. Vasko
Editors

**THE ANNUAL PUBLICATION
OF THE COLLEGE THEOLOGY SOCIETY
2022
VOLUME 68**

ORBIS BOOKS
Maryknoll, New York 10545

Founded in 1970, Orbis Books endeavors to publish works that enlighten the mind, nourish the spirit, and challenge the conscience. The publishing arm of the Maryknoll Fathers and Brothers, Orbis seeks to explore the global dimensions of the Christian faith and mission, to invite dialogue with diverse cultures and religious traditions, and to serve the cause of reconciliation and peace. The books published reflect the views of their authors and do not represent the official position of the Maryknoll Society. To learn more about Maryknoll and Orbis Books, please visit our website at www.orbisbooks.com

Library of Congress Cataloging-in-Publication Data

Names: Punsalan-Manlimos, Catherine M., editor. | Sayuki Tiemeier, Tracy, 1975- editor. | Vasko, Elisabeth T., editor.
Title: "Why we can't wait" : racism and the church / Catherine Punsalan-Manlimos, Tracy Sayuki Tiemeier, and Elisabeth T. Vasko, editors.
Description: Maryknoll, NY : Orbis Books, [2023] | Series: College theology society ; 68 | Includes bibliographical references.
Identifiers: LCCN 2022057378 (print) | LCCN 2022057379 (ebook) | ISBN 9781626985193 (trade paperback) | ISBN 9781608339815 (epub)
Subjects: LCSH: United States—Race relations. | Racism—Religious aspects—Christianity. | Race relations—Religious aspects—Christianity
Classification: LCC E185.61 .W65 2023 (print) | LCC E185.61 (ebook) | DDC 200.89—dc23/eng/20230110
LC record available at https://lccn.loc.gov/2022057378
LC ebook record available at https://lccn.loc.gov/2022057379

For Shawnee

Contents

Part II
Embodied Pedagogy and Spirituality

Part III
Racial Justice and the Church

Part IV
From "I Can't Breathe" to the Breath of Life:
Reimagining Our Theology and Practice

Call to Action

Introduction

Catherine Punsalan-Manlimos,
Tracy Sayuki Tiemeier, and Elisabeth T. Vasko

"Why We Can't Wait":[1]
Yesterday, Today, and Tomorrow

On January 16, 1963, eight White Christian and Jewish clergy penned "An Appeal for Law and Order and Common Sense." The open letter, printed in the *Birmingham News*, challenged White segregationists and affirmed seven principles, including "every human being is created in the image of God and thus due just respect."[2] Four months later, they changed their minds.[3]

In April 1963, the Southern Christian Leadership Conference (SCLC) and Rev. Dr. Martin Luther King Jr. joined Birmingham's local campaign, organized by Fred Shuttlesworth, to address segregation in the city. The SCLC chose Birmingham as opposed to

---

[1]This phrase directly refers to Martin Luther King Jr.'s *Why We Can't Wait* (Boston: Beacon, 1964).

[2]This was an open letter penned by a group of Christian and Jewish White clergy after the election of Governor George Wallace. The group articulated seven principles, which are outlined along with the process of discussion in S. Jonathan Bass, "Not Time Yet: Alabama's Episcopal Bishop and the End of Segregation in the Deep South," *Anglican and Episcopal History* 63, no. 2 (June 1994): 235–259. The open letter was originally published in the *Birmingham News* on January 17, 1963.

[3]The White clergy's support of desegregation in the South wavered over time. But in this particular case, the gubernatorial election of George Wallace prompted a response.

larger cities in the South like Atlanta, partly due to the reactionary nature of its leadership: Bull Connor. On April 3, 1963, civil rights leaders launched a campaign to shut down the city during the Easter holiday with marches, sit-ins, and protests. The residents of Birmingham responded by participating in full measure.[4] One week later, the local government was granted a state court injunction against the protests, making participation illegal. White clergy issued a second open letter, urging King and the SCLC to halt the demonstrations, calling them "unwise and untimely."[5]

Despite the injunction, on April 12, 1963, King and Rev. Ralph Abernathy decided to participate in the demonstrations and were arrested. On May 2, 1963, more than one thousand Black students attempted to march down the street. Hundreds were arrested. The next day, the city commissioner Bull Connor directed the police and fire departments to use force to stop the demonstrations. Images of children being beaten by police, blasted by high-pressure fire hoses, and bitten by police dogs were broadcast across the nation.[6] While in solitary confinement in the Birmingham jail, King addressed the nation:

> We know through painful experience that freedom is never voluntarily given by the oppressor; it must be demanded by the oppressed. Frankly, I have yet to engage in a direct action campaign that was "well timed" in the view of those who have not suffered unduly from the disease of segregation. For years now I have heard the word "Wait!" It rings in the ear of every Negro with piercing familiarity. This "Wait" has almost always meant "Never." We must come to see, with one of our distinguished jurists, that "justice too long delayed is justice denied."[7]

---

[4]Glenn T. Eskew, "Birmingham Campaign of 1963," *Encyclopedia of Alabama*, last updated October 9, 2017, http://encyclopediaofalabama. org; "Letter from Birmingham Jail," *King Encyclopedia*, The Martin Luther King, Jr. Research and Education Institute, https://kinginstitute.stanford.edu/.

[5]"White Clergymen Urge Local Negroes to Withdraw from Demonstrations," *Birmingham News*, April 13, 1963.

[6]Eskew, "Birmingham Campaign of 1963."

[7]Martin Luther King Jr., *Letter from Birmingham City Jail* (Philadelphia: American Friends Service Committee, May 1963).

Justice is not an abstract reality to be debated in academic circles. Justice is freedom from oppression actualized in human history. In the six decades since, King's words remain pertinent: too many are living in a world where "justice is denied."

We continue to live in a fractured and racially segregated America. Black and Brown children bear the brunt of criminalization in the United States today. Black girls are body slammed in the school cafeteria (Jasmine Darwin, 2017) and arrested for having temper tantrums in kindergarten (Kaia Roelle, 2019). Black and Brown people of all genders are killed by the police: Eric Garner (2014), Michael Brown Jr. (2014), Ahmaud Arbery (2020), Breonna Taylor (2020), Dominique Fells (2020), and George Floyd (2020). Migrants are detained in overcrowded and unsafe conditions at the US-Mexico border and separated from their families. Anti-Asian violence has risen in the wake of the COVID-19 pandemic. Anti-Jewish hate crimes continue to rise across the nation.

Racism persists in deeper, less obvious ways. Subtle acts of exclusion or avoidance, racial "jokes" and stereotyping, implicit racial bias, and racialized microaggressions are all acts of covert racism propping up racist structures and seeping into every facet of society, including religious life. As King stated, "The judgment of God is upon the church as never before."[8] Moreover, he expressed greater frustration over the "shallow understanding of people of good will" than the "absolute misunderstanding of people of ill will."[9]

While some may have seen our theme as passé, we find it fitting for the College Theology Society (CTS) in the present moment. The year 2022 was the first time the CTS devoted an entire convention to the theme of racial justice. Given the CTS's emphasis on education and its inception in an era of segregation in the United States, such attention is long overdue. The CTS was founded in 1954 by religious and lay women and men. Central to its mission is the training and formation of those who teach theology in Catholic institutions in the United States. While the society has focused on many social and political issues in its seventy-year history, it

---

[8]Martin Luther King Jr., *Why We Can't Wait,* Legacy ed. (Boston: Beacon, Kindle ed.), 105.

[9]Ibid., 96.

has yet to give sustained, systematic attention to the problem of racism in the United States. In 1954, the very same year of the CTS's founding, the US Supreme Court ruled in *Brown v. Board of Education* that "separate but equal" based on race in public schools was unconstitutional. The Court's 1954 decision ignited waves of White resistance across the country for decades that could not be ignored. Moreover, Catholic education benefited economically from *Brown v. Board*, with all-time high enrollments in the 1960s.[10] The reality is that any historically White institution (HWI) born in the 1950s that did not center (and has not centered) racial justice is part of the problem.

White liberal Christians continue to change their minds about the rules of belonging and engagement. Scholars of color have developed significant work that sheds greater light on the sin of racism and draws theological richness from experiences of communities of color. Yet their contributions have remained peripheral in the academy, church, and world. Theologians and scholars of religion must take on the process of self-examination and articulation of complicity in the sin of racism, as well as work in all areas of thought and practice to develop a faith defined by racial justice.

We are grateful for the CTS's willingness to host this conference and annual volume. In particular, the CTS board allowed us to play a prominent role in shaping the liturgy and the convention during the COVID pandemic. Yet there is much more work to be done. As an HWI, the CTS must begin where it is. At the conference, the CTS started to take a few steps forward with an amendment to the constitution to include an emphasis on diversity and the creation of three Diversity, Equity, and Inclusion (DEI) board positions. Yet there is still so much more that needs to be done. This work, if taken up by all in the community—not just a select few—will genuinely transform the way theology is done.

What Next?
For Those Not Ready for Healing

The convention was held during Pentecost weekend. As a part of our preparation, we invited Antonio Eduardo Alonso and Kim

---

[10]See Shannen Dee Williams, *Subversive Habits: Black Catholic Nuns in the Long African American Freedom Struggle* (Durham, NC: Duke University Press, 2022), 137–140.

R. Harris to develop an online Pentecost Vigil Evening Prayer. In the planning, we spoke together about our hope that the convention theme and annual volume not be used to "check off a diversity box" or be an occasional topic for discussion without deep discernment and change.

The liturgy was a true highlight of the convention, bringing together the Spirit's fire for truth and honoring the need for lamentation and repentance. We have included Kim Harris's powerful homily in this volume, which calls us to do the work of racial justice. Yet we also believe it important to note Antonio Alonso's use of Yolanda Pierce's "Litany for Those Not Ready for Healing." It reads in part:

> Let us not rush to the language of healing, before understanding the fullness of the injury and the depth of the wound.
>
> Let us not rush to offer a band-aid, when the gaping wound requires surgery and complete reconstruction.
>
> Let us not offer false equivalencies, thereby diminishing the particular pain being felt in a particular circumstance in a particular historical moment.
>
> Let us not speak of reconciliation without speaking of reparations and restoration, or how we can repair the breach and how we can restore the loss . . .
>
> Let us not be afraid to sit with the ugliness, the messiness, and the pain that is life in community together . . .
>
> Instead . . .
>
> Let us lament the loss of a teenager, dead at the hands of a police officer who described him as a demon.
>
> Let us weep at a criminal justice system, which is neither blind nor just . . .
>
> Let us . . . sit in the ashes of this nation's original sin.
>
> Let us be silent when we don't know what to say . . .

Let us listen to the shattering glass and let us smell the pu-
rifying fires, for it is the language of the unheard.

God, in your mercy . . .
Show [us our] own complicity in injustice.
Convict [us] for [our] indifference.
Forgive [us] when [we] have remained silent.
Equip [us] with a zeal for righteousness.
Never let [us] grow accustomed or acclimated to unrigh-
teousness.[11]

As we think of what is next, we call on the College Theology
Society and all who read this volume to continue to lament and
to repent—to sit with the "ugliness, the messiness, and the pain
that is life in community together." The wounds of the sin of
racism are deep, and the healing cannot be forced as wounds are
still being inflicted.

Map of the Volume

The volume represents numerous areas of research in varying
stages of development. We have been mindful of including this
variety to highlight the wholesale need to rethink our theologies,
pedagogies, and practices in light of racism. Racial justice work
requires continuous questioning, self-reflection, and discernment.
Whereas some of our authors specialize in race, theology, and
religious studies, others are taking up the challenge to examine
and reexamine their fields.

One of the many challenges in discussing race today is what
linguistic conventions to utilize. Language is power, and the
terms that we use matter. It is now common practice to capitalize the "b" in "black" when used as a racial designation to
signify "personhood, culture, and history."[12] A trickier question
is whether to capitalize the "w" in "white" when discussing race.

---

[11]Yolanda Pierce, "A Litany for Those Not Ready for Healing," Prayers
for Racial Justice and Reconciliation, xavier.org.

[12]Kristen Mack and John Palfrey, "Capitalizing Black and White: Grammatical Justice and Equity," MacArthur Foundation, August 26, 2020,
macfound.org.

Whereas a number of scholars and organizations have chosen not to capitalize "white"—either because there isn't seen to be a shared cultural history or because the organizations do not want to reinforce supremacists who capitalize "white" to assert their power—others capitalize "white" to highlight that there indeed is a shared construction of "whiteness" that needs to be made visible.[13] Another common practice is to italicize non-English words. However, scholars, writers, and activists, such as Khairani Barokka, have questioned this convention. Barokka argues that italicization reinforces cultural (English) hegemony.[14] We have asked authors, therefore, to be deliberate about their linguistic choices. Many authors offer explanations for their choices in the notes, especially those not following Orbis Books house style. We capitalize both Black and White, as Whiteness is neither neutral nor normative; it is culturally specific. We also have chosen not to italicize non-English words.

The volume is organized with an Introduction and Epilogue (authored by the editors), an Invocation and Call to Action (written by our 2022 annual convention homilist and award recipient representative), and four parts (authored by our volume contributors, including plenary speakers and some presenters from the 2022 annual convention). The Invocation, by Kim R. Harris, connects our current time with the Pentecost. Harris reminds us that the Spirit is already in our midst, and we cannot hide. We must "proclaim, lament, and rejoice in the Spirit." In her Call to Action, Joan F. Neal offers an inspiring message to CTS members, theologians, and religious scholars. For Neal, scholarship and teaching provide a foundation, a language, for justice. Our work is an essential vocation and resource for building a just society.

Part I of the volume focuses on colonialism and the (de)construction of Whiteness. Three plenary panelists—SimonMary A. Aihiokhai, Karen B. Enriquez, and Karen Teel—underscore the ongoing imaginary of European colonialism as entangled religious, racial, and cultural projects. Aihiokhai deconstructs the production of Whiteness in the European colonial project and offers a

---

[13]See, for example, ibid. See also David Bauder, "AP Says It Will Capitalize Black but Not White," Associated Press, July 20, 2020, apnews.com.

[14]Khairani Barokka, "The Case against Italicizing 'Foreign' Words," Dialek::Dialect, *Catapult*, February 11, 2020, catapult.co.

decolonial vision of radical encounter and Eucharistic humanity. Enriquez examines how the academy is colonized, how this colonization shapes her imagination and the need for conversion to truly see and love. Teel develops a Whiteness inventory, drawing on her own self-examination in order to draw out how Whiteness thinks. Christina Astorga examines the ways Iberian Catholicism imposed Western patriarchal binaries in Philippine colonization; yet even with the diminishment of the status of women during and after colonization, Babaylans (shamans) resisted. Victoria Basug Slabinski also focuses on the Philippines, arguing for an archipelagic approach that resists colonial and nationalistic interpretations of the quincentennial celebration of the introduction of Christianity to the Philippines.

Part II examines embodied pedagogy and spirituality, positioning ourselves as intellects and embodied persons with emotions, spirits, psyches, and more. Emilie M. Townes offers an excerpt from her plenary presentation, calling for a new model of theological education that resituates educators as learners grounded in fully embodied joy. Charles A. Gillespie, Emily Bryan, and Rachel E. Bauer develop an embodied pedagogy and antiracist spirituality based on the theater practice of table work, a practice of conversation, bodily encounter, and unfinished process. La Ronda D. Barnes proposes the affirmative mysticism of Howard Thurman as a practice for cultivating empathy and bridging racial divides. Finally, George Faithful wrestles with problematic passages in Juan de la Cruz, pushing notions of spiritual perfection and sainthood.

Part III considers racial justice and the church, offering assessments of Christian efforts for racial justice and suggestions for more effective ecclesial work. Cecilia A. Moore's plenary focuses on Black Catholic efforts in the last hundred years. Even as they experienced racism in the Church, Black Catholics fought for liberation, made space for themselves, and found creative and spiritual nourishment. Daniel Cosacchi challenges the current resistance to antiracist (and other) movements like Black Lives Matter among many US bishops by offering the example of Bishop Gumbleton. John N. Sheveland looks at how Whiteness prevents many Catholics from embracing Islam and the Muslim-Christian dialogue integrated into Pope Francis's magisterial teaching. Vincent Lui reads Acts through the lens of the racial geography of Baltimore, the racist legacy of Christian colonialism, and integral liberation.

"I can't breathe." The last words of Eric Garner (a Black man killed by police in 2014) and so many others.[15] Part IV reimagines theology and practice, lamenting the cries of "I can't breathe" and seeking pathways for the Breath of Life to flow. In her plenary, Shawnee Daniels-Sykes examines the ways adverse childhood experiences (ACEs) are behind the fear driving implicit racial bias in law enforcement and domestic terrorists. She proposes fear of the Lord to inspire the Church to protest in the streets, stop partisan politics, and address the greater public health crises within racism. Melissa Pagán's plenary applies a decolonial feminist analysis of el grito and vincularidad to construct a new way of relating, a decolonial intimacy beyond solidarity. Héctor M. Varela Rios argues for Latinx as theological microintervention, a linguistic mestizaje/mulatez. John Sniegocki explores Black veganism as a resource for deepening notions of integral liberation and integral ecology in Catholic social teaching. Maureen H. O'Connell draws on the urban alchemy of Mindy Thompson Fullilove to reimagine and transform Catholic campuses and their communities, spaces that have been fractured by racism.

Acknowledgments

We are grateful for the many people who helped make the 2022 College Theology Society annual convention and volume successful. First, we thank the authors of this volume, particularly the plenary convention speakers whose chapters anchor each section (SimonMary A. Aihiokhai, Karen B. Enriquez, Karen Teel, Emilie M. Townes, Cecilia A. Moore, Shawnee Daniels-Sykes, and Melissa Pagán). We also thank everyone who submitted essays for the annual volume. We could not include many due to our space

---

[15]Mike Baker, Jennifer Valentino-DeVries, Manny Fernandez, and Michael LaForgia, "Three Words. 70 Cases. The Tragic History of 'I Can't Breathe,'" *New York Times*, June 29, 2020, nytimes.com. More than half of the persons identified by the *New York Times* who died in custody after saying "I can't breathe" were Black.

limitations, and we hope they will find their way to publication to continue the many rich conversations begun at the annual convention. We are grateful to the many peer reviewers of the essay submissions. This volume could not have been completed without their close reading, careful review, and constructive feedback. We also would like to thank every participant at the meeting, especially the conveners and presenters, for planning such engaging sessions. We owe a special note of gratitude to Brian Flanagan (CTS president), Daniel Rober (executive director of national conventions), Dana Dillon (executive coordinator of digital media), and Katherine Schmidt. Their work to ensure a successful online convention was extraordinary. Reid Locklin has been a supportive advocate as CTS director of research and publications. Thomas Hermans-Webster has been a patient and helpful guide at Orbis Books.

We want to extend a special note of appreciation to our Action Collaborative co-conspirators (you know who you are). These dear colleagues were the support that helped us propose and develop the theme for our convention and volume. What started as a conversation over drinks led to a year (and then some) of processing and planning, venting and strategizing, deconstructing and reconstructing. We are especially thankful for the gift of your friendship.

Finally, we owe a great debt to Kayla Ray, our graduate assistant funded through Loyola Marymount University's Rains Research Assistant program. We could not have finished this volume without Kayla's organizational and editorial talents. To her, we are most grateful.

INVOCATION

"Why We Can't Wait"

Racism and the Church

Kim R. Harris

"I'm Gonna Do What the Spirit Says"

I'm gonna do what the Spirit says do
I'm gonna do what the Spirit says do
And what the Spirit says do,
   I'm gonna do Lord, Lord
I'm gonna do what the Spirit says do
I'm gonna pray when the Spirit says pray
I'm gonna pray when the Spirit says pray
And when the Spirit says pray,
   I'm gonna pray Lord, Lord
I'm gonna pray when the Spirit says pray
I'm gonna sing when the Spirit says sing
I'm gonna sing when the Spirit says sing
And when the Spirit says sing,
   I'm gonna sing Lord, Lord
I'm gonna sing when the Spirit says sing
I'm gonna march when the Spirit says march
I'm gonna march when the Spirit says march
And when the Spirit says march,
   I'm gonna march Lord, Lord

1

I'm gonna march when the Spirit says march
Traditional Negro Spiritual (adapted)[1]

I wonder, as we retell the Pentecost story from the Acts of the
Apostles (Acts 2:1–11), if the early friends and followers of Jesus
were having similar discussions in that upper room to the ones
we are having; why we can't wait. . . . We don't have a video or
DVD. We can't livestream their pre-Pentecost experience, but we
know how they eventually told the story and can imagine some
possibilities and conversations.

"Why can't we wait?"

"Why should we wait? This would be a great time!"

"We're counting the Omer (Leviticus 23:15–16; Deuter-
onomy 16:9-12)."

"It's almost Shavuot."[2]

"Yes! This is a holy time. Yes! We're scared, and we don't
want to be the next ones crucified. But some amazing things
have been happening."

"Yes! We saw Him, alive! He told us not to leave Jerusalem.
But He also told us to wait (Acts 1:4)!"

"But maybe we can't wait. Maybe we shouldn't wait. What
great timing this would be. Think of it. We're closing in on
Shavuot! So many people are coming to town on pilgrimage, for the festival. So many others are already here. You
know it's always one of the biggest crowds of the year in
the city. Yes, we're scared and can barely sleep. But on these
nights, we'd be awake anyway, keeping vigil, studying To-
rah, and waiting for the feast. I know we're not supposed

---

[1]"I'm Gonna Do What the Spirit Says," in *Rise Up Singing: The Group
Singing Songbook*, 15th ann. ed., ed. Peter Blood and Annie Patterson (Beth-
lehem: Sing Out!, 2005), 210, www.riseupandsing.org.
[2]"Shavuot 101," My Jewish Learning, www.myjewishlearning.com.

to celebrate as we wait. But I'm feeling so many things: scared, amazed, confused. We saw Him, crucified, then alive and then lifted right up into the air (Acts 1:9). I have a feeling that *something* incredible is going to happen. He said something about a spirit, and we'll be the witnesses. Well, we're already witnesses. That's why we can't wait! It is good to be here together. It's a relief, really, and almost sweet. But now we must get ready, we have to get going, we can't wait!"

I grew up hearing this story about Pentecost in church and thinking that it was only about God's timing! That it was all about the Holy Spirit deciding when to descend. But perhaps the followers of Jesus had something to do with the timing as well. And perhaps we also have something to do with the Spirit's timing. This is why we, in our moment, can't wait. The Pentecost story has something to tell us about timing, and spirit and gathering and breathing together, right here, right now, in our own day, and in our own time! We could tell a similar story as they did about Pentecost, as we reflect on racism in the Church, and why we can't wait.

Jesus' friends were fearful, living in an occupied land, where civil authorities might arrest and kill them at any time with impunity. We are certainly living in fear. In this nation, it's not only fear of civil authority, but also fear of each other. People come into grocery stores hunting for African Americans. People shoot Latinx children and teachers in the schools and attack Asian Americans and Pacific Islanders on the streets. Indigenous communities remember and face the aftermath of growing up in American Indian Residential Schools and the present reality of widespread poverty and the lack of necessary resources.

We are in fear, even as people of faith—not only fear of those outside of our communities, but also fear of leaders and members within our faith communities. They don't have our backs as we endure racist attacks. They often work against us, against our cultures, our liturgies, our scholarship, and our very existence. We can't breathe. We can't wait!

Why can't we wait? I am sure that you have heard several answers to that question, in presentations, papers, and prayers. We can't wait because we are asking and answering hard questions that need to be addressed prophetically and immediately.

We can't wait because our church membership is declining. And in my community, Black Catholic churches are closing or being closed due to institutional neglect and racist policies. We can't wait because young people, the same ones whom we are called to teach, are asking us difficult questions and telling us why they can't breathe and won't wait. We can't wait because we must train, accompany, and be challenged and led by the next generations of students, scholars, and faith leaders. We can't wait because our children, partners, colleagues, and elders are dying. We can't wait because our liturgies are unconnected in words, music, and actions to justice, whereas many were connected to justice in the past. We can't wait because the newest protests are not coming out of or being supported by our faith communities, as they were in the historic and recent past. We can't wait because peoples of many tribes, languages, heritages, orientations, and abilities are gathering in movements for freedom inside and mostly outside of our faith communities. And the Spirit is coming for us. She's coming for us, hiding in our offices, upstairs meeting rooms, and sanctuaries. He's coming for us to send us out to them, to speak to all, each in their own language. We can't wait, we won't wait. We have to do what the Spirit says do! We have to sing, dance, pray, and march! We have to research, study, learn, write, speak, and shout! We have to follow the lead of the mother of Jesus, as she spoke words of revolution reflecting her tradition (Luke 1:46–55; 1 Samuel 2:1–10).[3] We can't wait because we must proclaim, lament, and rejoice in the Spirit and commit ourselves to action. The time is now. The Spirit is here. We can't, we must not, and we won't wait!

---

[3] M. Roger Holland II, "Magnificat" (Chicago: GIA, 2022), giamusic.com.

PART I

COLONIALISM

AND THE (DE)CONSTRUCTION

OF WHITENESS

Deconstructing the Myth of Whiteness

A Decolonial Turn to a Eucharistic Humanity

SimonMary A. Aihiokhai

In the face of systemic and structural racism, is there any more legitimacy in our work as theologians? After centuries of enduring traumas caused by systemic racism, how much of a role has the Catholic Church in America and beyond played in undoing such systems that perpetuate the erasure of communities of color and their legacies in our collective psyches? These are questions that we can no longer ignore if we hope to be relevant in the world that is unfolding before us in the twenty-first century. The ignorance that defines the white psyche in matters related to the existential suffering of communities of color in our religious and secular institutions calls for collective lamentation. In 2020, as the United States rose up to condemn systemic violence perpetrated against communities of color, some of our religious leaders were more interested in defending doctrinal orthodoxy by resisting the Black Lives Matter movement.[1] In this work, I problematize the humanity that whiteness produces in order to articulate a corrective anthropology of surplus—Eucharistic humanity.

---

[1] See Megan Carroll, "Spokane Catholic Bishop Says Black Lives Matter Movement Is 'In Conflict with Church Teaching,'" *KREM2*, July 8, 2022, https://www.krem.com.

Whiteness as an Anthropology Rooted
in Scarcity

The birth of whiteness as a socio-anthropological positionality in the world goes back to the debates in the City of Valladolid, Spain (1550–1552), when Juan Ginés Sepúlveda and Bartolomé de Las Casas debated over the humanity of the Indigenous people of what is today called the Americas. It is often the case that scholars would want to take the side of Las Casas on this debate. After all, he took the side of the Indigenous people and argued for their humanity. It is important to problematize that preference if we are to free our imaginations from the urge to erase otherness that whiteness evokes in all of us. Las Casas argues that the natives cannot be called "barbarians" because of their "gentleness and decency," qualities that are expressed in them "more than the other nations of the entire world."[2] However, reading closely his argument on who and what constitutes a barbarian, one immediately notices that his point of reference is based on his understanding of European societies. In other words, non-European cultures and societies are considered civilized or barbaric insofar as such cultures and societies can be judged by social categories that define European cultural and social systems.[3] It is important that one poses the following question to Las Casas: Whose sociopolitical system is the yardstick for deciding who falls within such a category of people?

The othering of the natives holds supreme in the consciousness of the Europeans in the so-called New World. Even a benevolent approach to relating with the natives falls apart because, in the eyes of the Europeans, the natives will always be the other—an identity that cannot rise to the level of that of the Europeans. Whenever the parameters of civilized society are conditioned by the European experience, all that is non-European (white) will always be suspect. This point is buttressed by the apt analysis of Albert Memmi in his reading of the labels ascribed to the colonized by the colonizer. Memmi argues: "Nothing could better justify the colonizer's privi-

---

[2]Bartolomé de Las Casas, *In Defense of the Indians*, trans. Stafford Poole (DeKalb: Northern Illinois University Press, 1992), 28.

[3]Ibid., 32.

leged position than his industry, and nothing could better justify the colonized's destitution than his indolence. The mythical portrait of the colonized therefore includes an unbelievable laziness, and that of the colonizer, a virtuous taste for action."[4] When we look at contemporary society, we see the enduring dominance of whiteness in full display at the expense of the flourishing of all persons. It prompts me to ask the question: Can whiteness create a world of radical hospitality that allows for all to flourish?

Whiteness is an ideology inherently conditioned to subjugate and never to liberate. Interestingly, this ideology holds captive even white bodies. Its power to hold everyone captive is the very source of its legitimization in the world it creates. In other words, whiteness is a double-edged tool of subjugation. Both white and non-white bodies are held captive by it because it validates only one way of being human. Such a monolithic identity is rooted in deception.

Whiteness, as the hermeneutic expression of racism in the new social landscape that has defined the global context, while refusing to acknowledge the uniqueness of locality, must be evaluated within the broader framework of transnational racial consciousness. In doing this evaluation, one immediately sees an intricate intersectionality between the hierarchy of sense of self and trans-locality that is upheld by such systems as capitalism. What does this mean? The social landscape redefined by the forceful entrance of Western Europeans into other localities around the world brought about a sense of group identity not defined by previous notions of social identities such as place, language, or religion. This time around, group identity was defined by the myth of racial superiority that is primarily defined by skin color. This myth has been used to appropriate the religious meanings inherent in the symbols of Christianity. The holy is depicted as white. If the holy is white, then all who embody whiteness are themselves holy and elevated to take possession of the world. After all, did Yahweh not command true humanity to be the Lord of creation (Genesis 1:28–29)?[5] If whiteness embodies authentic humanity

---

[4]Albert Memmi, *The Colonizer and the Colonized*, expanded ed. (Boston: Beacon Press, 1967), 79.

[5]All biblical citations in Part I of this book are taken from *The New American Bible* (Wichita, KS: Catholic Bible Publishers, 1970).

that is blessed with the mandate of planetary dominion, then place must be constructed to mean that which whiteness sets its gaze on. On that note, the acquisition of other parts of the world by those who see themselves as white is in and of itself inherently valid. When the European imperialist comes to the Americas and recites the deeds of acquisition of the lands and peoples, they are doing what they believe to be blessed by the Christian God. Thus, it is the right of the European Christian to evangelize the "pagans" and "barbarians" found in those parts of the world. This is the underlying argument defining the papal interventions to resolve the tensions between Spain and Portugal over the "New World" and their claims to them.

The Church stands guilty in allowing itself to be part of the territorial ambitions of the European powers. Even when the claim is made that evangelization was the main interest of the Church, the same vessels carrying the imperialistic agents of Europe also brought Christian missionaries to the "New World." The Church cannot turn around to say it was innocent. Also, the Church's response to the evils of colonialism and imperialism cannot wash off the guilt it has brought upon itself in validating whiteness as a transnational imperialistic identity marker that favors Western Europeans and their descendants. The guilt goes beyond material resources. Intellectual institutions, the so-called Roman Curia and its members, prominent ecclesial positions and episcopal hierarchies in the Church in the United States are still the monopoly of the white clergy. It ought to be stated clearly that African Americans are not new to the faith. Many enslaved Africans were taken from ancient Christian communities in Mali, Sudan, and East Africa, and the Christian Kingdoms and Empires of Kongo, Benin, Warri, and Axum and brought to the "New World."

Looking closely at our own intellectual community, one has to confess that the College Theology Society lacks racial diversity. Even after all the work that continues to be done to create a more diverse society, we are still held captive by the imagination of whiteness as it plays out in our world. Why is this the case? Whiteness, as a way of being in the world, produces a form of scarce imagination that can be referred to as the coloniality of imagination. Coloniality of imagination operates with the assumption that non-whites are incapable of possessing epistemic freedom because they are creatures without a history, without a civilization, without the correct cognitive abilities to ask questions that lead to liberation. After all, they are simply creatures made from the fantasy of whiteness. What is so powerful about the structural system of the coloniality of imagination is that it does not need white bodies to constantly replicate it. Once one is assimilated into the matrix of whiteness, it replicates itself in a cyclic manner. As it validates and perpetuates the intentionality of whiteness, its victims are drawn deeper into the center of the system where they are systematically stripped of their cognitive abilities to free themselves. Can one ever escape from such a matrix of manipulation? I opine that it is possible through an embrace of a Eucharistic humanity.

A Radical Turn
to a Eucharistic Humanity

For Christians, the starting and ending place for any discourse on what it means to be human must necessarily be the Eucharist. The Eucharist is a ritual of awareness of the power of evil done by the powerful to the innocent. The Eucharist is the place where the community of the followers of Christ sits with and allows itself to be an active victim with the suffering innocents of our world. It is a ritualized place where our solidarity with others becomes the source for experiencing the fullness of our humanity as a gift that can be attained only when we choose to become one with the victims of systems of erasure.

Furthermore, if authentic humanity is to be realized, a Eucharistic humanity must necessarily reorient us to a hermeneutic framework that is centered on what M. Shawn Copeland calls "difference and interdependence rather than exclusion." Our humanity must also be grounded in "solidarity with the exploited, despised, [and] poor 'other.' "[6] This radical reorientation entails not just how we conceive and perceive our humanity; it invites us to embrace new ways of understanding how God operates in God's world.

A Eucharistic humanity involves an embrace of radical encounters with otherness that helps one to become an embodi-

---

[6]M. Shawn Copeland, *Enfleshing Freedom: Body, Race, and Being* (Minneapolis: Fortress Press, 2010), 89.

ment of *koinonia* (fellowship). *Koinonia* goes beyond the simple understanding of community; rather, it entails an embrace of a new way of being that allows one to be ethically responsible for others. To become an embodiment of *koinonia* is to take seriously one's ethical duties of being a source of flourishing for all that one encounters. Thus, one can argue that authentic *koinonia* involves an embrace of *kenotic* existence—dying to oneself so that one can be present for others. There can be no passivity in how we understand, tell, and live out our lives in this *kairos* and the *kenotic* moments of salvific encounters with God in and through others in God's world.

If human personhood is defined by solidarity in difference, and oneness with the *hypostatic* reality of the Second Person of the Trinity that is radically on full display within the Eucharistic ritual, then the pain and suffering of the marginalized ones of our world stand as a witness to how God conceives of our humanity when God chooses to be one with us in a world defined by evil—a vulnerable God-in-solidarity-with-otherness. In other words, *hypostatic* union that exists in the relationship of the Second Person of the Trinity with all of creation points to and is validated by divine solidarity with creation. All of us who are made in God's image and likeness and who embody the *hypostatic* identity in the likeness of the new humanity in Christ are ethically bound to embrace radical solidarity with others. Thus, this gifted identity in Christ is always an invitation to become responsible for the well-being of others. In the words of Emmanuel Levinas,

> [T]he epiphany of the absolutely other is the face where the Other hails me and signifies to me, by its nakedness, by its destitution, an order. Its presence is this summons to respond. The Ego does not only become conscious of this necessity to respond as if it were a demand or a particular duty it must decide on. The Ego is through and through, in its very position, responsibility.[7]

In other words, to speak of a Eucharistic humanity is to take seriously the gift of identity which the other brings to us through

---

[7]Emmanuel Levinas, *Humanism of the Other*, trans. Nidra Poller (Urbana: University of Illinois Press, 2006), 33.

our encounters with them as an iconic *epiphany*, an epiphany that keeps revealing insights of who and what we are becoming in the context of our relational encounters with otherness.

In conclusion, identity is never insularly constructed. It comes to us always through the medium of encounters. The legitimate question we are supposed to ask always is not, "Who am I?" Rather, it ought to be, "Who am I through the eyes of the other that I am encountering?" Such an approach demands of us to take seriously and to see all our encounters as graced moments of revelation. Revelation is understood here as a call to act in an ethical manner that allows for others to experience God's life in abundance. While a Eucharistic humanity points to an abundance of imagination that orients one to always see others as sources of abundant grace and surplus of meanings, whiteness invokes limited stories of scarcity, competition, manipulation, and exploitation of otherness whenever difference is encountered.[8]

---

[8]See Charles W. Mills, "White Ignorance," in *Race and Epistemologies of Ignorance*, ed. Shannon Sullivan and Nancy Tuana (Albany: State University of New York Press, 2007), 11–38.

Whiteness, White Christian Privilege, and Decolonizing the Academy

Karen B. Enriquez

As we are discussing decolonizing the academy, I would like to first acknowledge how many of our institutions were built on colonized lands. In the case of Loyola Marymount University, in Los Angeles, it is the Gabrielino-Tongva peoples who were the traditional land caretakers, dispossessed by colonial settlers and the Catholic Church. Beyond acknowledgment, I hope we can also reflect on what real justice and solidarity look like in the face of the recognition of this reality.

I approach racism and the Church from my own experiences as a Filipina, feminist, comparative theologian, and an immigrant to the US. And from my perspective, it is impossible to decolonize the academy, unless we as persons and educators start with a decolonization of our own selves first—not our syllabi, not our pedagogy. This includes addressing the spaces of our own privilege and the presumed centers of our theological imaginations. I say this as someone who is still continually waking up to how deeply entrenched the colonial imagination has been embedded within me and realizing its role in the academy in the process.

In his acclaimed essay "The Mis-education of the Filipino," historian Renato Constantino argued that "[t]he most effective means to subjugate people is to capture their minds," and that "education, therefore, serves as a weapon in wars of colonial conquest."[1] Not surprisingly, education became part of the Ameri-

---

[1] Renato Constantino, "The Mis-education of the Filipino (1959),"

can military strategy in the Philippines, with Lieutenant General Arthur MacArthur Jr. declaring that "the matter of public education is so closely allied to the exercise of military force in these islands, but in my annual report, I treated the matter as a military subject and suggested a rapid expansion of educational facilities as an exclusively military measure."[2] As part of that program, English became the language of instruction[3] in the Philippines, and a canon of exclusively Anglo-American literature became part of the curriculum that was used to promote myths about colonial reality. This made natural and legitimate the illusion that colonialism existed for the sake of the colonized and not the colonizers.[4] I am a product of this inherited colonial education, and I acknowledge the privilege and access it has given me. This is part of why I'm able to be here today. It allowed me to assimilate and approximate whiteness to a certain degree. I learned to speak, read, and write in English. I became familiar with Christianity, the canon of European and white American theologians, and American culture more broadly.

Over time, I started teaching and writing out of this frame, taking as a given that courses in theology would entail primarily white authors (but maybe with a sprinkling of some Latin American liberation theologians for good measure). I would shape discussions of Catholicism from the perspective of Europe, or European immigrants to the US, bypassing discussions of how Christianity was part of the colonial enterprise, and how such frames continue to silence and marginalize the presence and voices

---

Journal of Contemporary Asia 1, no. 1 (1970): 21, https://doi.org/ 10.1080/00472337085390031.

[2]MacArthur Jr. quoted in Isabel Pefianco Martin, "American Education and Philippine Literature," *Philippine Studies* 49, no. 1 (2001): 113. To understand how colonialism has shaped schooling and education in the US, see Eve Tuck and K. Wayne Yang, "Decolonization Is Not a Metaphor," *Decolonization: Indigeneity, Education and Society* 1, no. 1 (2012): 1–40.

[3]Since then, the policy has been criticized, upheld, denounced, sustained, eventually modified, and is still being debated at all levels of educational policy-making. See Allan B. I. Bernardo, "English in Philippine Education: Solution or Problem?," in *Philippine English: Linguistic and Literary Perspectives*, ed. M. A. Lourdes, S. Bautista, and Kingsley Bolton (Hong Kong: Hong Kong University Press, 2008).

[4]Pefianco Martin, "American Education and Philippine Literature," 248.

of othered Catholics, othered Christians, and non-Christians—
therefore unwittingly still following the colonial agenda that
centered dominant European and white American Christians.[5]

And yet in these same institutions with great mentors, I started
to find and appreciate my own voice and contexts as a Filipina
theologian doing theology between the Philippines and the United
States. I found the company of others who were in that same process. While finding inspiration and encouragement together, we
also suffered through an academy that still questioned whether
our work was scholarly enough, and whether it was universal
rather than niche.[6] I have sat on panels exclusively on Philippine
and Philippine American theology that were poorly attended,
where the few people in the audience were mostly other Filipino
Americans or other scholars of color. And so while we were in the
academy, we did not really fully belong. Many academic spaces felt
and still do feel both welcoming but also alienating at the same
time, and it is exhausting to try to constantly navigate such spaces.

And so I argue for the need for a radical and continuing conversion, both personal and structural, within the academy. This
begins with the need to awaken to the reality of the insidiousness
of the legacy of colonialism and white supremacy in this country,
and how it has shaped our personal and social imagination, limiting our ability to fully see each other and to respond with love.[7]

Bryan Stevenson, lawyer and author of *Just Mercy*, in a recent

---

[5]Here, I think about the works of Tim Matovina and Natalia Imperatori-
Lee, among many Latinx theologians, the contributions of Black Catholics
and Filipinx migrants and Fil-Americans to the life of the Church. Yet so
much of their work and so many of their contributions have still remained
invisible and unacknowledged in the academy and the Church.

[6]On the issue of what counts as "scholarly," see, for example, the arguments from Asian/Asian American theologians such as C. S. Song on the
importance of story or narrative theologies, and of feminist and Latinx
theologians about going beyond religious "texts" in the study of religion, and
looking at practices, such as the emphasis on popular religiosity.

[7]Nancy Pineda-Madrid has described the social imaginary worldview as
one that "tends to much more implicit than explicit, operative at the subcon-
scious level rather than on the plane of awareness. It concerns our precogni-
tive, prethematic grasp of the world and the ways this grasp orients how we
perceive the world around us and our place in it." *Suffering and Salvation in
Ciudad Juarez* (Minneapolis: Augsburg Fortress, 2011), 40.

incisive interview with Jon Stewart, explains that our history of slavery, segregation, and racism has so shaped us that to

> live in this country, you live in a space where the air has been polluted by, contaminated by, these narratives that have been shaped over centuries. And . . . no matter where you go, you're in a space where there are these narratives [of racial difference and hierarchy] that undermine our ability to look at each other in a healthy and whole way.[8]

In other words, the dominant narrative of white supremacy has placed our minds and hearts in bondage, to limiting views of self and other that lead to our social conditioning to not see certain others. Jon Sobrino has described them as the "non-person" because they have no practical consequence to anyone. James Cone talks about those whose existence is threatened by the power of non-being.

Hence the need for the intentional practice of paying attention to those whose voices have been made invisible from our consciousness and our history. To see this full truth of humanity, especially those erased from our history, which in itself is a kind of death, comes close to Jon Sobrino's invitation that spirituality must begin with a profound honesty about the real.[9] This includes, he says, the acknowledgment of our own, active, sinful tendency to "not want to know—we don't want to see, because at least subconsciously, we know we benefit from the system. We have had something to do with bringing about such a crucified world."[10]

This personal conversion cannot simply be a kind of cognitive or intellectual exercise, but instead requires contemplative practice in order to truly understand the bondage of our imagination to the narrative of white supremacy. And thus the need to unlearn what we thought we knew in order to recognize things as they

---

[8] Bryan Stevenson, interview with Jon Stewart, "America Needs to Admit How Racist It Is," *The Problem with Jon Stewart*, YouTube, February 21, 2022, 7:50–8:14, www.youtube.com.

[9] Jon Sobrino, *Spirituality of Liberation: Toward Political Holiness,* trans. Robert R. Barr (Maryknoll, NY: Orbis Books, 1988), 26–29.

[10] Jon Sobrino, *The Principle of Mercy: Taking the Crucified People from the Cross,* ed. Robert R. Barr (Maryknoll, NY: Orbis Books, 1994), 5, 26–29.

are, and to act in accordance with that. In dialogue with liberation theologies, we then have to reflect on the ways of our academy, our ways of teaching and scholarship, and the very model and structure of our academic institutions, conferences, and publications: What are the ways that we are complicit in this kind of social conditioning that upholds white supremacy and thus the disability of others?

Sobrino, discussing his own conversion, reflects on how it was absurd to go about trying to *Rahnerize* or *Moltmannize* the people of El Salvador. Rather, he says, the task was the reverse; if it all possible, he argued, we needed to *Salvadorize* Rahner and Moltmann.[11] In light of that, one could ask: What does that look like in our particular contexts? What does it look like to resist and actively unlearn the dangerous and harmful legacy of colonization? How do we center the voices that have been left on the underside of history? How is this work to decolonize self and academy not merely additive, but also actually a constitutive element of work within our institutions?

James Cone argues that, in order to be free, a person must be able to make choices that are not dependent on an oppressive system, and that to do this requires becoming part of and participating in oppressed communities.[12] And yet, he asks if it is possible to change communities. To change communities involves a change of being. It is a radical movement, a radical reorientation of one's existence in the world.[13] Christianity, he says, calls this experience conversion.[14] And in this time, when so much of the destructive patterns of the twentieth century seem to be repeating themselves—the rise of hatred, racism, antisemitism, dictatorship, and tyranny—we are reminded that this call for radical conversion must be constant, a never-ending reflection,

---

[11]Ibid., 3.
[12]James Cone, *A Black Theology of Liberation*, 40th anniversary ed. (Maryknoll, NY: Orbis Books, 2010), 103. For a fuller analysis of James Cone's call for white conversion, see Matt R. Jantzen, "Neither Ally, nor Accomplice: James Cone and the Theological Ethics of White Conversion," *Journal of the Society of Christian Ethics* 40, no. 2 (2020): 273–290.
[13]Cone, *Black Theology of Liberation*, 103.
[14]Ibid.

analysis, and transformation; it is not simply a reaction when particular events arise.

In the end, I came to the US and pursued my doctoral degree because I wanted to be a teacher. I truly saw how an education could be a powerful tool to help shape one's mind, one's perspectives of the reality of the world, and one's imagination of how the world could be. But I'm no longer naïve in thinking that education is neutral. Education is power. As educators and scholars, we have power and we have privilege to uphold or disrupt the dominant narratives in the academy and society—to reshape, create, and produce knowledge that shapes the social imagination. And as educators in the field of theology and religion, we also have the depths of the riches of the practices of our different religions to guide in ways to interrupt our normalized ways of thinking and being in order to elicit a radical conversion to decolonize the self and the academy.

Whiteness Inventory

Karen Teel

Several years ago, some faculty at the University of San Diego began incorporating a land acknowledgment into our syllabi. Having formulated and offered these plenary reflections while a guest on Kumeyaay land, I include it here:

> I want to acknowledge that the land on which we gather is the traditional and unceded territory of the Kumeyaay Nation. I want to pay respect to the citizens of the Kumeyaay Nation, both past and present, and their continuing relationship to their ancestral lands.[1]

To honor our debt—mine and the College Theology Society's—to the Kumeyaay Nation, I contributed to a local organization for Native youth. Going forward, I hope that the CTS will regularly offer a "land tax" or "rent" to the nations on whose land we meet each year.[2]

---

[1] This acknowledgment was developed in 2019 by Kumeyaay leaders together with Persephone Hooper-Lewis, then University of San Diego's tribal liaison.

[2] While land-back efforts are more common in Canada, US models exist: residents of San Francisco's East Bay can pay the Shuumi Land Tax; Seattleites can join Real Rent Duwamish. The College Theology Society leadership could research Native nations on whose land we meet, contact tribal governments, and respectfully offer a contribution acknowledging our use of their land. I first heard this idea from Theresa Rocha Beardall and Theresa Stewart-Ambo during an Indigenous Peoples' Day event at USD in 2020.

In the year 2022, the CTS still needed a convention theme and annual volume based on the work of Martin Luther King Jr. Why? Because our discipline remains firmly within the grip of whiteness and because, like most organizations related to higher education in the United States, the CTS is a predominantly white institution. It is historically white: it was founded and its basic character formed in 1954, during the era of legal segregation, when many white people in the US openly celebrated white supremacy. And it remains culturally white, both in terms of our numbers and in terms of our practices.

It may seem odd to say that the CTS remains culturally white when clearly the membership has diversified. Scholars of color have gained access, and many white scholars have welcomed them. We have made space for them to present papers, to dialogue with us, to join us at Eucharist. Moreover, plenary speakers, from James Cone in 1974 to Willie James Jennings in 2018, have proclaimed our need to renounce racism and whiteness.[3] While we may have received them graciously and listened attentively, "the[ir] joys and the[ir] hopes, the[ir] griefs and the[ir] anxieties" have not become our joys and our hopes, our griefs and our anxieties.[4] Our space has not been collectively transformed. It remains our space.

The problem is not that white scholars remain intellectually or morally unconvinced that racial injustice is a problem. We know that it is. Rather than belabor that point, I want to invite us to notice the quality of our attention when we are reminded of this problem. We hear about it over and over, and each time, many of us white scholars receive the information as though we've never really heard it before. We seem perpetually stunned by how bad it is. I think this is because we never fully metabolize the fact that white supremacy is relevant to us personally. It is true that many of us now are writing paragraphs, articles, and books drawing

---

[3] See James H. Cone, "Freedom, Hope, and History," in *Liberation, Revolution and Freedom: Theological Perspectives*, ed. Thomas M. McFadden (New York: Seabury, 1975), 59–75, and Willie James Jennings, "Teaching and Living toward a Revolutionary Intimacy," in *"You Say You Want a Revolution?": 1968–2018 in Theological Perspective*, ed. Susie Paulik Babka, Elena Procario-Foley, and Sandra Yocum (Maryknoll, NY: Orbis Books, 2019), 3–15.

[4] "Pastoral Constitution on the Church in the Modern World (*Gaudium et Spes*)," in *Vatican II, Revised Edition in Inclusive Language*, ed. Austin Flannery, OP (Northport, NY: Costello, 1996), para. 1, 163–282.

on the work of nonwhite scholars. We have learned to demonstrate awareness of their ideas, to critique white supremacy as a
problem. But we don't really grapple with our own whiteness. As
philosopher George Yancy observes, we are "whites (academic and
intellectual types) who are able to engage race and racism critically at the *conceptual* level, but appear to fail at challenging [*our*]
own whiteness at a deeply interpersonal level."[5] We "approach
the problem of race/whiteness as a mere *intellectual* pursuit."[6] We
have yet to realize that the political is personal.

Jennings exhorted the CTS to "renounce the way whiteness thinks." To do that, he said, "We need to do a whiteness
inventory."[7] I take this as a call to examine how whiteness manifests in our private thoughts, in what goes on inside our heads.
I often teach the work of Peggy McIntosh, whose numbered list
of everyday experiences of white privilege—her "invisible knap-
sack"—has empowered many whites to see that white privilege
exists and that we personally use it.[8] In this now-venerable tradition, I propose to offer an "inventory" of thoughts and feelings
that I have had during my life and scholarly career. You don't have
to be racialized as white to demonstrate these thought patterns;
I am speaking as one white person, trying to pin down the way
whiteness thinks. Exposing whiteness in this way "feels terrible,"
as Jennings observes.[9] It isn't pretty. But we can't "renounce the
way whiteness thinks" if we can't hear what it says. And what I
hear in these fourteen thought patterns is that the whiteness is
strong with me. As you read them, I invite you to notice whether
whiteness is strong with you, too.

1. When someone states that racism is unacceptable, and I rush
    to agree, I feel that we have been engaging in deeply mean-
    ingful antiracist action, rather than mouthing platitudes.

---

[5]George Yancy, *Look, a White! Philosophical Essays on Whiteness* (Philadelphia: Temple University Press, 2012), 26.

[6]Ibid., 27.

[7]Jennings, "Teaching and Living," 9.

[8]See Peggy McIntosh, "White Privilege: Unpacking the Invisible Knap-
sack," in *White Privilege: Essential Readings on the Other Side of Racism*,
5th ed., ed. Paula S. Rothenberg with Soniya Munshi (New York: Worth,
2016), 151–55.

[9]Jennings, "Teaching and Living," 10.

2. When I take the initiative to assert that racism is unacceptable, I feel that I am taking a courageous stand on the right side of history, rather than stating the obvious.

3. When I hear of incidents of racial violence, I sigh and mournfully shake my head, maybe donate a little money, and then go about my business, feeling that I have done what I can.

4. When I hear of continuing racial inequities in the academy, I assume that someone else will form a committee to address them, perhaps by writing a statement that I can sign.

5. I think that inviting scholars of color to present in regular and plenary sessions, enduring their admonishments, and electing some of them to the board basically satisfies our society's collective responsibility for white supremacy.

6. I assume that writing a paragraph or article about the ideas of scholars of color basically satisfies my professional and personal responsibility for white supremacy; I may even think that doing so marks my work as antiracist.

7. When I attend conference sessions in which nonwhite colleagues are giving papers, and I listen carefully and really try to take them seriously, I secretly congratulate myself for my exceptional generosity and broad-mindedness.

8. In professional societies and at my home institution, participating in programs or hiring processes that increase racial, ethnic, or gender diversity makes me feel noble and far-seeing.

9. I believe that my institution or department can reach a point at which we have "enough diversity" even while we remain predominantly white, whether demographically or through maintaining a culturally white environment.

10. I sometimes feel proud of myself when I support my colleagues of color; meanwhile, I support my white colleagues without thinking about it.

11. I sometimes forget that colleagues and students of color face different struggles than white colleagues and students not because people of color are deficient in any way, but because the university was built by and for white people.

12. When I attempt to call a white person's attention to their racism, I bend over backwards to be nice about it, desperately hoping that they won't feel bad or stop liking me.

13.   When I acknowledge my own white privilege or complicity in white supremacy, especially if I speak in a repentant or self-flagellatory tone, I feel certain that I am doing better than 99 percent of white people; I am in the antiracist 1 percent.

14.   When I admit that I personally have done something racist, apologize, and pledge to do better, I feel like I should be canonized immediately. What more could possibly be expected of me?!

In considering this whiteness inventory, I notice that, while I am having a lot of intense feelings, I am doing very little that has any measurable effect on systemic racism or white supremacy. My way of being in the world remains much the same as it was before I had any inkling of the problem. I have learned to nod knowingly and sigh regretfully, to wish that things were different. Yet I still exhibit this remarkable ability to maintain an attitude of self-satisfaction and benevolent detachment in the face of pervasive racial injustice. I exhibit whiteness.

I suggest to you that in our society and our discipline, white scholars exhibit whiteness collectively. We acknowledge the problem, but we have scarcely begun the process of transformation. We bring in scholars of color, allow them access and airtime, and we feel virtuous and magnanimous. But we don't change the deep structure of our work, our meetings, our society, our discipline, our institutions.

What would change look like? I don't know. With my whiteness, I don't think I can adequately imagine it, much less achieve it. To make genuine progress, I think we have to try something new. I propose that we cede power formally to our colleagues of color and ask them to take charge of reshaping everything. (While this idea is not new, executing it in a predominantly white academic context might be.) I am not claiming that our colleagues of color are immune from whiteness. We are all human, and we all trained in the same academy; there are no guarantees that this will work. But having what standpoint theorists call the epistemic advantage of oppression can render people of color more likely to be able to recognize and resist the "way whiteness thinks."[10] And when

---

[10]Ibid., 9. Emilie Townes names this the "fantastic hegemonic imagina-

they cultivate this ability—and many do—they see how different things could be. Anyway, the chance that they will make things worse is vanishingly small. I say we give it a try.

This does not mean, however, that we white scholars get to sit back and do nothing. Here in San Diego, and in other cities, there is a delightful means of transportation that is a cross between a party bus and a tandem bicycle. This "party bike" has a driver in the front and a lot of riders in the back pedaling. The driver is sober, and the riders are not. The driver controls the route, the steering, and the destination, and the riders contribute the labor of pedaling to get everybody there.

As a white person, including as a theologian, I am drunk on whiteness. My vision, my judgment, my reaction times, all are severely impaired by my white privilege and my participation in white supremacy. As my whiteness inventory tries to show, many white people's ideas of what constitutes antiracist action are strikingly ineffectual. We're just riding in circles, having a good time. If we want our racial justice efforts to have a chance of going somewhere meaningful, then those of us with a whiteness problem should get out of the driver's seat.

The beauty of this plan is that even though I am severely impaired, I can still help. I just have to let my colleagues of color take the wheel. Then I need to get in the back of the bus, pun intended, and pedal when they say pedal.[11]

tion"; see Townes, *Womanist Ethics and the Cultural Production of Evil* (New York: Palgrave Macmillan, 2006).

[11]Much gratitude to Jamall Calloway and my Black colleagues at the University of San Diego, whose July 2020 open letter to our administration catalyzed racial justice efforts campuswide and inspired me to develop this metaphor. This "party bike" metaphor is intended to help white scholars shift our frame of reference, to realize that we should not be leading all or even most racial justice efforts. Of course, the metaphor is limited. Racial justice work does not always feel like a party, and white people do need to take the initiative to sober up as best we can, to learn to contribute more effectively. As for the drivers, they don't get paid enough; and although some may manage to enjoy their work, many might prefer to use their talents for something other than managing impaired white folks. Ultimately, while I hope that the party bike metaphor serves to move some of us along, I also hope that it reminds us that this situation remains far from ideal.

Colonialism, Racism, and Gender

The Case of the *Mujer Indigena* and the *Babaylans* in the Philippines

Christina Astorga

When colonialism is connected with racism and gender, it brings into sharp light the evil that it wreaks. Colonialism, to put it simply, "marks the historical process whereby the 'West' attempts to systematically cancel or negate the cultural differences and values of the 'non-West.'"[1] Colonialism intersects with race when persons canceled or negated as persons and their cultures are regarded as inferior by virtue of their race. And if these persons are women, colonialism intersects with race and gender. The intersectionality of colonialism, race, and gender was a lived reality in the case of the *mujer indigena* and the *Babaylan*s in the Philippines, when the country was under Spain for more than four hundred years.

Based on the Doctrine of Discovery, the popes in the fifteenth century granted authority to European kings to invade, capture, vanquish, enslave, and subjugate native lands and peoples outside of Europe.[2] In the Philippine archipelago, Spanish colonialism and Catholicism were inextricably linked as twin institutions that delivered to the male clergy power, authority, and control. Those

---

[1]Leela Gandhi, *Postcolonial Theory: A Critical Introduction*, 2nd ed. (New York: Columbia University Press, 2019), 16.

[2]Linda Tuhiwai Smith, *Decolonizing Methodologies: Research and Indigenous Peoples* (London: Zed Books, 2004), 42–43.

who resisted the Spanish authority were charged with treachery and treason. The conquest and colonization of the Philippines were marked by a peace treaty that lasted until 1895.[3] With the signing of the treaty agreement, the Cebuano people surrendered their land to the Spaniards.[4] What defined the boundary was a line of trees, one side of which was assigned to the natives, where they could "build their houses and till the fields."[5] The boundary signified that the indigenes were those who tilled the soil to produce food while the Spaniards were the rulers. On the side of the line of trees where the Spaniards lived, Governor Miguel López de Legazpi built a fort, to serve as a bulwark against chaotic forces, and a Spanish town that he named Villa de San Miguel.[6] The treaty stipulated against any native coming into or near the Spanish settlement with any kind of weapon, none whatsoever. Nevertheless, the boundaries did not only serve as protection, as Jonathan Z. Smith argues, "The concern for limits, borders, and boundaries is a far more subtle and pervasive thing."[7] For the Spaniards to be safeguarded from the possibility of any form of hybridization with heathen influences,[8] a clause was added to the treaty that forbade any native from entering the Spanish settlement after dark. This was to avoid what Smith terms "the mingling of

---

[3]Ibid.

[4]Control of people rather than seizure of lands signaled power and wealth. Throughout Southeast Asia, "land was abundant [and] buildings impermanent," and the objective of frequent raiding parties was to "seize people rather than territory." See Anthony Reid, *Southeast Asia in the Age of Commerce, 1450–1680*, vol. 1: *The Lands below the Winds* (New Haven, CT: Yale University Press, 1988), 120–22.

[5]Cited in Carolyn Brewer, *Shamanism, Catholicism, and Gender Relations in Colonial Philippines, 1521–1685* (London: Ashgate, 2004), 19. This and other symbolic *actos de posesion* were not enacted only in the Philippines, but were also done in Latin America and Spain, wherever the Roman law was imposed.

[6]This town was eventually to become Santisimo Nombre de Jesus, in memory of the *imagene* of the Santo Nino, given to the "queen" by the members of the Magellan expedition.

[7]Jonathan Z. Smith, "The Influence of Symbols upon Social Change: A Place on Which to Stand," *Worship* 44, no. 1 (October 1970): 457–74.

[8]In relation to purity, see Mary Douglas, *Purity and Danger: An Analysis of Concepts of Pollution and Taboo* (London: Routledge and Kegan Paul, 1979 reprint), esp. 49 and 53.

seeds,"[9] which, however, could not be stamped out by Legazpi, as the sentinels which he posted could not stop the women who "prostituted themselves freely throughout the camp."[10]

The diminution, discrimination, and cancellation were particularly directed toward women. Gender rather than women, however, is addressed in this essay for both theoretical and practical reasons. Although the essay is constructed mostly around women and women shamans, "woman" and "gender" are not synonymous terms. In this study, "the focus on gender relations strategically allows for the demarcation between biological categories based on genitalia and reproduction and socially constructed categories imposed upon a sexed body"[11] "that are both historically defined and culturally contingent."[12] "The study of gender roles refers to the more fundamental question relating to the way a group of human beings are made to become 'women' or 'men' and on the power relationships that are authorized between the two."[13]

In the collision of the cultures of Iberian Catholicism and the natives, women were caught in the crossfire. This essay addresses the question of how Iberian Catholicism canceled and erased the native women (*mujer indigena*) in general, and *Babaylans* in particular. I will present the status of *mujer indigena* and the *Babaylans* before and after they were canceled or erased by Iberian Catholicism.

Mujer Indigena:
Before and After Hispanic Catholicism

The women in the Philippines, when the country was not yet called such, enjoyed a singular status not shared by other women during the period. The *mujer indigena* enjoyed an egalitarian

---

[9]Smith, "The Influence of Symbols upon Social Change," 465.

[10]Cited in Brewer, *Shamanism, Catholicism, and Gender Relations*, 20.

[11]Joan W. Scott, "Gender: A Useful Category of Historical Analysis," *American Historical Review* 91, no. 5 (December 1986): 1056.

[12]Studies focusing on cross-cultural notions of power and gender in a Southeast Asian context include Shelley Errington, "Recasting Sex, Gender, and Power: A Theoretical and Regional Overview," in *Power and Difference: Gender in Island Southeast Asia*, ed. Jane Monnig Atkinson and Shelley Errington (Stanford, CA: Stanford University Press, 1990), 1–58.

[13]Brewer, *Shamanism, Catholicism, and Gender Relations*, xviii.

relationship with her husband. When married, she did not lose her name. In fact, among the Tagalog-speaking Filipinos, when a woman was distinguished due to her family's fortune or connections or due to her personal merits, the husband took her name. So people were heard to refer to a man as the "husband of Ninay or Isang."[14] In this egalitarian society, the woman had an honored place in the family, whether as a daughter or as a wife. Her birth was welcomed as the birth of a son; she received equal opportunity for education[15] and enjoyed a great measure of freedom in decision-making, particularly having children.[16] The mother enjoyed the sole prerogative of naming her child.[17] She was not, however, confined to domestic affairs. Her presence and approval were necessary in the signing of formal contracts, as she was considered the more serious and formal partner in the making of contracts. A man would not enter into them without the presence and consent of his wife.[18] The purse was also entrusted by the husband to the wife, as she was known to exercise more wisdom and prudence in terms of the economic management of the home. The wife enjoyed equal rights with her husband with regard to divorce before the law. If the wife was at fault, the bride's dowry was returned by her family. The custody of the children, however, was granted equally, and properties were also equally divided.[19]

The sexual culture was such that men took no heed of the relationships of their wives before their marriage, as virginity was

---

[14]C. F. Pedro Paterno, *La Antigua Civilizacion Tagalog* (Madrid: Tipografia de Manuel G. Fernandez, 1887), 244.

[15]Mary John Mananzan, "The Filipina Women: Before and After the Spanish Conquest of the Philippines," in *Essays on Women,* ed. Mary John Mananzan (Manila: Institute of Women's Studies, 1987), 6–35 at 13.

[16]Ibid., 12.

[17]Most of the studies indicate a tradition of egalitarian child preference in the Philippines. Marie Loy Frias Bautista aims to provide a "basis for understanding the Filipinos' egalitarian child preference patterns and to examine the historical factors which influenced its formation." Marie Loy Frias Bautista, "Historical Influences on Gender Preference in the Philippines," *Journal of Comparative Family Studies* 19, no. 1 (Spring 1988): 143–53.

[18]R. Gonzáles y Martin, *Filipinas y Sus Habitantes* (Béjar: Establecimiento Tipografico de la Viuda de Aguilar, 1986), 222.

[19]Mananzan, "The Filipina Women: Before and After the Spanish Conquest of the Philippines," 13. See Anthony Reid, "Female Roles in Pre-Colonial Southeast Asia," *Modern Asian Studies* 22, no. 3 (1988): 629–45.

not valued, and the loss of it was only regarded as misfortune.[20] Adultery was accepted. If a wife committed adultery, action was not taken against her, but against the adulterer in the form of fees. Adultery was not mentioned unless in relation to a child born of the extramarital union. The fine levied against the adulterous male by the father made the child fittingly legitimate, and the paternity fine was considered a dowry. Without an underlying notion of proprietary ownership of the woman's body, the wife was not punished for a perceived transgression, nor did her husband leave her. The adulterous male was also not shamed and disgraced.[21]

In the realm of politics, women were not barred from becoming village chieftains because, in the absence of a male heir, daughters succeeded their fathers. Women were as capable of governance as the men, or even better. They wielded political power directly, or indirectly through the influence over their husbands, if the latter were the ones holding the positions of power.[22] Some of the women were very able leaders, and their roles in precolonial politics were so distinguished that the archipelago was known as the Queen Country of Ancient Asia.[23] Performing important economic, political, and religious roles, precolonial Filipina women, unlike many of their Asian sisters, were not made to walk behind their men; on the contrary, it was the men who walked behind them, as a sign of deep respect.[24]

When Spain conquered the Philippines, women were stripped of all the privileges they used to enjoy, by the power of the sword and in the name of the cross. European thought, tempered in the crucible of Christian ideology, had resolved what David Stannard explained as "immoderate enjoyment of the pleasures of the flesh [which] belonged to the world of the brute. . . . Abstinence, modesty, strictness, and sobriety are to be treasured above all

---

[20]Cited in Emily Sanchez Salcedo, "From Urduja to Maria Clara; From Pura Villanueva to Lola Rosa—Face of the Filipina Across Phases of History," SSRN (2013): 8, http://dx.doi.org/10.2139/ssrn.2214224.

[21]Brewer, *Shamanism, Catholicism, and Gender Relations*, 23–24.

[22]Cited in Salcedo, "From Urduja to Maria Clara," 8–9.

[23]L. Gleeck, *American Institutions in the Philippines: 1898–1941* (Manila: Historical Conservation Society, 1976), 46.

[24]Cited in Salcedo, "From Urduja to Maria Clara," 12.

else."[25] Using ideological persuasion backed by power, Iberian Catholicism enforced the transformation of indigenous sexual culture. For men, women's bodies as objects of temptation were to be avoided, and women were to think of themselves as good or bad, based on their sexual behavior, according to the tenets of the Catholic Christian teachings.[26] Modesty and chastity, based on self-control and bolstered by religious piety, defined a good woman. Women should be properly covered to hide their charms lest they tempt the men to commit sin. They should not be seen in public except in church, where they were holy figures with rosary beads in their hands. Confined to domestic chores, they were refused admission to universities, except if they desired to train as teachers, the only course open to women.[27]

In the documents and accounts, the *mujer indigena* was negatively presented in any aspect of her being that did not align with the Ibero-Catholic notions of the good woman. Her authority, power, and agency were either misrepresented or erased. For Iberian Catholicism to be successful, it was necessary to introduce a new image of woman in which the virgin/whore dichotomy was paramount. According to the Gospels, the Virgin Mary—the sublime model of chastity, the humble and obedient woman—declared at the Annunciation: "I am the handmaid of the lord, let what you have said be done to me" (Luke 1:38). "This image of obedience was crucial to a church which sought to locate Mary's place, and by analogy the position of all women within the confines of the sexually approved behavior of passivity, timidity, docility and compliance that typified the good woman."[28] This it did at the expense of the iconoclastic image of Mary in the Lukan

---

[25]David E. Stannard, *American Holocaust: The Conquest of the New World* (New York: Oxford University Press, 1992), 154. See Ann Laura Stoler, *Carnal Knowledge and Imperial Power: Race and the Intimate in Colonial Rule* (Berkeley: University of California Press, 2002).

[26]Brewer, *Shamanism, Catholicism, and Gender Relations*, 39. The Virgin Mary looms large as the image of "good" Filipina. The Church reinforces such imagery to highlight the madonna-whore dichotomy. See Jeane C. Peracullo, "Maria Clara in the Twenty-First Century: The Uneasy Discourse between the Cult of the Virgin Mary and Filipina Women's Lived Realities," *Religious Studies and Theology* 36, no. 2 (2017): 139–53.

[27]Salcedo, "From Urduja to Maria Clara," 14.

[28]Brewer, *Shamanism, Catholicism, and Gender Relations*, 46.

Magnificat (Luke 1:46–55)—the image of Mary as prophetic and liberating, breaking the patriarchal constructs of feminine silence and submission.

The sacraments of Baptism and Penance were used to enforce the moral life that women should live, against the forbidden life of a sexually dangerous woman.[29] The rituals of the sacraments, along with the practice of flagellation, imposed restraint, repression, containment, and control of the body, in view of what was licit and illicit, permitted and forbidden. Although Baptism was the entryway to the faith, confession and flagellation were used to curb the obsession with sexual desire,[30] and to submit the body to the newly constructed moral will.[31] Instilling guilt in the convert's mind, along with flagellation's scarification of the body, Iberian Catholicism imposed the "relations of power" through what Foucault refers to as the sexual "repressive hypothesis."[32] Flagellation or ritual floggings were widely accepted by converts in the seventeenth century as acts of voluntary contrition.[33]

In the various missionary accounts, however, men and women differed in their conversions. Women internalized the teaching that they were evil by nature, while men separated their sins from their essential selves, and blamed women as the cause of their sins.[34] This meant that men sinned without being diminished as essentially worthless and damned. The scars of flagellation on men reminded them of the danger of women, while those on women reminded them that they were dirty and evil.[35] "As the woman's finger contacted bruises and scarred areas on the back of the man, both lovers were reminded that her beauty was only skin deep and that he was embracing a sack containing nothing but bile, dung, mucous and pestilent odours."[36]

---

[29]Ibid., 63.

[30]See Lois McNay, *Foucault and Feminism: Power, Gender, and the Self* (Cambridge: Polity Press, 1992).

[31]See Michel Foucault, *Discipline and Punish: The Birth of the Prison,* trans. Alan Sheridan (London: Penguin, 1977).

[32]See Michel Foucault, *The History of Sexuality:* vol. 1: *An Introduction,* trans. Robert Hurley (London: Penguin Books, 1990), 15–50.

[33]Brewer, *Shamanism, Catholicism, and Gender Relations,* 70.

[34]Elizabeth Reis, *Damned Women: Sinners and Witches in Puritan New England* (Ithaca, NY: Cornell University Press, 1997), 39.

[35]Brewer, *Shamanism, Catholicism, and Gender Relations,* 63.

[36]Ibid., 76.

The *Babaylans*:
Before and After Hispanic Catholicism

The role of women in the political field during the precolonial period has been disputed in particular because it was claimed by some to have only been based "merely" on legends. But it is in the religious field that the predominant role of women as leaders in the pre-Spanish Philippines was unquestioned. Religion was at the center of life, and the woman was a recognized leader who presided over rites of life and death. The *Babaylan* was usually a female, but when a male assumed such a role, he dressed as a woman.[37] This privileging of the female, however, is not reflected in the Filipino concept of God or *Bathhala*, who is imaged as neither man nor woman, but as a Spirit that encompasses the characteristics of both genders. In the Filipino creation account, it is told that the Creator split a bamboo, and created simultaneously male and female, not separately, with one following the other as told in the Genesis account. A bilateral egalitarian kinship is at the root of the indigenous Philippine culture.[38]

Before the arrival of Catholicism, a form of shamanistic animism was the spiritual substratum or bedrock upon which the communities relied. Shamanism is typified by the ability of the adept to enter into an altered state of consciousness. Under this state, the shaman is able to heal the sick, communicate with the spirits of the dead, and perform supernatural feats. In the sixteenth and seventeenth centuries in the Philippines, the adepts were mostly women, but there were also men who dressed as women, at the time when throughout much of the rest of the world, the adepts were men.[39] Animist religions were more localized than universal; they were not missionary oriented. Each tribe has its own beliefs, traditions, and rituals, which were influenced by other religions. Strong similarities between the animist traditions of Southeast Asia show Indic influence as the common link, albeit with regional variations.[40]

---

[37]Ibid., 84.

[38]Mary John Mananzan, *The Woman Question in the Philippines* (Manila: Institute of Women's Studies, 1997), 4.

[39]Brewer, *Shamanism, Catholicism, and Gender Relations*, xvii.

[40]Ibid.

The *Babaylan* stood for an integral and embodied spirituality. Her psyche, her body was the channel of the divine, as she danced the healing movements, both literal and metaphorical.[41] She "presided over all the rituals of her people, from planting to harvest, from birth, disease to death, from weddings, hunts, wars to victory."[42] The realms that she navigated and internalized in her dance encompassed her multiple roles. "Aside from being a priest, she was an empowered healer, midwife, herbalist, a trusted confidante, a reputed and wise counselor/adviser, a mediator (between humans), a medium, or bridge (between humans and the spirit world), a historian, a visionary/clairvoyant, an environmentalist, and cosmologist."[43] Grounded in all spheres of life, she was the community's leader and wisdom figure.

But so-called dualisms like the spirit and the body/earthly/ sensual, the ancient and the new, the mystical and the scientific, the beginning and the end, the rational and the intuitive, conscious and unconscious, (with) in and (with) out, light and dark/shadow, god and goddess, female and male, anima and animus, nature and culture, sexuality and spirituality, immanence and transcendence, certainty and mystery—all imply each other, are brought into balance, in the babaylan's dance. And she, with her people, dances not only in joyous thanksgiving and celebration, but even in the most precarious conditions, like during an epidemic, to ward off or propitiate the dis-ease-causing spirits.[44]

In the *Babaylan*'s dance flows the whole of life, intertwining, interconnecting, and intersecting, in a spirituality that is holistic and integral.

In the collision of Iberian Catholicism and animist religion at

---

[41]Agnes Miclat-Cacayan, "She Dances in Wholeness," in *Babaylan: Filipinos and the Call of the Indigenous*, ed. Leny Mendoza Strobel (Santa Rosa, CA: Center for Babaylan, 2010), 116. Grace Nono, *Babaylan Sing Back: Philippine Shamans and Voice, Gender, and Place* (Ithaca, NY: Cornell University Press, 2021), examines current religious, social, and feminist constructions of Filipino shamanism.

[42]Miclat-Cacayan, "She Dances in Wholeness," Ibid., 117.

[43]Ibid.

[44]Ibid.

the same time as thousands of women in Europe, especially from the lower classes, were being tortured, hanged, and burned on charges of witchcraft, the Spanish colonizers called the *Babaylans* by the same names and similarly charged them. They were called *hechicera* (witch, sorceress, old hag), *diablesa* (she-devil), *sacerdotisa del infierno* (priestess of hell), and *bruja* (witch, old hag).[45] Considered a threat to the colonial and Christianization project, they were marginalized and taken over by a patriarchal, male-dominated clergy. Carolyn Brewer, in *Holy Confrontation*, writes about the "disappearance" of the *Babaylan* tradition within the first hundred years of colonial conquest.[46] The *Babaylans* fled to the mountains and led their people in fierce resistance against the colonizers, and they made it extremely difficult for the Spanish friars to take their culture, religion, and way of life from the indigenous Filipinos. The Spanish mounted an Inquisition-like pursuit, as they hunted the *Babaylans* down, confiscated their ritual instruments, and put them to death.[47]

In 1587, Friar Diego Aduarte boasted, "By the punishment of a few old women, who acted as priestesses . . . the idolatry of the whole region was brought to an end."[48] Juan de Plasencia also reported, "May the honor and glory be God our Lord's that among all the Tagalogs, not a trace of this is left. . . . Thanks to the preaching of the holy gospel, which has banished it."[49]

---

[45]Domenico Pietropaolo, "Alcina in Arcadia," *University of Toronto Quarterly* 72, no. 4 (2003): 864. Brewer, *Shamanism, Catholicism, and Gender Relations*, 86.

[46]See Carolyn Brewer, *Holy Confrontation: Religion, Gender, Sexuality in the Philippines, 1521–1685* (Manila: Institute of Women's Studies, 2001).

[47]Milagros C. Guerrero, "The Babaylan in Colonial Times: Bodies Desecrated/Body Narratives, Metaphors, and Concepts in the Philippine Indigenous Religion," in *Gender/Bodies/Religions*, ed. Sylvia Marcos (Mexico City: ALER, 2001), 175–76, citing Gaspar de San Agustin, OSA, *Conquistas de las Islas Filipinas, 1565–1615*, ed. Manuel Merino (Madrid: Consejo Superior de Investigaciones Científicas Instituto, "Enrique Flores," 1975), 660.

[48]Diego Aduarte, "History of the Dominican Province of the Holy Rosary," in *The Philippine Islands, 1493–1898*, vol. 33 (1519–1522), ed. Emma Helen Blair and James Alexander Robertson (Cleveland: Arthur H. Clark, 1903), 173–97, 196. Richard L. Deats, *Nationalism and Christianity in the Philippines* (Dallas: Southern Methodist University Press, 1967), 16. Brewer, *Shamanism, Catholicism, and Gender Relations*, 89.

[49]Juan de Plasencia, "Customs of the Tagalogs," in *The Philippine Islands,*

They were pushed by the Spanish to the underground, and their religion was condemned as pagan, superstitious, and a form of fanaticism. The coming of the colonizers changed the colonized Filipino perception of their religious heritage. What was sacred was now the work of the devil, something to be ashamed of, and to be condemned. The *Babaylans* reemerged during the revolutionary war between Spain and the Philippines, when many of them who were once spiritual warriors, turned into military warriors, leading local revolts against Spain.[50]

Reflections and Analysis

Iberian Catholicism canceled the gender symmetry—the mutual power and authority enjoyed by indigenous Filipino women and men. The pre-Hispanic women were strong in sexual matters, as they were strong in other aspects of life as well. It is necessary to look beyond the genitals to the position of women in society as a whole. The gender symmetry of pre-Spanish men and women contradicts Sherry Ortner's Eurocentric model of a devaluation of women, which holds that a woman is to a man as nature is to culture, with woman and nature as inferior.[51] Janet D'Urso claims that as "one ruling class supersedes the others, so do myths accommodate the new reality."[52] As far as the construction of gender, women were not always inferior to men as shown by indigenous cultures, but as men assumed power and control in society, there was a progressive masculinization of myths, which "altered over

---

1493–1898, vol. 33 (1519), ed. Emma Helen Blair and James Alexander Robertson (Cleveland: Arthur H. Clark, 1903), 173–97. Deats, *Nationalism and Christianity in the Philippines*, 16. Brewer, *Shamanism, Catholicism, and Gender Relations*, 89.

[50]Leny Mendoza-Strobel, Introduction to *Babaylan: Filipinos and the Call of the Indigenous*, ed. Leny Mendoza Strobel (Santa Rosa, CA: Center for Babaylan, 2010), 2. Alicia Magos writes of the continuing influence and presence of the Babaylan tradition in *The Enduring Ma-Aram Tradition* (Quezon City: New Day, 1992).

[51]See Sherry B. Ortner, "Is Female to Male as Nature Is to Culture?," in *Woman, Culture, and Society,* ed. Michelle Zimbalist Rosaldo and Louise Lamphere (Stanford, CA: Stanford University Press, 1974), 71–83.

[52]Janet D'Urso, "The Social Construction of Woman: Western Mythic and Religious Stereotypes," *Hecate* 1, no. 1 (1975): 24.

time to become means of psychological coercion and means of maintaining control over a reality to favour men."[53]

In the Philippines, the changeover of a largely symmetrical gender arrangement to one in which men dominated women in spiritual and political realms, the masculinization of the myth did not only occur where Jewish and Christian myths were imposed on indigenous culture, but also where the Spaniards read indigenous culture through their own gendered lenses. In the latter, the colonizers rewrote the indigenous myths to reflect their own. The indigenous woman who was not expected to be chaste must reconstruct herself to fit the image of a moral woman, which means a chaste woman.

In the confrontation between animism and Iberian Catholicism, a new worldview was imposed on the indigenous Filipinos—a worldview that negated women's bodies and women's positions in society. The status of woman was diminished and her self-perception was altered. Rather than elevate women's already high status, Iberian Catholicism denigrated women, taking away from them their agency over their own bodies, sexuality, and their reproductive processes. Developing their self-identities based on their sexual behavior, they were to judge themselves according to a good woman / bad woman binary predicated on Catholic myth and tradition. Through confession and the practice of flagellation, Iberian Catholicism imposed its repressed sexual ethics through the internalization of guilt.

It was the women shamans (*Babaylans*) who resisted the new religion with ferocity, but then they had the most to lose. They were faced with a triple negative. Their status as women was degraded, their role as religious practitioners was usurped, and they were vilified as priestesses of hell. Banished to the periphery of society, they lost their status and their source of livelihood. And many lost their lives. "The power and the authority of the church and state was consolidated, further pushing to the deepest recesses of people's minds the 'dangerous memories' of a time when women had autonomy and when shaman women exercised considerable influence in the spiritual realms. By the late 19th century . . . men

---

[53]Ibid.

were able to take over the religious and spiritual roles left vacant by the demonized women."[54]

The story of the *Babaylans* was a story of resistance, which, in the end, was vanquished by the power and control of clericalism, which continues to rear its ugly head in the Catholic Church in the Philippines, even as it seeks reform of its structures of leadership and participation. And in the world today colonialism and its tentacles in racism and gender injustice continue to cast a long and dark shadow.

[54]Brewer, *Shamanism, Catholicism, and Gender Relations*, 193.

Beyond Grand Narratives

Toward an Archipelagic Approach to the Philippine Quincentennial

Victoria Basug Slabinski

The year 2021 marked five hundred years since the arrival of Ferdinand Magellan's crew on the shores of what are now the Philippine islands and the beginnings of Christianity's presence in the archipelago. On March 14, 2021, Pope Francis prompted an online discussion by posting the following message on Twitter in commemoration of the quincentennial: "Dear brothers and sisters from the Philippines, five hundred years have passed since the Christian message first arrived in your land and you received the joy of the Gospel. And this joy is evident in your people. Thank you for the joy you bring to the whole world!"[1] The Philippines-based news source *Rappler* reported that some Filipinos responded to the tweet by thanking the Pope for celebrating the Philippines, others reframed it by acknowledging Spanish colonization and celebrating the "Filipinization" of Catholicism, and others condemned celebrations of the "Arrival of Colonizers" by calling instead for atonement and reparations.[2] The varied reception with which the Pope's celebratory message was met reveals the existence of competing narratives framing the remembrance of 1521.

---

[1]Pope Francis (@Pontifex), Twitter post, March 14, 2021 (8:30 a.m.), https://twitter.com.

[2]Mikaela De Castro, "Filipinos Debate: 500 Years of Christianity or Centuries of Colonization?" *Rappler*, March 17, 2021, https://www.rappler.com.

As this essay will explore, some framings of the quincentennial celebrate it as the moment the peoples of the Philippines first received Christianity, and alternative framings commemorate it as an event of colonial contact against which one might honor the Philippine peoples' centuries of anticolonial victories. Through an exploration of visual imagery and artwork created to remember 1521—in the examples of, first, the baptismal imagery promoted by the Catholic Bishops' Conference of the Philippines for celebrations of 500 Years of Christianity, and second, the Philippines' governmentally sponsored Quincentennial Art Competition—this essay analyzes the colonialist and nationalist narratives of Philippine history through which the quincentennial has been framed and examines the harmful consequences of both. Next, this essay considers the diverse works of art displayed at the Pintô Art Museum's *History of Struggle* exhibition as examples of artistic creations that resist consolidation into a coherent grand narrative. Inspired by this exhibition, Sarita E. See's use of archipelagic metaphor, Nelson Maldonado-Torres's explanation of colonial heterogeneity, and Emilie Townes's account of countermemory, this essay proposes an archipelagic approach to the Philippine quincentennial that rejects colonialist and nationalist grand narratives. Developed from and with attention to a Filipino American positionality, yet with hopes of expansive adaptability for others contending with the entangled histories of Christianity and colonialism, this archipelagic approach offers an alternative means through which the quincentennial might be remembered and its significance contended with in the present.

Colonial Gift, Colonial Debt:
Narratives of Christianity's Arrival in the Philippines

In *Brown Skin, White Minds: Filipino-/American Postcolonial Psychology*, E. J. R. David challenges the persistence of colonial myths. One of these myths, labeled "The Golden Legend," involves the belief that Spain colonizers "civilized" the once-savage Filipinos through "the gifts of Spanish culture and Catholicism."[3]

---

[3]E. J. R. David, *Brown Skin, White Minds: Filipino-/American Postcolonial Psychology (with commentaries)* (Charlotte, NC: Information Age, 2013), 20.

The message of this colonial myth is that Philippine peoples "had nothing before Western colonialism" and therefore owe a debt to their colonizers.[4] Today, the Philippines is frequently characterized as a majority-Catholic nation, and Catholicism continues to have a strong influence on many Filipino and diasporic-Filipino lives, but David cautions that unnuanced narratives of Spain "gifting" Catholicism to the Philippines serve to reinforce a colonial myth.[5]

Fernando C. Amorsolo, *The First Baptism in the Philippines*, 1949. Reproduced by permission of the Filipinas Heritage Library.

The narrative of Christianity's origins in the Philippines conveyed by the Catholic Bishops' Conference of the Philippines (CBCP), evident in baptismal imagery used to represent the theme of "Gifted to Give" chosen for the quincentennial celebrations, reinforces the idea of Catholicism being a gift from Magellan and his crew. The "500 Years of Christianity" logo on Gifted to Give websites, which draws from a scene depicted within Fernando Amorsolo's painting *The First Baptism in the Philippines* (1949),[6] prominently features the cross that Magellan planted

---

[4]Ibid., 13, 76.

[5]Ibid., 13–14. Also see Ricky Manalo, "A Look at 500 Years of Christianity in the Philippines—and Counting!" *Catholic Review*, March 25, 2021, https://catholicreview.org. According to Paulist priest Ricky Manalo, eight in ten Filipinos profess a Catholic faith.

[6]Fernando C. Amorsolo, *The First Baptism in the Philippines*, 1949,

on the island of Cebu.[7] The vertical beam of the cross marks a central line through the logo. On its left side is a kneeling figure with brown skin and a face turned away from the viewer. On its right is a standing European priest with a calm facial expression and a gaze directed toward the sky. One of his hands points upward, and he extends his other to the kneeling figure. Behind the two figures is the Philippine sun derived from the Philippine flag, and beneath them is a ship for which Magellan's cross functions doubly as the mast.[8]

The various Gifted to Give websites explain that the scene from Amorsolo on which the logo is based presents the baptism of Rajah Humabon of Cebu by Magellan's accompanying priest, Father Pedro de Valderrama.[9] As in the logo, the original scene in Amorsolo's painting depicts Indigenous Philippine peoples positioned in postures of reception and attention as the European priest administers a baptismal ceremony. The sky appears bright, and the blue waters of the ocean are populated by large ships in the background of the painting. A red flag flows in the wind and frames the raised face of Pedro de Valderrama, marking him—rather than Humabon—as the work's focal figure. While sunlight falls on the priest's uplifted countenance, Humabon's facial expression is turned away from the viewer and cast in shadow.[10]

The bishops' conference distinguishes the arrival of Christianity from colonization;[11] however, when framed by Gifted to Give messaging, the logo and the painting that inspired it appear to convey a colonial gift narrative involving benevolent Spanish activity and Philippine receptivity. The CBCP's 2021 pastoral

---

oil painting on canvas, 34½ x 51½ inches, Insular Life—FGU Collection, Filipinas Heritage Library, Makati City, Philippines (reproduction: painting, photographed by the Ayala Museum Research Team). A clearer image of the painting may be seen at https://www.filipinaslibrary.org.

[7]"Philippine Church Releases Logo for 500 Years of Christianity," *Vatican News*, September 23, 2019, https://www.vaticannews.va.

[8]Ibid. An image of the logo may be seen at https://500yoc.com.

[9]Marvin Mejia, "1521–2021: 500 Years of Christianity (YoC) in Cebu," Gifted to Give (Archdiocese of Cebu), https://500yoccebu.ph, and "About: 500 Years of Christianity," Gifted to Give (Archdiocese of Toronto), www.ph500toronto.com.

[10]Amorsolo, *The First Baptism in the Philippines*.

[11]"Philippine Church Releases Logo."

letter about the quincentennial, which provides additional textual context for the interpretation of this baptismal imagery, reinforces this narrative: "Five centuries ago we received the marvelous gift of the Christian faith; our hearts overflow with joy and gratitude."[12] Additionally, the Gifted to Give website attributes the Philippines' historical progress to the institutions developed by early Christian missionaries.[13] The most prominent message conveyed by the Gifted to Give theme is that through the introduction of Christianity, the Philippines received a gift from Magellan and his crew, for which Filipinos ought to express gratitude and joy in the present. The narrative underlying the CBCP's visual imagery, as deployed to represent this message, approaches that of the Golden Legend.

David writes that the colonial myth of the Golden Legend has led to the development of a colonial mentality among Philippine peoples and diasporic Filipinos, a form of internalized oppression in which the oppressed feel a sense of inferiority in relation to their oppressor and may accept historical injustices as "the natural cost for progress or civilization."[14] As David explains, colonial debt—a psychological experience in which one feels grateful for colonization and "indebted toward their past colonizers"—remains one of colonial mentality's overt manifestations.[15] Although it is true that Catholicism in the Philippines has not only served colonial ends but has also historically received anticolonial and anti-oppressive expression,[16] overly simplified narratives of Christianity being a gift from European colonizers contribute to feelings of colonial debt in the present. David's work on the healing of internalized oppression emphasizes that critiques of colonialist narratives and the promotion of more nuanced views of Philippine history

---

[12]Romulo G. Valles, "CBCP Pastoral Letter for the 2021 Year of *Missio Ad Gentes*: Becoming Jesus' Missionary Disciples," *CBCP News*, November 29, 2020, https://cbcpnews.net.

[13]"500 Years of Christianity in the Philippines: The Elements," Gifted to Give, https://500yoc.com.

[14]David, *Brown Skin, White Minds*, 19, 70.

[15]Ibid., 76.

[16]For instance, see Rebecca C. Asedillo and B. David Williams, eds., *Rice in the Storm: Faith in Struggle in the Philippines* (New York: Friendship Press, 1989), and Kathleen M. Nadeau, *Liberation Theology in the Philippines: Faith in a Revolution* (Manila: De La Salle University Press, 2004).

play a vital role in the unlearning of colonial mentality and the facilitation of antiracist collective empowerment.[17]

In addition to acknowledging and challenging the psychological impact of colonial gift narratives of Christianity, critiques of the myth of the Golden Legend also prompt a recognition of the ways that the narrative of the Philippines being a Catholic nation has historically resulted in harmful consequences for inhabitants of the archipelago who do not claim a Christian faith or who do not adhere to the official stances of its Catholic leadership. As noted in the *New York Times*, the Philippines is "the only state aside from the Vatican that still bans divorce," and the Catholic bishops' conference there has long opposed reproductive healthcare and sex education initiatives.[18] Activists in the Philippines have protested the inaccessibility of contraception for families in precarious financial situations and warned of the danger posed to women by their inability to leave abusive marriages.[19] The imagination of the Philippines as a Catholic nation has also fueled acts of internal colonialism against Indigenous peoples and the predominantly Muslim peoples of the Philippines' southern islands, as scholars analyzing racial-religious hierarchies in the Philippines have noted.[20] Awareness of the continued prevalence of colonial mentality, harmful policies, and the enduring existence of internal colonialism reveals a need for approaching uncritically celebratory narratives of the Philippine quincentennial with caution.

[17]David, *Brown Skin, White Minds*, 178, 196.

[18]Jason Gutierrez and Amisha Padnani, "Carlos Celdran, 46, Philippine Activist and Performance Artist, Dies," *New York Times*, published October 11, 2019, and updated October 14, 2019, www.nytimes.com.

[19]Ibid., and Menchu Macapagal and VJ Bacungan, "Gabriela Refiles Divorce Bill," *CNN Philippines*, published August 3, 2016, and updated August 4, 2016, https://cnnphilippines.com.

[20]For instance, see Tisa Wenger, "Making Empire in the Philippines: Filipinos, Moros, and the Ambivalence of Religious Freedom," in *Religious Freedom: The Contested History of an American Ideal* (Chapel Hill: University of North Carolina Press, 2017), 54–100, and Paul A. Kramer, *The Blood of Government: Race, Empire, the United States, and the Philippines* (Chapel Hill: University of North Carolina Press, 2006), esp. 160–163. My usage of the term "racial-religious" follows Wenger in *Religious Freedom*.

Victory and Humanity: Nationalist Narratives
in the Quincentennial Commemorations

In 2018, Philippine President Rodrigo Duterte created the National Quincentennial Committee (NQC) to oversee the nation's 2021 commemorations of the Magellan-Elcano expedition's arrival, Lapulapu's victory over Magellan at the Battle of Mactan, and other historical events that took place from 1519 to 1522.[21] Although the introduction of Christianity is listed as one of the major historical events to be commemorated,[22] the title of "500 Years of Victory and Humanity" provided by the committee reveals a reliance on a different narrative framing than that employed by the bishops' conference—one that emphasizes nationalism and patriotism rather than the reception of colonial gifts.[23]

In their comprehensive plan, members of the NQC indicated their desire to ensure that commemorations would be "Filipino-centric," "pro-Filipino," and historically grounded.[24] The committee's first listed aim is to implement projects that "[r]einvigorate Filipino nationalism, unity, and international comity through history, culture, and media."[25] One event designed to realize this aim was the Quincentennial Art Competition, which called for representational paintings on the themes of sovereignty, magnanimity, unity, and legacy, and offered cash prizes equivalent to approximately US$10,000 to the grand winners of each category.[26] The competition's specification of delineated themes provided a

---

[21]National Quincentennial Committee of the Republic of the Philippines, "Comprehensive Plan for the National Quincentennial Commemoration of the Victory at Mactan and Related Events," ed. Rene R. Escalante, printed by the National Historical Commission of the Philippines (Malacañang, Manila, Philippines: January 28, 2019), xi and 4, https://nqc.gov.ph. For consistency, this essay follows the NQC's spelling of "Lapulapu."

[22]Ibid., xi.

[23]National Quincentennial Committee Secretariat, "Victory and Humanity," Quincentennial Commemorations in the Philippines, August 27, 2021, https://nqc.gov.ph.

[24]National Quincentennial Committee, "Comprehensive Plan," xi, 11.

[25]Ibid., 4, 9.

[26]"About the Quincentennial Art Competition" and "Quincentennial Art Competition: Guidelines," Quincentennial Commemorations in the Philippines, https://nqc.gov.ph.

means of ensuring that winning artworks provided clear depictions of scenes including Queen Juana's reception of the *Santo Niño* in Cebu, the Philippine peoples' compassion and contributions to world navigation, and "the gallantry of Lapulapu and his warriors."[27]

Matthius B. Garcia, *Hindi Pasisiil,* 2021. Copyright © 2021 by Matthius B. Garcia. Reprinted with permission.

Winning paintings from the competition, including Matthius B. Garcia's *Hindi Pasisiil* (or *"Never to Be Conquered"*),[28] have received international praise for "flip[ping] colonial history on its head by focusing on Indigenous resistance" and offering a Philippines-centered perspective that counters imperial versions of history.[29] Unlike Amorsolo's baptismal scene, in which benevolent Europeans gift Christianity to Indigenous Philippine peoples,

---

[27]Ibid.

[28]Matthius B. Garcia, *Hindi Pasisiil,* 2021, oil on canvas, 3 x 4 feet. Image from Garcia, attached in e-mail message to author, June 28, 2022. A clearer image of the painting may be seen at the Quincentennial Art Competition website at https://nqc.gov.ph.

[29]Kate Fullagar and Kristie Patricia Flannery, "Ferdinand Magellan's Death 500 Years Ago Is Being Remembered as an Act of Indigenous Resistance," *The Conversation,* April 25, 2021, https://theconversation.com.

Garcia's painting depicts a beach battle in which Lapulapu leads "a force of Indigenous warriors to defeat Magellan's crew—and the Spanish threat to their sovereignty."[30] As in Amorsolo's painting, a splash of red color frames the face of the work's central figure. The story that Garcia conveys, however, is imagined with an Indigenous protagonist in mind. In *Hindi Pasisiil*, Lapulapu's expression of determination and heroic rage is prominently illuminated by the glow of a torchlight, while the facial expressions of Magellan and his men are de-emphasized and scarcely perceptible, cast in the shadows of smoke clouds and helmet brims.[31] Garcia's painting offers a decisively anti-Spanish-colonial image that rejects the Golden Legend of colonial gifts. Positioned within the context of the NQC's efforts to strengthen nationalism and unity, however, the framing of the image by the themes outlined by the Quincentennial Art Competition also allows it to be mobilized in support of a "pro-Filipino" nationalist narrative.

Although the NQC's approach challenges colonialist grand narratives by centering the subjectivity and agency of peoples of the Philippines, its patriotic and nationalistic narrative framing of the quincentennial introduces other dangers. Journalists and academics have long critiqued the Philippine government for "silencing 'unpatriotic' criticism of national leaders," rendering contemporary movements for Indigenous peoples' autonomy and sovereignty invisible, sustaining "threats and attacks against critics and human rights defenders," and discouraging dissent.[32] In a column discussing the remembrance of the quincentennial, artist Igan D'Bayan comments on the frequent use of revisionary histories to support dictatorships and anti-democratic propaganda: "History is malleable, dictators know this. Stalin was a walking Adobe Photoshop: having enemies erased from photographs and having them deleted from existence. . . . Revising history has become an integral part of the modus operandi of politicians."[33] Although

---

[30]Ibid.

[31]Garcia, *Hindi Pasisiil*.

[32]Fullagar and Flannery, "Ferdinand Magellan's Death," and "For Many Filipinos, Maria Ressa's Nobel Prize Win Is More Than Just an Award," *Rappler*, December 12, 2021, www.rappler.com.

[33]Igan D'Bayan, "The History of Struggle Is a Struggle against Oblivion," *Philippine Star*, May 29, 2021, https://philstarlife.com.

the remembrance of histories of anticolonial resistance is vital for countering colonial gift narratives, triumphalist nationalist narratives that only allow space for anticolonial victories serve to project an image of Philippine strength that predicates itself on the concealment of ongoing stories of oppression, struggle, and dissent within the archipelago.

Scholars such as historian Vicente Rafael have warned against the simplistic replacement of colonialist grand narratives with nationalistic ones. Rafael critiques the ways that nationalist narratives of Philippine history, while capable of inspiring acts of anticolonial resistance, have also historically "provided an alibi for self-serving collaboration with new regimes and the systematic repression of those opposed to them."[34] Additionally, in turning to diasporic Filipinos, Rafael cautions against the ways that nationalism has so often provided the "language" for efforts to organize against racism and challenge colonialism's legacies. He emphasizes that nationalism relies on a homogenized and commodified view of "Filipino identity" that "situates Filipinos abroad in a touristic—that is to say, neocolonial—relationship with the Filipinos at home."[35] While nationalist commemorations of the quincentennial may appear to provide an empowering anticolonial alternative to the Golden Legend, such commemorations construct another grand narrative that risks reinforcing dynamics of internal colonialism and neocolonialism, as well as obscuring or silencing the anti-oppressive efforts pursued by minoritized groups within the archipelago.

Countermemory: An Archipelagic Approach to the History[/ies] of Struggle

Conscious of the dangers of both colonialist and nationalist grand narratives, the remainder of this essay develops an alternative "archipelagic" approach to the Philippine quincentennial and applies this approach to the recognition of expressions of countermemory present at the Pintô Art Museum's *History of*

---

[34]Vicente L. Rafael, "Introduction: Episodic Histories," in *White Love and Other Events in Filipino History* (Durham, NC: Duke University Press, 2000), 13.
[35]Ibid., 13–14.

Struggle exhibition. As Filipino American scholar Sarita E. See notes, Filipino and Filipino American theorists have frequently drawn from the metaphor of the archipelago.[36] In her own work, See advances an "archipelagic sensibility" for contending with the "wild heterogeneity" of the Philippines and its diasporas, a heterogeneity that exists in terms of gender, sexuality, race, religion, culture, and the multiplicity of colonial histories. She argues that attention to these heterogeneous particularities is necessary for opening up alternatives to "the fundamental tension between anti-imperialist collective action and the exclusionary practices of any group formation."[37] This essay's constructive framework, developed from a Filipino American positionality, references and situates itself within the Filipino and diasporic-Filipino theoretical tradition cited by See in taking up the term "archipelagic." This usage is not intended to posit any singular perspective as universally valid or to imply that archipelagic metaphors are always or exclusively applicable for those with heritage from the Philippines. Rather, inspired by See's application of the metaphor, I view archipelagic imagery as helpful for visualizing the breaking-apart of homogenizing grand narratives and attending to heterogeneity and particularity.

In attending to the heterogeneity of the Philippines and its diasporas, I draw from Nelson Maldonado-Torres's discussion of colonial heterogeneity from his essay "Liberation Theology and the Search for the Lost Paradigm." Following Walter Mignolo, Maldonado-Torres argues that a critical response to the structures of colonial difference must involve an analysis of colonial heterogeneity, which in his explanation involves "a set of interrelated forms of oppressions articulated not only through class but through race and gender as well."[38] In response to the historical exclusions enacted by elite mestizo formations of Latin American liberation theology, he proposes a decolonial perspective that

---

[36]Sarita Echavez See, *Decolonized Eye: Filipino American Art and Performance* (Minneapolis: University of Minnesota Press, 2009), xxx.

[37]Ibid., xxx, 124–125.

[38]Nelson Maldonado-Torres, "Liberation Theology and the Search for the Lost Paradigm: From Radical Orthodoxy to Radical Diversality," in *Latin American Liberation Theology: The Next Generation*, ed. Ivan Petrella (Maryknoll, NY: Orbis Books, 2005), 46–47, 55.

would advance epistemic justice by privileging the experiences of women, Black and Indigenous peoples, and non-Christians whose struggles have been treated as peripheral.[39] Although this essay speaks to a different geographic context, its archipelagic approach strives to take seriously Maldonado-Torres's proposals and to contribute to decolonial conversations from a perspective also shaped by legacies of Spanish colonialism. Resistance against grand narratives of Philippine history requires a recognition of the uneven impact of Spanish colonization within the archipelago and attention to the particularities that have formed through differentiations of class, race, gender, and religion.

In constructively applying an archipelagic approach to narrative, this essay is inspired by Emilie Townes's account of countermemory. In *Womanist Ethics and the Cultural Production of Evil*, Townes works within a tradition of womanist ethical reflection, which begins with a focus on the radical particularity of Black women's lives before moving outward toward the expansive consideration of the particularities of others, an expansion informed by the knowledge that "the story of Black women's moral lives . . . can only be understood in relation to other stories."[40] Townes's womanist attention to particularity allows her to reveal both history and memory as subjective, ideological constructions that too often exclude marginalized voices and lives from their narratives.[41] In response to such exclusions, Townes proposes countermemory as a subversive strategy that counters essentialism and seeks "to force a reconsideration of flawed (incomplete or vastly circumscribed) histories."[42] Countermemory reconstitutes history "such that we begin to see, hear, and appreciate the diversities within our midst as flesh and blood rather than as cloying distractions."[43] In Townes's account, justice requires attending to the particularities of those who are most marginalized and resisting exclusionary, oppressive, and universalizing narratives.[44] With recognition of

---

[39]Ibid., 55, 57.

[40]Emilie M. Townes, *Womanist Ethics and the Cultural Production of Evil* (New York: Palgrave Macmillan, 2006), 23.

[41]Ibid., 16–17.

[42]Ibid., 8, 53.

[43]Ibid., 7–8.

[44]Ibid., 135, 138.

the wide-ranging significance of Townes's approach to history and memory, this essay imagines her constructive theoretical work in dialogue with other particularities, applying her strategy of countermemory to the context of Philippine quincentennial commemorations. In attending to colonial heterogeneity and the existence of diverse particularities, especially the marginalized particularities so often excluded from grand narratives, this essay's archipelagic approach seeks to recognize and prioritize expressions of countermemory.

Ambie Abaño, "*. . . reza por ellas de las Filipinas, rezar por las Filipinas . . .* ," 2021. Copyright © 2021 by Ambie Abaño. Reproduced with permission.

Many expressions of countermemory can be located in the exhibition *A History of Struggle: Philippine Art Remembers 1521* that was displayed in the summer of 2021 at the Pintô Art Museum in the Philippine city of Antipolo. The exhibition, curated by Patrick Flores, featured works by contemporary artists that addressed topics such as the travels of Magellan, the victory of Lapulapu at Mactan, and the beginnings of Catholicism's presence in the archipelago. Unlike the Quincentennial Art Competition, however, the exhibition did not impose restrictions based on artistic medium and did not require that artworks present a patriotic historical narrative. Instead, Flores selected artists whose works engaged the relations among "image and reality, narrative and so-called fact" and who, from their own diverse commitments and positionalities, offered reflections "on the entangled history of colonization, Christianization, and struggle of all kinds between then and now."[45] Artists responded heterogeneously to the events surrounding 1521 through creative and critical uses of "allegory, counter-history, [and] alternative mythology" presented through a wide range of media. Their artworks offered expressions of rage, grief, frustration, and the imagination of alternative histories and worlds.[46]

One piece displayed in the exhibition was Ambie Abaño's woodcut on canvas created with collage, acrylic, and cut-outs, titled "*. . . reza por ellas de las Filipinas, rezar por las Filipinas . . .* " (or "*. . . pray for the women of the Philippines, pray for the Philippines . . .*"). The piece features the black/sepia-and-white portrait of a Filipino woman's face in order to center, as Abaño explains, those "who suffered most the oppression in the time of colonization."[47] According to Abaño, the piece draws from the concept of the estampita, a holy card with a prayer, but in contrast to a typical estampita that bears the image of a religious figure to whom a prayer is addressed, Abaño's artwork is "representative of the one who needs to be prayed for."[48] Abaño's sword-and-crosses imagery, in which small crosses crown the woman and a sword is positioned vertically in her forehead, challenges colonial gift narratives of Christianity in its representation of the long-

---

[45]Igan D'Bayan, "The History of Struggle Is a Struggle against Oblivian," *The Phillipine Star*, May 29, 2021.

[46]Ibid.

[47]Ambie [Ma. Victoria] Abaño, email correspondence with author, June 29, 2022.

[48]Ibid.

term effects of intergenerational trauma.[49] The woman carved by Abaño stares directly into the eyes of the viewer as if to call for acknowledgment, repentance, and action against the future transmission of such trauma. By presenting the face of a Filipino woman and refusing to frame her anticolonial critique through the proposal of a triumphalist nationalist narrative, Abaño's art resists categorization into either the colonialist or nationalist grand narrative and instead challenges both.

Understood through the archipelagic approach of this essay, Abaño's piece and other artworks displayed in the *History of Struggle* exhibition may be recognized as expressions of countermemory that push for a reimagining of the events of 1521. Through their heterogeneous explorations of particularities so often excluded from colonialist or nationalist grand narratives, the works of this exhibition break apart exclusionary, oppressive accounts of history and call for their reconstitution. They offer an alternative to simplistic celebratory narratives that fail to contend with the complicated role of Christianity in colonial histories, or that conceal minoritized communities' ongoing stories of harm and resistance. For Filipino American Christians and those of other positionalities seeking to grapple with the legacies of moments like the Philippine quincentennial, an archipelagic attention to countermemory provides a starting point from which questions of decoloniality, religion, and justice might be explored in the present.

---

[49]Ibid.

PART II

EMBODIED PEDAGOGY

AND SPIRITUALITY

Recentering the Theological Canon and the Future of Religious Education

Emilie M. Townes

i think we must develop enhanced, or better yet, new models of theological education that do not hold racism as a problem distinct from our scholarship and teaching

> but rather it is a deeply theological conundrum that we must integrate into our work with vigor

>> yes, it will be hard and painful; but i argue that it will free us if we take it on and will eventually bring us to joy and relevance

> this new model begins by considering what it is that students and faculties need to learn in order to respond to the kind of racisms that think little of killing old folks and young folks, praying folks, dancing folks, learning folks, and more

>> we are in a world of fast-paced change and a sometimes-stagnant status quo—an enigma if there ever was one

>> of wars and peace agreements

>> of protests and stand your ground

>> of justice and no peace

income inequality and conspicuous consumption

food deserts and gourmet grocers

poverty and wealth

"isms" abounding and works of justice-making and more

i suggest that we lay down our brains and intellect as our *first* move in tackling racism

instead, i encourage us to begin by practicing antiracist behavior and scholarship that will help us pick up our scholarship in fresh ways that deepen it, ripen it to face the challenges of our day and the worlds that enter our classrooms that want to learn and grow

and let me hasten to say that i am not arguing for throwing out the various disciplines that make up theological education

what i *am* arguing for is the need to put our actions first and then pour our considerable mental power into how to theorize and explicate the intent and effect of our actions

many of us here

and throughout the whole of the academy

have been told to live in split, if not fractured bodies

to deny the gift that God gives us body and soul

to treat our bodies as suspect

almost illegal

and worse—illicit

and sometimes you and i have been told this is holy

we must refuse to rip ourselves apart or to invite colleagues and students to perform this demonic shake dance

> based on a notion of universals that are really particulars that are threatening not to sit next to you, me, or others in a scholarly pew that is little more than a postmodern auction block

we must look for spaces—faithfully, rigorously, methodologically, and theologically—to understand how and why gender, class, race, sexuality, and more are deeply theological and moral categories that should command our attention

> because they do affect our work profoundly

>> it matters that kierkegaard had an overbearing father and that the niebuhrs survived an abusive one

>> it matters that luther had bowel problems

>> it matters that nietzsche was a pampered only son

>> it matters that tillich had a rather healthy libido

>> it matters that kant had racist ideas and eventually moved to a more egalitarian worldview

>> it matters that wittgenstein felt the power of his argument or the lack of a decent argument in others that he could be driven to near violence

these are not things that we should treat as interesting points we drop into our lectures to keep students' attention

> they represent the thick isness of life and thought

> and who we are and what we have become and are becoming in our work and in the work of others

these are the dancing minds we inherit and we become their interlocutors as the generations behind us will become ours and this makes all of us human and perhaps even humane

as we engage the work of recentering the theological canon

this is why we must try to hold ourselves accountable for the methods and modes of our scholarship as well as its content (or lack of it) and subject matter when it comes to race and the whole matrix of oppression that gets formed by living in the unexamined hegemonic imagination

i urge us to make better and more healthy use of our time by learning new things as we practice reading new material, diverse material, material that throws us off balance like our early days in the classroom as students

because we have placed ourselves in the role of learners once again

and we have to admit that although we know many things, there is so much more to know and incorporate in our work

and just like the study groups we formed as students, form them again with colleagues and other scholars who want to be a part of doing the new, the relevant, the necessary

because we are in a world of trouble and what we don't know about race, income, gender, sexual orientation, sexuality, age, and more are literally killing folks—if not ourselves

we must, absolutely must, walk away from the scholarship of death and destruction that is so terrified of the complexity of existence that it shapes answers before hearing the questions

it crafts reading lists that look like the high side of misery

it sanctions curricula that believe it's a good thing to segregate the mind, body, and spirit

it rolls over and plays dead when faced with disasters—natural and human-made it tries to respond to life and living but spends too much time primping in front of funhouse mirrors of academic jabber- wocky

. . . .

let me suggest 2 challenges

THE FIRST CHALLENGE: CAN WE BE FAITHFUL REPRE- SENTATIVES OF THE GOSPEL AND HAVE SUCCESS BE THE ONLY WORD IN OUR VOCABULARY?

the agenda of scholarship and ministry (lay or ordained)

> must be more than the number of students in our programs

> more than being the influential voice in professional meetings and gatherings

> more than the number of placements we do

> the number of local churches, parishes, and agencies associated with our seminaries or departments

these concerns are minor notes to our world of chaos and hope

> yes, they are important in the life of any school, *but they are not the heart of our ministry*

education means we are more concerned about those who come to our doors seeking to discern and answer their call

> and yes, even the ones who are simply there to get the piece of paper

our curricula, which are also our ministries and profound theo- logical statements, must be, where they are not, an active witness

> to the power of God working *in life* to change us body, mind, and soul

there is much to contend with if we are to know the promise of
our call

> and we cannot deal with the kinds of principalities and pow-
> ers we face

> by remaining focused only on the next institutional move as
> if this is the only reason why we are in theological education

we have to look for partners in the struggle

> they may come in different colors

> they may come with different agendas

> they may come with a variety of gifts and liabilities

> and they may well be other faith traditions

CHALLENGE TWO: WHAT ARE WE DOING FOR OUR SPIRITUAL HEALTH?

in all the ways we can get in touch with the spirit

> are we telling ourselves and others

>> that we are less than

>> and not even realizing it

are we seeking to draw closer to God or are we using faith to
abuse ourselves and others

living and working in partnership requires joy and hard work

> it takes tolerance and conviction

> it demands love and stubbornness

such a daunting task

does not just happen one-to-another

it means giving ourselves

some slack

while we demand the very best of who we are

and who we hope to become with God's grace

taking time to sort through

your center

to explore your deepest longings

your most heartfelt needs

means doing so

in the context of a community of faith

you must return to

and help mold

let's move toward experientially *and* intellectually embracing a new future, a more robust theological canon that is more vibrant, more life bringing and giving, more welcoming, more humane

more alive with possibilities that engage others and ourselves

hell, i love what i do and it is nothing but sheer and utter joy to walk into the classroom and see what we will learn

to have the time and space to have a sustained thought and to have it long enough to recognize its strengths and weaknesses

to work with faculty colleagues on joint projects or to be a listening ear or guiding voice with them as they work through a tough classroom situation or research idea or how to get published or how to survive

to work with administrators and staff to create and maintain a structure where students and staff can do their best work and be challenged and find some measure of nurture

to spend time with younger scholars and be thankful to God almighty that the next generation *is* coming and i should get ready to retire and let it and you step to the fore

because regardless of how tough it gets some days, i am encouraged to live my work with joy, to always keep the learning wheel turning, and to remind myself that i want to be *very* old when i die

because dying of old age is the ultimate ornery womanist move

Table Work as Antiracist Spirituality

Reflections on *Untitled Othello*,
Embodied Pedagogy, and Spiritual Productivity

Charles A. Gillespie,
Emily Bryan, and Rachel E. Bauer

Can one discover a route toward an antiracist spirituality by
reading a nontheological text?[1] What if that text operates as a
whitewashed "classic" of the literary canon? In order for antiracist
practices to be considered "productive," the drive toward a white
capitalist product needs to be resisted.[2] Work to decenter whiteness requires unlearning that pressure for a finished product. This
essay has two key goals and emerges from a much larger and still
ongoing collaborative project.[3] First, the essay will introduce, in

---

[1]We are indebted to and thankful for co-conspirators far too numerous to
list who make this continuing collaboration possible, including our anonymous reviewers. We approach antiracism along the lines articulated by George
J. Sefa Dei as an "action-oriented strategy for institutional systemic change
that addresses racism and other interlocking systems of social oppression.
Antiracism explicitly names the issues of race and social difference as issues
of power and equity, rather than as matters of cultural and ethnic variety."
George J. Sefa Dei, "Critical Perspectives in Antiracism: An Introduction,"
Canadian Review of Sociology / Revue Canadienne de Sociologie 33, no. 3
(1996): 252.

[2]In choosing to capitalize "Black" but not "white" in this essay, we follow
the *Untitled Othello* Project's conventions.

[3]The three of us teach in different departments, but we share interests
in theatre. We have increasingly sought ways to collaborate around what

broad strokes, the *Untitled Othello* Project (UOP) via its 2021 residency at Sacred Heart University.[4] The second aim of the essay is to offer a theologically informed framework for thinking about UOP's table work as a model for an embodied pedagogy that invites an antiracist spirituality.

UOP is an open ensemble of professional actors led by the project's founder and director, Keith Hamilton Cobb, and associate director, Jessica Burr, working on the Shakespeare play purportedly about "the Moor of Venice." *Othello* remains a staple of the anglophone theatrical, literary, and curricular canon, but the script features overt anti-Black racism, rampant misogyny, and xenophobia. The play's performance history makes a well-documented contribution to the formation of the racial imaginary.[5] But contemporary productions of *Othello* rarely, if ever, manage to tell Othello's story in Shakespeare's words without also recirculating the play's violent and dehumanizing treatment of its characters, its performers, and its audiences. Ayanna Thompson makes this argument in an episode of National Public Radio's *Code Switch*.[6] Thompson argues that *Othello* should no longer be performed, and that it causes psychological damage to the actors who play *Othello*. Yet she maintains that studying the play in an academic context may be profitable. UOP holds out hope for a more humane meaning in performances of this play

---

we call the "dramatic humanities"—attention to dramatic literatures and performance practices as productive of knowledge and skills that are human centered and text based.

[4]Please visit www.untitledothello.com to learn more about them.

[5]See Dennis Austin Britton, *Becoming Christian: Race, Reformation, and Early Modern English Romance* (New York: Fordham University Press, 2014); Urvashi Chakravarty, *Fictions of Consent: Slavery, Servitude, and Free Service in Early Modern England* (Philadelphia: University of Pennsylvania Press, 2022); Imtiaz Habib, "Othello, Sir Peter Negro, and the Blacks of Early Modern England: Colonial Inscription and Postcolonial Excavation," *Lit: Literature Interpretation Theory* 9, no. 1 (1998): 15–30; Kim F. Hall, "Virtual Book Club: Othello Was My Grandfather: Shakespeare, Race, and Visions of Freedom in the African Diaspora," http://nationalhumanitiescenter.org; Arthur J. Little, "'An Essence That's Not Seen': The Primal Scene of Racism in Othello," *Shakespeare Quarterly* 44, no. 3 (Autumn 1993): 304–324; Ayanna Thompson, *Passing Strange: Shakespeare, Race, and Contemporary America* (New York: Oxford, 2013).

[6]Gene Demby and Shereen Marisol Meraji, "All That Glisters Is Not Gold," *CodeSwitch*, podcast audio, August 19, 2021, https://www.npr.org/.

through its unique table work method, which is deeply informed by humanist practices.

The *Untitled Othello* Residency:
Providing a Room Where It Happens

At the end of September 2021, Dr. Emily Bryan connected with Keith Hamilton Cobb, a professional actor and the creator of a play called *American Moor*.[7] The play features a middle-aged Black actor reflecting on his audition to play the role of Othello for a white director half his age. Could theatre help counter the gravitational pull of whiteness away from uncomfortable conversations about race? Why not use this contemporary play about Shakespeare to ask pressing contemporary questions about race and our life together? Instead, Cobb shared about his latest project: *Untitled Othello*. Here, Cobb envisions a search for whether a more humane production of *Othello* is even possible by slowly, deliberately, and deeply reading and interrogating the script. Cobb's descriptions of the project, its goals, and some clips are readily available on the project's website: www.untitledothello.com.

Shakespeare's *Othello* claims an authorial figure coded as a white English poet and perpetuates (perhaps even inaugurates) many racist, misogynist, and colonial tropes.[8] (Similar arguments can be made about misogyny in *Taming of the Shrew* and anti-Judaism in *Merchant of Venice*.)[9] The script fates this great Black character to be duped by Iago and to murder his wife, Desdemona, on stage, in full view of a complicit and conventionally silent audience. To perform *Othello* seems to recycle and uncritically sanction images of violent Blackness, imperial grandeur, forced conversion, erasures of women's agency, and punished love. To stage *Othello* in our moment means potential replication and

---

[7]See https://americanmoor.com.

[8]On professional actors grappling with *Othello*, see Catherine Conroy, "There's a Whole Group of Black Actors Who Won't Do Othello," *Irish Times*, June 1, 2016, https://www.irishtimes.com.

[9]Eric Brinkman claims that Iago was never the leading man of the play until Black actors took on the role of Othello instead of white actors in blackface. See "Iago as the Racist Function in *Othello*," *Shakespeare Bulletin* 40, no. 1 (2022): 23–44.

perpetuation of these problematic images. If the play is infected by racism, then gathering to perform the play simply risks a superspreader event. Some might think it better to keep such contagion isolated and hermetically sealed in the sterility of a textual laboratory. Scholars and classrooms can continue to study this canonical text, but too much danger arises when bodies give breath to Shakespeare's words.

Cobb holds a decidedly different view. While he acknowledges that the play could be too toxic to stage, he wants to find out for himself. He opened the *Untitled Othello* residency with a reflection on the construction of a "safe space" open to "authentic discussion, unflinching dialogue" that "includes everybody in the room."[10] In addition to acting the words of the script, participants were to pause and discuss these words' meanings both historically and for the present community. Could or should the word "Moor," for instance, carry the weight of our era's worst racial slurs? "Nothing about Shakespeare's *Othello* is comfortable," Cobb explained, and the work needed to confront the linkages between the racism recognizable in Shakespeare's text and the racism experienced in our contemporary world.[11] That is, the play's language reflects racist attitudes and behaviors that persist in ways that can be felt by those present in the room.

Performance history, including the legacies of racialized trauma on the American stage, plays a major role. UOP responds not only to the inherited language of the Shakespeare script but also the systems and contexts of production that have performed this play for centuries. Historically, the role of Othello has been played by countless white actors in blackface. According to Ayanna Thompson, "*Othello* was one of the most popular plays on the early American stage, but there were various other popular plays that contained Black characters who were portrayed by white actors."[12] Any encounter with *this* play in the lived context of the United States, then, includes an encounter with its performance

---

[10]Keith Hamilton Cobb, Residency Opening, Sacred Heart University, November 29, 2021. See News Room, "SHU Hosts Playwright, Theatre Residency Program Exploring Shakespeare's 'Othello,' " Sacred Heart University, November 12, 2021, sacredheart.edu.

[11]www.untitledothello.com.

[12]Ayanna Thompson, *Blackface* (New York: Bloomsbury, 2021), 20–21.

history: *Othello* is inextricably linked to the wounds of minstrel shows and recirculating images of violent Black men offered as entertainment, and disturbingly as tortured entertainment.[13]

In a retort and refutation of the performance of a tortured Othello, Cobb favors a methodical process of table work that is being done over the course of three years. UOP avoids rushing the transition from textual study to theatrical production. The phrase "table work" derives from professional theatre practice. Prior to "putting a scene on its feet," actors and directors and designers begin by reading a script together around a table. But the real benefits of table work derive from the fact that it is, by definition, collaborative.[14] In table work, the individual's reflections and intellectual labor collide with the choices and insights of others. Theatre requires the labor of different people—writers, actors, directors, designers, producers, house managers, stage hands, caterers, and others. Table work usually marks the first gathering of the ensemble, an emergent artistic collective more than the sum of its component parts.

As modeled in the Sacred Heart residency, UOP conducts slow, close reading with frequent pauses for conversation, investigation, and re-imagination. Table work has room to breathe. At Sacred Heart, the entire residency was open to student and faculty participation. The residency was recorded on video to be archived at the Folger Shakespeare Library and live-streamed. Across the project's sixty hours around a boardroom table, the ensemble only made it to the first scene of Act II.

Antiracism and Embodied Pedagogy in *Untitled Othello*

The *Untitled Othello* Project's table work offers a pedagogical model that foregrounds the embodied possibilities for reading texts together. Table work can be indistinguishable from certain

---

[13]See Timothy Turner, "Othello on the Rack," *Journal for Early Modern Cultural Studies* 15, no. 3 (July 1, 2015): 102–36.

[14]Table work expands on the "read-through" at the start of a rehearsal process. For one description of table work's benefits in a professional theatrical context, see Kathleen Eddy, "The Power of Theatre," *Stage Directions* (December 2013): 17–19.

forms of seminar-style teaching. Table work invites collaborative close reading and interpretive improvisation in mutual dialogue by showing care for the enfleshed humans performing reading and conversation. In many ways, this form of teaching/theatre echoes bell hooks's approach that values "everyone's presence" and where participants are interested in one another.[15] UOP includes the university community and beyond. Students and faculty alike can sit at the table alongside and with the ensemble. The subject matter for table work is both the script *and* the ensemble. Questions arise not only about what the text means but also about how this script becomes manifest through living bodies in community. Such a manifestation begins "in the room" even as it operates against the horizon of hope for a fully staged performance.

But the work of *Untitled Othello* does not seek a predetermined end: it leaves outcomes open.[16] UOP generates a striking case study for embodiment as the starting point for antiracist teaching and learning. Confronting racial oppression raises complicated and difficult emotions felt in the body.[17] Antiracist work is therefore an ongoing and self-reflexive process for both educators and learners. UOP's "unflinching dialogue" and conversation externalized the process in ways that could be observed and emulated by students.

Antiracist approaches call for overt and critical attention to how racism and white privilege operate structurally, institutionally, and spiritually. Even the most diverse university spaces, like the professional American theatre scene, are not race neutral or "colorblind." Indeed, antiracism work goes further in its response to "institutional whiteness" than praise for the appearance of

---

[15]bell hooks, *Teaching to Transgress: Education as the Practice of Freedom* (New York: Routledge, 1994), 8.

[16]Scholars who reflect on antiracist pedagogy call for educators to resist the temptation to predict a post-racial future; see Karen Teel, "Getting Out of the Left Lane: The Possibility of White Antiracist Pedagogy," *Teaching Theology & Religion* 17, no. 1 (2014): 17. For a critique of journey and road metaphors in antiracist pedagogy, see Audrey Thompson, "Anti-Racist Work Zones," in *Philosophy of Education: 2003*, ed. Kal Alston (Urbana, IL: Philosophy of Education Society, 2004), 387–95.

[17]Anna Floerke Scheid and Elisabeth T. Vasko, "Teaching Race: Pedagogical Challenges in Predominantly White Undergraduate Theology Classrooms," *Teaching Theology & Religion* 17, no. 1 (2014): 31ff.

diversity.[18] Scholarship on antiracist pedagogy explains that work that begins with self-awareness can become an "organizing effort for institutional and social change that is much broader than teaching in the classroom."[19] *Untitled Othello* does not seek an immediate product, but its presence on campus generated immediate questions about racial inclusion and representation at the institutional level. How can a predominantly white institution (whether American theatre or a Catholic college) invite new collaborators to read canonical stories, bodies, and meanings differently?

"A Better Piece of Theatre": Beauty and Justice

Cobb's vision for UOP avoids any recycled production of *Othello*. UOP does not offer a product that may be paid for and consumed by an audience. In the language of its marketing tagline, visible on websites and banners: "with all due reverence to Shakespeare, there is a better piece of theatre to be discovered here, and any number of better ways to give the work, the worker, and the product the justice they deserve."[20] *Untitled Othello* subsists, entirely, in slow, deliberate, and justly compensated table work on the play. As a result, the process seeks to do justice both to Othello the character and justice to the working conditions of the artists making the play. Cobb's gambit remains that such work will produce better theatre.

Critical to Cobb's project is the use of an academic space in conversation with academics who actively pursue antiracist pedagogy. Kim Hall, the author of *Things of Darkness: Economies of Race and Gender in Early Modern England,* wrote the foreword to Cobb's play *American Moor.* As a member of the UOP ensemble, David Sterling Brown, professor at Trinity College and a fellow with Claudia Rankine's Racial Imaginary Institute, provides a pedagogical lineage of antiracist work within the field of early

---

[18]Sara Ahmed, *On Being Included: Racism and Diversity in Institutional Life* (Durham, NC: Duke University Press, 2012).

[19]Kyoko Kishimoto, "Anti-Racist Pedagogy: From Faculty's Self-Reflection to Organizing within and beyond the Classroom," *Race Ethnicity and Education* 21, no. 4 (2018): 540–54.

[20]www.untitledothello.com.

modern studies. Brown's essay, "Things of Darkness: 'The Blue-print of a Methodology,'" reminds scholars of Hall's expansive work to apply Black feminist methodology to the study of early modern literature, echoing Toni Morrison's call in *Playing in the Dark* to attend to whiteness as a racial formation.[21] Hall's epilogue addresses the need of scholarship and pedagogy to reframe its relationship to race:

> Our scholarship on race should be accompanied with a discussion of new teaching strategies and pedagogical issues such as: how in class do we stop regarding only people of color as racial subjects? How do we generate discussions that are intellectually rigorous, historically sensitive, and meaningful to the students' own lives? Regardless of our critical positions or pedagogy, the ethnic composition of the United States and its classrooms is changing. This means that scholar-teachers can either reexamine our scholarship and teaching or continue to play the role of Prospero-teacher to passive students. We can create a cultural narrative for the white student based on a family tale of glorious origins and lost (but soon to be regained) power and make the student of color a Caliban, fit only to serve the psychic and social needs of those in power. Or, we can acknowledge the ongoing legacy of "this thing of darkness" and use that knowledge to create new ways of thinking about difference that let students approach the texts of Western culture as equals. If we are successful, we can give students the critical tools for a more meaningful and complex dialogue on race, one that comprehends the intersection of categories without disregarding our differences and that moves beyond racial guilt—but not beyond justice.[22]

As the inheritor and advocate of Hall's methodology and attention to Black feminist thought, Brown challenged the UOP ensemble to interrogate its own positionality and to hold whiteness account-

---

[21]David Sterling Brown, "Things of Darkness: 'The Blueprint of a Methodology,'" *The Hare* 5, no. 1 (2020), https://thehareonline.com.

[22]Kim F. Hall, *Things of Darkness: Economies of Race and Gender in Early Modern England* (Ithaca, NY: Cornell University Press, 1995), 268.

able for the systemic racism of the text.[23] Brown's inclusion as project dramaturge complements Cobb's search for justice and truth in the text.

Already *Untitled Othello* comes fraught with language that invites theological interpretation. Shakespeare demands "reverence." These scripts operate like scripture; Shakespeare's poetry is a creative logos from which springs our contemporary life.[24] Othello, so certain of himself and Desdemona's love for him, asserts, "My life upon her faith" (1.3.295), and the play hinges on Othello's fervent devotion to those he trusts. It is about "a prayer of earnest heart" (1.3.152), "perdition catch[ing] [the] soul" (3.3.90), and "soul and fortunes consecrate" (1.3.255). Shakespeare sets up an early evocation of witchcraft and magic, but quickly replaces the tenor of the play with Christian language, evoking the medieval *Everyman* in Iago's vice-like figure, and Othello's fall from grace. How might concern for interpersonal justice craft more beautiful art and community, so that the process, not just the play, engages the human condition?

Cobb's idea of "good theatre" invokes the long-standing alignment in philosophical and theological aesthetic theories between justice and beauty. UOP proposes that good theatre (theatre of high aesthetic quality) will and must also do good (theatre of high moral quality). Better theatre will be more beautiful. Cobb's approach aligns with M. Shawn Copeland's reply to Frantz Fanon's rhetorical question "Who then can tell me what beauty is?" Copeland writes, "I answer that beauty is consonant with performance—that is, with ethical and moral behavior, with habit or virtue. In other words, beauty is the living up to and living out the love and summons of creation in all our particularity and specificity as God's human creatures."[25] Copeland's stirring account of the beautiful aligns well with Cobb's notion of "good theatre." This work begins in attending to the full humanity of actors *and*

---

[23]Also see David Sterling Brown, "'Hood Feminism': Whiteness and Segregated (Premodern) Scholarly Discourse in the Post-Postracial Era," *Literature Compass* 18, no. 10 (2020): 1–15, https://doi.org/10.1111/lic3.12608.

[24]Harold Bloom, *Shakespeare: The Invention of the Human* (New York: Riverhead, 1998), 3.

[25]M. Shawn Copeland, "Disturbing Aesthetics of Race," *Journal of Catholic Social Thought*, 3, no. 1 (2006): 19.

characters. The quest for a fully human portrait of Othello the character includes attention to the full humanity of the artistic ensemble. Performances that make good theatrical art intersect and interact with performances of good human living. In order to make "good theatre," UOP confronts the play's racism without permitting the text's racist distortions to render its characters or actors less than fully human in an eventual performance.[26]

Bodies, Breath, and Spirit

Untitled Othello demonstrates how antiracist table work may be spiritually productive without any overt intention to be so. Spiritual work need not occur in the presence of a theological text or a stated desire to "do what the church does." The conditions for spiritual productivity are the social contexts in which table work operates and attentive care for the human meanings it generates.

Human breath incarnates language. Ashon T. Crawley, writing about Blackpentecostal experience and Blackpentecostal aesthetics, identifies how breathing flesh invites the presence of Spirit and contests the reduction of fleshly experience to an enclosed point of "categorical coherence" for theology or philosophy. "But breathing flesh makes apparent the importance of openness, of otherwise grammars, against borders."[27] Crawley's reflections on Blackpentecostal aesthetics, while far from the lived experience of a Catholic university hosting religiously diverse actors reading a Shakespearean play, nonetheless illuminates what he calls the "otherwise possibilities" invited by UOP and its table work. Crawley locates Spirit in how "we share in the materiality of that which quickens flesh; we share air, breath, breathing through the process of inhalation and exhalation."[28] Bringing breath to Shakespeare's play will perform meanings both beautiful and fraught, meanings that can be both worthwhile and violent. Hall's book also reflects on this problematic, as she discusses Ossie Davis's

---

[26]UOP purposefully makes space in its process to address intersecting oppressions of misogyny, xenophobia, and colonialism, but we lack the space here to comment extensively on those dimensions of the project.

[27]Ashon T. Crawley, *Blackpentecostal Breath: The Aesthetics of Possibility* (New York: Fordham University Press, 2017), 59.

[28]Ibid., 40.

essay "The English Language Is My Enemy," which argues that the connotations of "darkness" and "black" in the English language are a trap and a means of debasement for Black Americans.[29] Cobb recognizes that we must share this language, look at it, acknowledge it, and grapple with it. Table work risks impurity to work toward performances that might be plausible across the multiple dimensions of a human life.

Table work does not produce a final stage production, but certain forms of table work might inspire new ways to think about productivity by emphasizing the spiritual gains of "process." *Untitled Othello*'s approach to table work addresses a similar reverberation of whiteness that Willie James Jennings addresses: "The tragedy is the narrowing of intellectual formation to a form of attention cultivated through brutality, through a design that demands Euro-masculinist gesture as the required carrier of this student's ideas, her creativity, and her search for understanding."[30] How might we design classrooms that leave room for Spirit to breathe and for attention to circulate incarnationally, across table work's unions of words and flesh?

In addition to sharing a space and its attendant meanings, table work also invites nonverbal reactions and gestures, parallel conversations, immediate feedback, and reduced barriers to conversational entry. Table work is communal rather than individual. How often do our pedagogies stifle these potential benefits to "being in the room"? As Jennings writes, "Unfortunately, the use of tradition in theological education has most often been to promote white self-sufficient masculinity in search of a coherence that would make us safe from seeing our fragment work and conceal what the fragment aims toward: communion, the working and weaving together of fragments in the forming of life together."[31] Table work structurally invites co-feeling to become an aspect of textual interpretation and conversation. The ways the shared text's words and ideas are experienced by the ensemble matter for the text's meaning.

Homiletics scholar James Henry Harris follows Paul Ricoeur's

---

[29]Hall, *Things of Darkness*, 265–66.
[30]Willie James Jennings, *After Whiteness: An Education in Belonging* (Grand Rapids, MI: Eerdmans, 2020), 59.
[31]Ibid., 44.

interpretation theory to argue that meaning happens "in front of the text."[32] Table work, like preaching, embraces this human meaning produced in front of the text rather than excavated from behind or within it. If there is a clue for antiracist spirituality at work in *Untitled Othello,* it resides at the level of shared bodily experience, shared breath, shared "being in the room." *Untitled Othello* foregrounds how bodies make meaning in relation to each other. This point is quite obvious in the theatrical context: Shakespeare's script must be performed. Actors allow words to move through flesh and so accrue more and more meaning. The event of theatre, then, also bears the meanings of the bodies of the actors. Theatrical representation matters: casting choices—what bodies play which characters—establish the boundaries of possibility for a given production's meanings. But, according to Jennings, "We live in the wake of a decision to limit loves, directing their flow in only one direction—away from nonwhite flesh and toward the European."[33] Such desires normalize casting choices as inevitabilities. Liturgical theologians grapple with such casting choices all the time: Who reads or sings what part during a dramatic recitation of the passion narrative? How might the meanings of the passion narrative be disclosed differently if the role of the Christ gets read by a woman, or the role of Peter by a priest? Casting does not change the words, but it certainly opens a new set of questions about human meanings.

Untitled Othello does not seek to rewrite Shakespeare's text. Instead, table work looks for places to make cuts in order to shorten the show's run-time; but the script cannot be discarded. Members of the project held a noticeable reverence for the beauty of Shakespeare's poetry. Throughout the residency, actors made frequent, quasi-religious connections between Shakespeare's influence on contemporary culture and the Bible's. Part of the UOP residency's work does seek to explore and nuance Othello's conversion from Islam to Christianity and how religious identities intertwine with colonialism and racialization. But because the company undertook table work in the context of a Catholic institution—a place open to the possibility of God—spiritual

---

[32] James Henry Harris, *Beyond the Tyranny of the Text: Preaching in Front of the Bible to Create a New World* (Nashville: Abingdon, 2019).
[33] Jennings, *After Whiteness,* 61.

questions resonated with contemporary relevance. Table work does not require an ostensibly "revelatory" theological text: a Shakespeare script is not holy scripture. Instead, the "room" testified to Spirit through newfound practices that seek, in Cobb's words, "the bravery of the academic community to stop speaking the language of anti-racism and anti-oppression and do."[34] Table work inspires a spiritual attitude for this action of embodied attention to creaturely particularity and resistance to the social sin of racism.

Still-Going Conclusions:
Audience Presence and Spiritual Productivity

There is, to be sure, some danger in theologically interpreting the spiritual work of the UOP ensemble. Embodied, antiracist work cannot be quarantined from risk. UOP demonstrates how spiritually productive work need not intend to be religious or ecclesial in order to be *spiritually* productive. That is, UOP demonstrates how antiracist spirituality might be *done* rather than *discussed*. As Bryan Massingale identifies: "a 'white' church and a 'white' theology, that is to say, a church and theology in (unconscious) complicity with white privilege and entitlement, is not and cannot be a carrier of a 'catholic' and truly universal faith."[35] Decentering the whiteness of an institutional Spirit can begin with something like the embodied practices of table work.

So, what about the audience? The *Untitled Othello* residency included our students watching, listening, and asking their own questions. How can we make sense of those persons present "in the room" but *not* doing the table work of an actor reading a specific role? Are students merely passive recipients, aloof observers to the "dissection theatre" of the actor-surgeons at work on this Shakespearean corpus? There is a physical distinction between those "at the table" with microphone and nameplate and those seated around the periphery. Sometimes, Sacred Heart students

---

[34]Keith Hamilton Cobb, "The Untitled Othello Project and Anti-Racist Solutions" (presentation, "Creating Anti-Racist Solutions" conference, Sacred Heart University, Fairfield, CT, August 10, 2022).

[35]Bryan N. Massingale, *Racial Justice and the Catholic Church* (Maryknoll, NY: Orbis Books, 2010), 172.

were invited to sit in with the actors and occasionally read a part of the play. Faculty were invited to add commentary. Anyone present is thus already playing a role. The Brazilian experimental theatre-maker Augusto Boal coined the term "spect-actor" to describe an audience aware and ready with their capacity to become part of the action.[36] UOP shows the minimum requirement for participation in table work and, by extension, antiracist spirituality, is presence.

The full depth of presence can be hard to measure empirically. Felt presence can be dismissed as private or interior and, according to materialist readings of performance, inaccessible for scholarly interpretation.[37] Actors must discover how to make manifest their interior thoughts, ideas, and emotions about the play. A brilliant interpretation offered during table work means little if its insights cannot be performed by a body and recognized by an audience. So too, antiracist sentiments and feelings mean little if not enacted. Table work creates a structure wherein the room holds such felt presences, including the felt presence of Spirit, in human meanings that struggle to find adequate translation into abstract language.

Table work on *Othello* led the actors into a discussion of the way the felt presence of whiteness and racialization haunts rehearsal spaces and affects the actor's work. In addition, those conversations modeled ways for students, as spect-actors, to take seriously how differing social locations might lead people to feel the presence of oppression differently. One of the longest and most powerful interventions regarded a discussion about how to perform racist characters without compromising the actor's own humanity, without allowing the character to render the actor complicit. The ensemble invoked the red herring of "technique"—bodily approaches that hold impacts on interiority at arm's length and treat the performance of the text as a job to be done. But rather than dismiss felt presences and human meanings, UOP required an interrogation of technique's limits. Appeals to technique—like appeals to scholarly "objectivity"—disregard the humanity of those present in the room who are doing the work.

---

[36]Augusto Boal, *Theatre of the Oppressed* (New York: Theatre Communications Group, 1985).

[37]Donnalee Dox, *Reckoning with the Spirit in the Paradigm of Performance* (Ann Arbor: University of Michigan Press, 2016).

Antiracist encounters with inherited texts will require spiritual practices alongside purely material or procedural interventions.

Table work prompted a richly human engagement about both the work necessary to make good theatre and the work necessary to create a space of mutual flourishing for the ensemble. The conversation embodied Massingale's invocation of hope: "That is why I speak of hope in the African American experience as that *inner orientation of the human spirit that motivates and sustains one to work for a nonguaranteed future in the face of formidable obstacles.*"[38] *Untitled Othello* does not move toward some guaranteed future in the form of a production or accomplishment. Rather, it offers an antiracist spirituality amid ordinary conversation and attentive bodily encounter, as part of ongoing and unfinished table work.

---

[38]Massingale, *Racial Justice and the Catholic Church*, 147, emphasis in original.

Cultivating Spiritual Empathy
for the Classroom

Howard Thurman Shows Us a Way

La Ronda D. Barnes

During Howard Thurman's time as leader of the Fellowship Church, an interracial and interfaith church he co-founded in 1944, he gave a sermon series on the mystics who influenced his spiritual development. One of those mystics was the late sixteenth/early seventeenth-century philosopher Jacob Boehme. Thurman speaks of Boehme's understanding that,

> [L]urking around in his spirit [was] a hunger . . . to be completely and inclusively saluted, cared for, loved. And in the magic of that vitalism my spirit begins to stir, and as it stirs it sets up processes that wash me clean of my fears, of my insecurities, of all the things that choke my life. Boehme says that it is possible for one human being to deal with another human being through . . . double vision, double view: seeing in time, in circumstance, in vicissitude but dealing with time, circumstance, vicissitude from a dimension outside of time, circumstance and vicissitude. An awkward and simple way to say it: to walk on the earth by the light in the sky.[1]

---

[1]Howard Thurman, *The Way of the Mystics*, Walking with God: The Sermon Series of Howard Thurman, vol. 2, ed. Peter Eisenstadt and Walter Earl Fluker (Maryknoll, NY: Orbis Books, 2021), 101–102.

As spiritual leaders, wherever our classroom or pulpit may be, how do we create or cultivate spaces in which our parishioners, in whatever form they may come, can "walk on the earth by the light in the sky,"[2] and how do we teach others to do so? How, in particular, do we lead classrooms in which Spirit speaks through us and through the other learners who inhabit these spaces? How can we be God's instruments of spiritual formational development for the current and future spiritual leaders who look to us for guidance? I believe affirmative mysticism, including the work of Howard Thurman, shows us a way.

Thurman was a twentieth-century mystic, preacher, and scholar who served as dean of Howard University's chapel, the first Black dean of Boston University's Marsh Chapel, and leader of a delegation of Black Christians to India to meet with Mahatma Gandhi.[3] In this essay, I explore with Howard Thurman how doing our own interior work identifies for us our open wounds, begins the process of healing, and expands our capacities for spiritual empathy.

Allow me to begin with an example. One of my small groups for an introductory preaching class in the US was composed of three Black women, three Black men, and one White woman. The stated and laudable goal of forming groups in which Black students would constitute the majority was to avoid making Black students the diversity in a classroom for White students while possibly generating feelings of isolation for the Black students. As a Black woman formally educated in primarily White institutions, I appreciated the need for such compositions to uplift the voices and gifts of students of color and to aid in their community-building. At about three weeks into the semester, I found myself feeling sorry for the one White woman. I will call her Sabrina for this story. "It must be hard for her," I found myself saying. To which God asked, "Why? Are you afraid the big, bad Black people are going to hurt her?" I guess for the person whom American society had indoctrinated, the answer was yes. After all, we all, White people, Asian people, and even "respectable" Black people, need to be protected from Black people, don't we? Nevertheless, God had

---

[2]Ibid., 102.

[3]In an effort at equitable naming, designations of racial and ethnic identity are capitalized throughout this essay, except in the quoted works of other authors.

nudged me out of my indoctrinated state at least for a moment, and I have learned to appreciate each one of those moments. I have also learned that those moments do not come without doing the interior work, the work that helps me dig below the stereotypes of others and misconceptions of self that society puts forth and that I have ingested over decades.

Flash-forward several months, and I'm reading Thurman's *The Luminous Darkness: A Personal Interpretation of the Anatomy of Segregation and the Ground of Hope.* While I was processing the depression, anger, and heartache that arose as I read the book, God brought the Sabrina story to mind. "Yes," says God, "I awakened you to the prejudices and self-hate with which you have been indoctrinated and that caused you to see your student Sabrina as a person in need of rescue simply because she was a White person in a class with people who look like you." "Yes," says God, "the feelings of guilt, shame, and sadness that arose with that awareness were real and needed to be processed."

Then, there was more. God sent forth what one of my former therapists would call a little lamb. Little lambs are those feelings and memories of experiences that rest in the recesses of our consciousness, things that may have been too overwhelming or traumatic to deal with in the past. She would say that little lambs want to come forth, and they will if they feel it is safe to do so. But if we scare them, reject them, or refuse to acknowledge them, they will go back in and go even further back than they were. At this moment, a little lamb came forth with the next set of questions, the ones I was now able to process if I allowed myself to do so: How much of what you were feeling for Sabrina was a reflection of what you as an adult feel for the child who rests within, for the child who sat in classroom after classroom over decades, feeling alone, different, less than—for the child who grew up in institutional systems where she rarely saw, read, or heard anything good about people who looked like her? Are you able now to recognize and thank her for her resilience and courage? Are you able to comfort her and help both of you heal deeply embedded wounds? Will you take this experience and these insights and be consciously aware of them when you encounter another Sabrina-like student or parishioner, regardless of racial or other identity markers? Can you articulate for others a process by which they can cultivate and teach others to cultivate spiritual empathy as a pedagogical gift? In this paper, I begin articulating a process in conversation with three of Howard Thurman's works: *The Way of the Mystics*, which is a collection of some of his sermons and lectures; *The Luminous Darkness: A Personal Interpretation of the Anatomy of Segregation and the Ground of Hope;* and *The Search for Common Ground: An Inquiry into the Basis of Man's Experience of Community.*[4] This process includes: (a) Finding Wisdom Within; (b) Properly Using Instruments for the Work; (c) Identifying the Walls; and (d) Connecting Human Spirits through the Spirit.[5]

Finding Wisdom Within

In *The Way of the Mystics*, Thurman states,

[There are] two pillars about which the whole mystical insights rest, that we are surrounded by an all-pervasive Spirit of God, which Spirit is the Creator of life and the

---

[4]Howard Thurman, *The Luminous Darkness: A Personal Interpretation of the Anatomy of Segregation and the Ground of Hope* (Richmond, IN: Friends United Press, 1989); Howard Thurman, *The Search for Common Ground: An Inquiry into the Basis of Man's Experience of Community* (Richmond, IN: Friends United Press, 1986).

[5]This chapter offers a close reading analysis of Thurman that contributes to the growing body of research on empathy in the classroom, race, and Howard Thurman. See, for example: Jessica L. Tinklenberg, ed., "Empathy and the Religious Studies Classroom: Spotlight on Teaching," *Religious Studies News*, January 2020, aarweb.org; Michalinos Zembylas and Elena Papamichael, "Pedagogies of Discomfort and Empathy in Multicultural Teacher Education," *Intercultural Education* 28, no. 1 (2017): 1–19; Chezare A. Warren, "Towards a Pedagogy for the Application of Empathy in Culturally Diverse Classrooms," *Urban Review* 46, no. 3 (2014): 395–419; Patrick Clayborn, "Preaching as an Act of Spirit: The Homiletical Theory of Howard Thurman," *Journal of the Academy of Homiletics* 35, no. 1 (2010): 3–16; Mark S. Giles, "Howard Thurman, Black Spirituality, and Critical Race Theory in Higher Education," *Journal of Negro Education* 79, no. 3 (Summer 2010): 354–365; Liza J. Rankow, "Pedagogy of Head and Heart: Teaching Howard Thurman in Community Settings of Exile," *Religious Thought* 60, no. 2/1–2 (2008): 195–206; Mark S. Giles, "Howard Thurman: A Spiritual Life in Higher Education" (PhD diss., Indiana University, 2003); Stephanie Athey, "Building on a Radical Foundation: The Work of Theologian Howard Thurman Continues," *Trotter Review* 10, no. 2 (1997): 31–34.

world, and which Spirit is in *me*. And that Spirit which is in me is the real thing, and I can make direct contact with that Spirit without going outside myself.[6]

Imagine being a scuba diver suiting up, diving into the water, and making your way into the depths of the ocean. In many ways you are entering another world with life-forms not seen on land or in the shallows of the waters. In other ways, this is simply another area of one world, intricately connected with shallow waters, land, and sky. Imagine exploring the ocean depths with a spirit of curiosity, not a sense of fear or disgust or need to make mental notes for later documentation, but simple, child-like curiosity. Imagine doing so, not like the child who is at play running from place to place, but the child who over time has observed or thought about exploring a specific area of the house and now has the opportunity to do so without fear of interruption. As Thurman observes, this is what the interior work or engagement with the Spirit within us looks or feels like. Awakening to the Spirit within us and consistently engaging Spirit in an interior realm is the beginning of cultivating spiritual empathy.

Interior work builds what Thurman calls personality. Personality is the manifestation of the self that God created, a self that lives, not merely exists, in the world. A strong sense of personality enables us to appreciate our uniqueness, tap into our innate sensibilities and gifts, and have the courage to use those gifts in life-empowering ways. Thurman scholar Luther E. Smith Jr. summarizes the importance of personality as follows:

> Thurman believes that the personality is a gift of God that enables individuals to interact creatively with social realities. Through personality one interprets meaning and derives purpose for living. Individuals come to know their worth as children of God, and their response-ability to life as persons of faith, when they have a proper sense of self. These matters of meaning, purpose, worth, and responsibility rely upon one's attentiveness to one's self. So Thurman expends considerable writing on the spiritual practices that

---

[6]Thurman, *The Way of the Mystics*, 6. Emphasis in original.

prepare the personality to discern what contributes to and what diminishes a proper sense of self.[7]

Interior work also puts us in touch with what Thurman calls the genuine, what Meister Eckhart calls the Godhead, what Quakers call the light within, and what I believe is the spirit and Spirit within. One of the major challenges for us in contemporary society is what Thurman calls "break[ing] down [our] misconstructed intellectual armor."[8] By the time many of us reach adulthood, we have been told in myriad ways by individuals and institutional mouthpieces that there is nothing within us that is worth a deep dive. We have been told that the mind controls what is within, and through reasoning, in conjunction with external stimuli, we learn all we need to know about engaging the world. Wisdom, so the teachings go, is the product of formal education, reason, self-discipline, and to a minor extent, observation of the world around us.

For Christians, there may be the added institutional church teachings of God as Wisdom or a source of wisdom that may be accessed through canonized Scripture and narrowly defined prayer. Outside of these channels of access, we are discouraged from believing in direct communication with God, and especially from believing that we "hear" or otherwise sense God speaking to us. I can imagine that some of you are wondering about my mental stability in posing questions from God earlier in the essay. Does she really think she communicates with God in this conversational way? The answer is yes, and the best part of the yes is that I believe any of us, any living being, can do the same if we are willing to break through the armor of which Thurman spoke and related in ways that inspired others to view their own spiritual encounters as legitimate ones. As Thurman notes, "[T]he great and first basic principle of the mystic's interpretation of life is that we are surrounded by and enveloped by an all-pervading Spirit and that Spirit is the reality."[9]

One of our roles as spiritual beings who are educators is to communicate and interact in spiritually informed ways, thereby

---

[7]Luther E. Smith Jr., in *Essential Writings*, by Howard Thurman (Maryknoll, NY: Orbis Books, 2006), 29.

[8]Thurman, *The Search for Common Ground*, 74.

[9]Thurman, *The Way of the Mystics*, 5.

opening the classroom space and students' hearts for the Spirit to move. This includes speaking of the spiritual in classrooms where the Holy Spirit may not be the focus of the curriculum. This communication is a manifestation of the interior work we have done. Imagine Howard Thurman, Saint Francis of Assisi, Julian of Norwich, Mahatma Gandhi, Simone Weil, or Archbishop Desmond Tutu, not only teaching a subject directly related to theology, but teaching calculus, anatomy, or pastry arts. Whatever their religious or spiritual beliefs, they would speak in spiritually informed ways and with effortless, inclusive, and intellectually liberating references to the spiritual realm. Thurman models this for us in his interviews, sermons, and other writings. When speaking of the "spiritual," he seamlessly weaves in examples and metaphors from myriad areas, including biology and history. When speaking of the "secular," including the horrors of segregation and the damage it does to all of us as individuals and communities, he seamlessly weaves in the "spiritual."

Instruments for Deep-Diving

Meditation, silence, and prayer are three of the instruments that can help us communicate with the Spirit within us. Thurman, however, cautions us that even when we use these instruments, exploration of the interior and encounter with the Divine is not a given. Thurman states, "The mystic uses meditation as a means. . . . [T]he temptation is to use it as an end."[10] In other words, with our focus on the mind and on the rational, we are tempted to view meditation as a way to ease the burdens of the mind or clear the mind in order to contemplate an issue. For the mystic, meditation becomes a way to detach ourselves from the masks and veils we wear, the fears of being wrong, the necessity of feeling we need to be somewhere else and/or doing something else at this very moment other than spending time with Spirit. Thurman states,

> One of the serious . . . roadblocks . . . to a sense of coming home to your center, which is for me coming to God, is my sense of private and personal guilt for injuries that I have perpetrated, sometimes deliberately . . . sometimes without

---

[10]Ibid., 137.

awareness of others for reasons that are private, that have to do with my own hurt. So that guilt and hatred and bitterness become—generate a climate, an atmosphere, a thickness by which I am surrounded psychically . . . something deep within me feels that I don't have the right to experience the Presence.[11]

In our interior work, we must be willing to open ourselves to our feelings of guilt, shame, and anger. We also must be willing to process those feelings as a part of our continual inner work and hone the ability to empathize with ourselves and others. It is important to practice these spiritual disciplines to be aware when our focus has shifted from the spiritual, gently guiding ourselves back to our focus without guilt or feelings of incompetence. It is also important to remember that disciplines that work at one point in our lives may not work at other times. We must be open to new ways of doing deep dives and of encountering the Divine.

Identifying the Walls

Identifying what Thurman refers to as the walls society continually builds to keep us focused on our identity groups and on naming others in destructive, life-debilitating ways is connected both to doing the interior work and to our observation of what occurs and has occurred in our personal lives and in the lives of our communities. In his writings, Thurman often discusses his search for places of genuine connection. For example, in discussing the harms of segregation, Thurman advocates having experiences that allow a person to identify with another being and to "listen for the sound of the genuine in another."[12] He states, "Such an experience cannot become a dogma—it has to remain experiential all the way. It is a probing process trying to find the opening into another. And it requires exposure, sustained exposure. One of the great obstacles to such exposure is the fact of segregation."[13] I envision these places of genuine connection as ones we enter after having reached a level of awareness in which we can, as Thurman would say, call a wall a wall.

---

[11]Ibid., 124–125.
[12]Thurman, *The Luminous Darkness*, 111.
[13]Ibid.

The walls are what divide us, at times, insulating us so we can begin developing community or begin healing from wounds received from reaching or trying to reach beyond them. One of the ways affirmative mysticism may be practiced is in taking action to help others tear down, cross, or see through life-diminishing walls. As people of faith, it could involve advocating for social justice causes, speaking or preaching about social injustices, or praying and marching with social justice activists. In our daily lives, regardless of vocation, doing our interior work may manifest itself in having the courage to name the walls we encounter or see others encountering whether in a supermarket, a classroom, a boardroom, or a worship gathering.

Identifying walls is also some of the most heart-wrenching work we can do, but it must be done if we are to live holistic lives and help others do so in ways that are not personally draining and debilitating. Family and community members may expose us to the walls or communicate with us about their existence at an early age. Or they may attempt to shield us from that awareness, so that we look at the world with limited prejudices, sorrow, or bitterness. In discussing the different perspectives in Black communities of the 1960s on addressing the walls, Thurman states,

> [T]his applies to the older generation of Negroes. . . . In many ways they have tried to shield their children from naked exposure to the worst and most damaging aspects of white society. They have stood guard on the walls that separate and divide, seeking always how to make a virtue of social necessity. Often with sacrifices of which they dare not speak, they have bought time for their youth to prepare for effective living with tools, skills, and knowledge of which they sometimes dreamed but they could never realize.[14]

I grew up in a household in which what Thurman speaks of was apparent and spoken of to some degree but which, in other ways, I am only beginning to be aware of and understand. Emphasis was placed on excelling in school, being a "respectable" member of society, and accepting personal responsibility for what occurs

---

[14]Thurman, *The Search for Common Ground*, 93–94.

in one's life with a trust that family and friends would understand and assist one in times of need. There was communication of the realities of needing to work harder as a Black person to receive opportunities comparable to those of White people and to realize that even in doing so, life can still be unfair. Phrases like "last hired and first fired" were gospel. As someone in primarily White schools with White friends, I received gentle reminders that, as teenage years approached, friendships may dissolve due to racist beliefs of my friends' families and/or their desire to protect their children from exposure to society's racism.

Although my family's shielding and protection allowed me, for the most part, to avoid exposure to overt acts of racism, they could not protect me from the covert racism that is indigenous to this nation. Racism has impeded my own strengthening of personality. Doing the interior work has helped me identify both the covert experiences of racism in my own life and the ways in which covert and overt racism and other isms or walls affect the other lives I encounter, including those of my parishioners and students.

Connecting Human Spirits through the Spirit

After doing the interior work and identifying the walls, connecting our spirit with the spirit of another is the next thing that Thurman's work guides us to. We begin by acknowledging the personality of the other being and the ways in which our individual uniqueness is a communal strength. Thurman states,

There is a spirit in man and in the world working always against the thing that destroys and lays waste. Always he must know that the contradictions of life are not final or ultimate; he must distinguish between failure and a many-sided awareness so that he will not mistake conformity for harmony, uniformity for synthesis. He will know that for all men to be alike is the death of life in man, and yet perceive the harmony that transcends all diversities and in which diversity finds its richness and significance.[15]

---

[15]Ibid., 6.

Acknowledging the personality of the other is also an account-ability checkpoint in our interior work as it helps us remember that what we are doing does not make us spiritual gurus. We have been given the same capabilities of encountering the Spirit as any other human or any other life. Every life can communicate with God, has been created by God, and is valued in and of itself by God. As we grow in celebration and affirmation of self, we should also grow in celebration and affirmation of other life. Thurman expresses the concept as follows:

> The ultimate meaning of experience is felt in such a way that all of oneself is included. It is total, it is unified and unify-ing. It is not the experience of oneself as male or female, as black or white, as American or European. It is rather the experience of oneself as *being*. It is at such a time that one can hear the sound of the genuine in other human beings. This is to be able to identify with them. One man's response to the sound of the genuine in another man is to ascribe to the other man the same sense of infinite worth that one has for oneself. When this happens, men are free to relate to each other as human beings—good, bad, mean, friendly, prejudiced, altruistic, but human beings. Whatever may be the nature of the shortcomings, they are seen from the view on the other side where the person lives whose shortcomings are encountered.[16]

"Hear[ing] the sound of the genuine . . . [and seeing] from the view on the other side where the person lives"[17] does not mean we understand their experiences or feelings. It means we attempt to understand. We recognize they are living beings with gifts, flaws, doubts, and challenges and that their experiences in life affect the way they interpret life. Only then can we take the next step of relating our experiences and feelings to theirs in ways that are mutually edifying and that build communities instead of walls.

In a sermon on Meister Eckhart, Thurman refers to this type of engagement with another being. He states,

---

[16]Thurman, *The Luminous Darkness*, 98–99. Emphasis in original.
[17]Ibid., 99.

[I]f it be true as Eckhart presupposes . . . that there is central in every living person a core which has at its core the eternally undifferentiated Godhead, then that means two things that are very important. One: that I am never permitted to say of another human being that he is anything that is a denial of the infinite worth of his personality, because his personality is the basket in which is carried this priceless ingredient . . . and therefore, in all of my primary, intimate face-to-face or secondary contacts with human beings my greatest and most insistent responsibility is to seek to develop with them the kind of relationships that will make it possible for core to salute core. The core in me to salute the core in you.[18]

To connect in this way is to imagine standing in someone else's shoes while at the same time realizing that they are not our own shoes. It is a posture or way of being that can only be attained through the Spirit and by opening our imaginations to the Spirit's work. Possibly, this is one of the reasons Thurman refers to imagination as "the agent of God."[19]

In the case of my White female student, Sabrina, I opened myself to the Spirit's use of my imagination to make a genuine and respectful attempt to experience what she was experiencing as the only White person in the class. My own embodied experiences, as having been the only Black person in classrooms, as a female, and in any related identifiable ways would assist in my endeavor. This allowed me to cultivate spiritual empathy for Sabrina as well as for the other Black people in the class who may be having save-Sabrina moments or experiencing feelings of guilt or anger for having those moments. If I was in the same classroom today, I would probably find ways to address those issues directly and share the ways in which doing our individual inner work and cultivating spiritual empathy can assist in making difficult moments and feelings lead us to more holistic living. At the very least, my interior work, and the questions raised within me, will result in an approachable posture that opens the door for students to discuss their feelings and potential ideas for adapting

---

[18]Thurman, *The Way of the Mystics*, 89.
[19]Thurman, *The Luminous Darkness*, 99.

the classroom and curriculum to be more hospitable to all while
learning from the experiences presented.

Conclusion

As educators doing our own interior work by utilizing spiritual disciplines and mystic thought and tapping into our unique
personalities and innate worth as God's creatures, we have an
awareness of self that strengthens personality in life-giving ways.
Doing our interior work helps us identify the walls that exist
within and between communities, reminds us to respect and seek
to uplift the personalities of other life, and opens our imaginations
through the Spirit so we may connect our spirit to the spirit in
another being and cultivate spiritual empathy.

Thurman's writings guide us to engage with each other at levels
that are deeper than the walls' foundations. They inspire us to
dig deep to experience a level of spiritual empathy in which we
not only see and respect the other in their uniqueness, but we are
able to think, speak, and act in ways that help us identify our
own wounds, avoid opening or deepening the wounds of others,
and generate imaginative and creative ways of nurturing all life.

As educators, part of our call is to create spaces and climates
for people to cultivate spiritual empathy. It begins with identifying practical elements or ways of encounter that help individuals
use their imaginations and move beyond any fear of or societally
induced embarrassment in delving into the interior, of being a part
of the mystery that is God.

Thurman's work challenges us to delve into the depths of our
souls, awaken to our uniqueness, appreciate the uniqueness of
others, and seek connection with other humans, other life, and all
of Creation in a spiritual place in which we appreciate the other
in their otherness. His work focuses our attention on the need for
spiritual empathy. It encourages us to empathize with others in
ways that are Spirit driven, helps us grow in our understanding of
their struggles, joys, and points of view, and assists them in what
Thurman refers to as "actualizing potential"[20] as empowered personalities. By doing so, we also gain a better understanding of self

---

[20]Thurman, *The Search for Common Ground*, 4.

and cultivate more creative ways of developing and implementing our methods of teaching, interacting with our students, viewing our roles as educators, and creating spaces in which spiritually informed leaders may flourish.

What to Do When a Saint Is Racist?

Wrestling with Saint John of the Cross

George Faithful

When have you heard something that stripped away some dearly held part of you? How often have you, too, perhaps with the best of intentions, spoken such poison into the world? And how many times have you, whether in the hearing or in the speaking, kept going about your day as if everything were fine? Even saints do such things.

The Poison

Shortly after I graduated from college, a mentor at church told me, "I never would have guessed you were Black. You're so smart. I always assumed you were Jewish."[1] I smiled, shrugged, and thanked him. But those words sat with me, heavy with the weight of death. As they sank in, I recognized their parts: the backhanded compliment, the lauded presumed genius of one group, the denigration of another.[2] In the coming years, I would grow to

---

[1] I have capitalized labels for discrete racial-ethnic groups throughout and prioritized the use of adjectives to convey that these identities are not totalizing. For example, "Jewish people." By contrast, "white" is more fluid and vague, thus rendered lowercase. Any exceptions to this are from direct quotes.

[2] From Latin *denigrare*, "to blacken, make dark." www.etymonline.com. Racial, color-based discourse marks the English language as we have received it.

understand how, through the internalization of false expectations, an accumulation of such words can hamper individuals' lives and diminish communities' flourishing.[3]

Racism isn't always a cross burning in the front yard. Polymorphous and adaptive, it varies in appearance in different contexts over time. It can be a system of assumed biases revealed in a casual remark or a hiring decision. Because of this, one might posit different points of origin for what has yielded its current forms, all of which bring death, whether literally-physically, socio-relationally, economically, intellectually, and/or spiritually. This death-yielding quality helps illuminate racism as a form of sin.

Ideological forms of racism have the power to poison the imagination. I offer the following as a brief working definition of racism, as it has developed historically in European and European-colonized and -occupied contexts: a conceptualization of a hierarchy of races that is, at least in part, complexion-based and which situates "whites" in the presumed position of intellectual, moral, and spiritual superiority. A racist, then, is anyone who promotes such ideologies. For present purposes, it will suffice to classify antisemitism as a form of racism due to the history of racialization of Jewish people in the West.[4]

Ideological racism does not need to be a deliberate, mean-spirited antipathy, such as Flannery O'Connor's well-documented disdain for Black people.[5] It could take on analogical forms, as in J. R. R. Tolkien's tacit assumption that the only good orcs and goblins were dead ones.[6] Racism might represent but a small portion of someone's moral impact, which, on the whole, might

---

[3]See discussion of "stereotype threat" and other forms of "internalized racial oppression" in Özlem Sensoy and Robin DiAngelo, *Is Everyone Really Equal? An Introduction to Key Concepts in Social Justice Education* (New York: Teachers College Press, 2017), 136–137.

[4]J. Kameron Carter, *Race: A Theological Account* (Oxford: Oxford University Press, 2008), 75–77.

[5]In 1964, Flannery O'Connor stated, "You know, I'm an integrationist by principle and a segregationist by taste anyway. I don't *like* negroes. They all give me a pain and the more of them I see, the less and less I like them. Particularly the new kind." Quoted in Paul Elie, "How Racist Was Flannery O'Connor?" *The New Yorker*, June 22, 2022.

[6]Anderson Rearick, "Why Is the Only Good Orc a Dead Orc?" *Inklings Forever* 4 (2004), art. 10.

be positive. It is one thing to appreciate their work, despite their flaws. It is another to whitewash those flaws in order to avoid cognitive dissonance. Like any persistent form of cultural oppression, racism has many roots and many branches. And all those who do not actively clear the soil of its weedy expanse contribute, however unwittingly, to its spread.

The Saint(s) in Question

Some years ago, I began a comprehensive analysis of the work of Saint Juan de la Cruz (1542–1591). I assumed that I would find consolation for the plight of people caught in between social categories, including, ironically, race. In short, I came seeking a remedy. I found that—and traces of poison, as well.

Saint Juan de la Cruz was a racist. Granted, he was also a mystic, a theologian, a mentor, a monastic reformer, a poet, a victim of persecution, a prisoner, a survivor, and other important things. But he was also a racist, as the following analysis will demonstrate. And that fact must not only shape how one perceives Juan's mystic, poetic, and other gifts, but also inform one's scrutiny of other saints as well as concepts of sainthood and Christian "perfection" generally.

Before confronting Juan's shortcomings, it would do well to acknowledge the limitations of our discourse in English, especially in the United States. The pervasive Anglocentrism of our context incentivizes against calling Juan de la Cruz by his actual name, although doing so would help distinguish him from the myriad other Saint Johns. Anglocentrism is a linguistic variant of racism, however subtle, inflecting and infecting our discourse. This helps illustrate how deeply ingrained bias can be, to the point of passing by invisibly. The English language has served colonial expansion, imperial domination, and global cultural hegemony to the point of excluding some voices and distorting others, even in such conversations as this.[7]

The following analysis illustrates Juan's racism by way of a handful of particularly problematic passages. They are not the

---

[7]Yan Guo, "The Hegemony of English as a Global Language: Reclaiming Local Knowledge and Culture in China," *Convergence* 40, no. 1 (2007): 117–132.

only fraught phrases in Juan's corpus. Including the others, the sum of all of them constitutes a minuscule fraction of Juan's complete works. Nonetheless, the words in question convey values egregious not only when judged by the standards of our era, but by the standards of Juan's own claims about himself, as one who purports to offer a path to spiritual "perfection."

Rhetorical Genocide in *The Living Flame of Love*

Saint Juan is premiere among mystical theologians for offering a method for achieving union with God. His approach is particularly notable in addressing a common experience among intermediate contemplatives: a perception of long-term lack of spiritual progress. *The Ascent of Mount Carmel* troubleshoots an earlier set of struggles ("the dark night of the senses") in the upward ascent. *The Dark Night* concerns a later set of struggles ("the dark night of the spirit"). *The Living Flame of Love* charts the final phase of the upwardly ascending contemplative soul's journey into union with God. Couching his mystical guidance in the form of commentary on some of his poems, Juan's work transcends the ordinary bounds of human language.

It is perhaps fitting, then, that it is at the apex of the ascent and in the realm of allegory that some of the most significant trouble occurs. In *The Living Flame of Love* (redaction B) 3.38, Juan states that "the Egyptians need to be drowned."[8] That is the translation offered by the standard contemporary translators of Saint Juan's work into English, Kieran Kavanaugh and Otilio Rodriguez, both of Juan's own Order of Discalced Carmelites. By rendering *gitano* as "Egyptian," they frame the passage as an allegorization of the Exodus narrative, in which Christians supplant the people of Israel as God's chosen people—part of a centuries-old practice.[9] One might also readily translate the term as "Gypsy."[10] After all, the conflation of the Roma people and

---

[8]*Llama de amor viva (B)* 3.38. San Juan de la Cruz, *Obras Completas* (Salamanca: Ediciones Sígueme, 2007), 832. Translation mine, as in all subsequent citations of this source.

[9]Ronald E. Diprose, *Israel and the Church: The Origins and Effects of Replacement Theology* (Downers Grove, IL: InterVarsity Press, 2004), 29–62.

[10]Kieran Kavanaugh, OCD, and Otilio Rodriguez, OCD, trans., *The*

Egyptians, along with the persecution of the former, has a long history, as well.[11] With whatever label one might apply to them, the group of people represents the senses in Juan's allegory. They need to be rendered inert so that the soul can continue its upward ascent into union with God.

Earlier in the same work (3.31), Juan had insisted on the need to "eliminate the Jews."[12] Here Kavanaugh softens the blow by rendering *los judíos* as "the Judeans," as if a matter of geographic location rather than racial/ethnic/religious identity were fundamentally in question. In Juan's schema, they represent the appetites. Like the senses, the appetites must be subdued in the soul's upward ascent. Juan's call to marginalize them is dispassionate, rhetorical, and not in any way reflected in hateful actions on record. And yet his words remain problematic.

Allegory, metaphor, and other forms of symbolic imagery are not value-neutral but reveal fundamental assumptions of their creators and interpreters. The appetite-driven "carnal Jew" is a long-standing trope in antisemitic Christian discourse.[13] And promoting genocide, even allegorically, is never acceptable. The fact that I feel obligated to explain this is an indication that this moral absolute is, perhaps, less self-evident than it ought to be.[14] One need not demonstrate the impact of the individual threads of such casual assertions to grasp their concrete, cumulative effects: the Shoah was an anomaly in its scale and severity but stands as a kind of culmination of long-standing physical and rhetorical violence committed by Christians against Jewish people.

Collected Works of Saint John of the Cross (Washington, DC: Institute of Carmelite Studies Publications, 1991), 688.

[11]Sydnee Wagner, "Outlandish People: Gypsies, Race, and Fantasies of National Identity in Early Modern England" (PhD diss., City University of New York, 2020).

[12]San Juan, *Obras Completas*, 811.

[13]Susanna Drake, *Slandering the Jew: Sexuality and Difference in Early Christian Texts* (Philadelphia: University of Pennsylvania Press, 2013), 19–37.

[14]Literature abounds regarding the divine injunctions to the Israelites to wipe out the Canaanites in the Hebrew Bible, especially in the conquest narratives in Joshua and Judges. See, e.g., Wes Morriston, "Ethical Criticism of the Bible: The Case of Divinely Mandated Genocide," *Sophia* 51, no. 1 (2012): 117–135.

Sexist Colorism (Misogynoir)
in *The Spiritual Canticle*

The Spiritual Canticle contains a slightly different set of issues. Like Juan's other substantial works, it takes the form of a prose commentary on his poetry. In this case, it is a commentary on his version of the Song of Songs. In contrast to Juan's other works, it encompasses the whole sweep of the soul's potential ascent. No wonder he was keen to polish it. Juan shuffled the order of some of the middle stanzas of the poem and then redacted and expanded his original commentary (dubbed *Canticle A* by later scholars) in order to produce a work more closely aligned with his understanding of the archetypal soul's journey (*Canticle B*). It is to this fuller, definitive version that I will refer, unless otherwise indicated.

In the earlier stanzas of the Canticle, the female protagonist has wandered far in search of her male Beloved. Juan explains that she represents the soul and that her lover represents God. She pleads with passing shepherds, resplendent fountains, and the surrounding greenery for guidance. Surely the trees must know where he is. After all, he planted them! The line blurs here and throughout between divine Creator and human lover, between allegory and reality.

Even once she traverses borderlands and past fortifications, she fails to find him. In despair, she turns into a dove and flies away—just as he, in the form of a wounded stag, finally reveals himself to her and urges her to return. They enter into a bower, a cave made of intertwined rose vines, and join in the utmost intimacy. In terms of gender, sexuality, and species, the lines blur, as well, shaping the potentially liberative dimensions of the text.

Astute observers might recognize that, in Stanza 32, the discourse has already turned to self-deprecation in ways that are problematic:

> When you looked at me,
> your eyes imparted their grace to me.
> That is why you came to love me so.
> That is how my eyes became worthy
> to adore what they see in you.

Even in their mutual adoration, her beauty is contingent on his gaze. She has no intrinsic value of her own. Womanist thought identifies such conceptualizations as profoundly unhealthy.[15] Because people have unconditional value, self-love is a viable first principle. This is especially true for groups that have historically tended to receive constant messaging through various channels that their value is always contingent, whether upon their own labor or upon the appreciation of someone else.[16]

The sexism of the text takes on a racist dimension in stanza 33:

> Please do not despise me if, before,
> you noticed my complexion was dark.
> You can see me well now,
> since you looked at me,
> bestowing grace and beauty to me.[17]

Juan's commentary on the passage represents a textbook case of colorism, that is, a variant of racism based primarily on color: God "no longer remembers her former ugliness and sin."[18] Darkness and sin were synonymous for Juan. He goes on to explain, speaking to God, "the grace of your loving gaze removed my dark complexion and made me worthy to be seen."[19] The fact that this is an allegory in which Juan identifies himself (viz., his soul) with her in no way exonerates him.

To be fair, this is based on the already awkward Song of Songs 1:5, which a thoughtful translator might render as "I am dark *and also* beautiful," but which English Bible translators have been consistently rendering some iteration of "dark *but* beautiful" for the better part of half a millennium.[20] The Latin Vulgate, with which Juan was working, is even more problematic: *nigra sum*

---

[15]See, for example, Melanie C. Jones, "The Will to Adorn: Beyond Self-Surveillance, Toward a Womanist Ethic of Redemptive Self-Love," *Black Theology* 16, no. 3 (2018): 218–219.

[16]Ibid.

[17]San Juan, *Obras Completas,* 729.

[18]Ibid., 730.

[19]Ibid.

[20]For example, ASV, ESV, GNV, KJV, MSG, NASB (1995), NCB, NIV, NKJV, NLV, NLT, RSV, and TLB all use some form of "dark *but* beautiful." By contrast, CEB, CEV, and NRSV offer some version of "dark *and* beautiful," as does NASB (2020).

sed formosa ("I am black but beautiful"). As historian Kate Lowe notes, in addition to its socially problematic dimensions, which would bear poison fruit in the centuries to come, Jerome's word choice falls short in a technical sense as good translation work.[21] This suboptimal interpretation of the Hebrew is among the roots of Juan's own problematic verbiage, with their own fraught lineage. Yet even in the Vulgate had Juan accounted for the narrative context of the surrounding chapter, it might have softened the blow. In Song of Songs 1, the darkness of the female protagonist is due to having been forced to do manual labor outdoors at the behest of her brothers, not due to her race as such.

Juan's contemporary Luis de León, an Augustinian friar, mystic, and professor of theology, produced his own commentary on the Song of Songs. They shared, too, an experience of imprisonment, for Luis de León's vernacular translation had raised the ire of the Inquisition.[22] Yet his approach, perhaps by virtue of being an early exemplar of historical-contextual rather than allegorical exegesis, interprets the woman's darkness matter-of-factly: "She says, 'I admit that I am dark [*morena*] but in every way I am beautiful and worthy to be loved.' "[23] Two of the five manuscripts interpolate "every other way," so this counterexample is not completely clear-cut.[24] Regardless, historical context alone isn't enough to explain away Saint Juan's transgressions.

Juan escalates the intensity of his rhetoric and of his theological aesthetic in his commentary on Stanza 34:

> The little white dove has returned
> to the Ark with a branch
> and already the turtledove has found
> her longed-for partner
> on the green riverbanks.[25]

---

[21]Kate Lowe, "The Global Consequences of Mistranslation: The Adoption of 'Black but . . .' Formulations in Europe, 1440–1650," *Religions* 3, no. 4 (2012): 545–547.

[22]Ilana Pardes, *The Song of Songs: A Biography* (Princeton, NJ: Princeton University Press, 2019), 130–135.

[23]Fray Luis de León, *El Cantar de los Cantares de Salomón* (Madrid: Cátedra, 2016), 112.

[24]Ibid., 79–81, 112. It is worth noting that they are later exemplars of the text.

[25]San Juan, *Obras Completas,* 733.

This beautiful description of the resolution of her earlier avian metamorphosis did not need to be about her allegorical race/complexion. In fact, in Canticle A, the earlier redaction of the commentary on this stanza, race was a non-issue. This chapter (32 in Canticle A) makes no mention of *morena* (the feminine or female dark-complected person or characteristics) from the preceding chapter. By contrast, see Juan's commentary on this stanza in Canticle B:

> In the preceding stanza, she belittled herself, calling herself dark and ugly, and lauded him for his beauty and grace since with his regard he gave her beauty and grace. And since he customarily exalts those who humble themselves, he fixes his eyes on her as she requested, and in the next stanza, he extols her and does not call her dark, as she called herself, but a white dove, praising her good characteristics that are like those of a dove and the turtledove.[26]

In this redaction, Juan has expanded the severity of his sexist, racist colorism (viz., misogynoir).[27] Under all of it lies the assumed whiteness of God.

The Stakes

Why does any of this matter? Consider where Juan stands at the crux of colonial-imperial history. Within living memory, *los reyes Católicos*, the King and Queen of a unified and officially Christian empire, Ferdinand and Isabella had "reconquered" Spain and sponsored the "discovery" of the "New World," both of which occasioned the institutionalization of cultural genocide; one might rightly, therefore, frame the Spanish Inquisition and Spanish colonization as two sides of the same lethal impulse to

---

[26]Ibid., 732.

[27]The combination of misogyny and anti-Black racism. Moya Bailey and Trudy coined "misogynoir" in 2008. Yet due to the phenomenon they sought to illuminate, their roles in contributing to contemporary discourse have been largely erased. They discuss this in "On Misogynoir: Citation, Erasure, and Plagiarism," *Feminist Media Studies* 18, no. 4 (2018): 762–768.

dominate.[28] It is essential for us to consider how Juan's voice numbers among those complicit in that twin enterprise. Even as he built on the roots from those who came before, his work laid a foundation for subsequent mystics, oppressors, and mystics-who-were-also-oppressors. Some may be tempted to forget that these can be the same people.

Consider, too, the radical nature of Juan's claims regarding Christian "perfection." Stated most clearly in *The Living Flame of Love*, in "perfect union with God [. . .] all the inclinations and activity of the appetites and faculties—of their own the operation of death and the privation of the spiritual life—become divine." The soul "lives the life of God," "the intellect becomes divine," "God's will and the soul's will are now one," and the soul's appetite "is no longer anything else than the appetite of God." In short, "it has become God through participation in God."[29] "Having been made one with God, the soul is somehow God through participation. Although it is not God as perfectly as it will be in the next life, it is like the shadow of God." For "it is no secret to the soul itself that has attained this perfection."[30] Underlying this, as the whole basis of Juan's authority to knowing the path up into union with God, is the implicit claim that he himself had arrived at its summit. Juan invites spiritual aspirants to embark on nothing less than the path to "the highest degree of perfection attainable in this life, which is transformation into God."[31] What is at stake is not merely Juan's legacy but, by implication, the notion of sainthood as proffered by the Catholic Church. After all, the Catechism proclaims that "the Church's holiness shines in the saints."[32] Similarly, at stake is any meaningful doctrine of Christian "perfection," of which iterations appear in various confessions.[33]

---

[28]Fernando Cervantes, *Conquistadores: A New History of Spanish Discovery and Conquest* (New York: Viking, 2021), 15.

[29]San Juan, *Obras Completas,* 811–813.

[30]Ibid., 851, 859.

[31]Ibid., 776.

[32]United States Conference of Catholic Bishops, *United States Catholic Catechism for Adults* (Washington, DC: United States Conference of Catholic Bishops, 2006), 138.

[33]*The Oxford Dictionary of the Christian Church*, 3rd ed., s.v. "perfection."

Wrestling for a Price

So, what are our options? Let's first dispense with two untenable extremes. First, the dismissive approach. "Maybe it's not that bad," one might argue. "After all, look at all the good in Juan's theology!" For many people, this can be a knee-jerk safeguard against facing uncomfortable facts and, flowing from those facts, an even-less-comfortable moral responsibility to transform the status quo. Remember, even if one could bracket out the passages where Juan promotes a sexist, anti-Black/anti-Brown colorism, he tacitly affirms the value of genocide. To ignore or whitewash such racism is to become complicit in it. In the face of such realities, one can either remain comfortable or maintain one's integrity, but not both.

At the other extreme, one might reject Juan's work in its totality. This is the more tenable of the extremes by virtue of confronting racism. However, this approach, too, has its problems. It seems likely that, due to their own personal shortcomings and the biases inherent in their respective contexts, every human source of theological insight is fraught, whether due to racism, sexism, or a litany of other issues. If one were to consistently and comprehensively eliminate perceived transgressors from consideration, one would be left with a very short list—and one probably closely resembling one's own preexisting preferences. I further hypothesize that if you were inclined to "cancel" Juan de la Cruz, there are slim odds that you would have opened this volume, much less that you would still be reading it.

Those who would neither ignore Juan's faults nor abandon their quest to embrace his good must wrestle with the tension he embodies. This comes at a price. The tension itself can be jarring and difficult to sustain, engendering its own kind of dark night. There may be lasting damage, whether in the forms of peace of mind lost, clear-cut conceptualizations abandoned, or some other forms. In Genesis 32, Jacob wrestled with an angel and prevailed, but suffered a lifelong injury. To wrestle with Juan is to acknowledge that, like any saint, he was no angel. That is, perhaps, the first bit of damage to accept.

The next is to expand, complicate, and contextualize our definitions of sin. There is an inherent paradox in recognizing that every saint is a product of their age and its mores, while simultaneously expecting them to stand apart from and above the rest. We historical theologians must seek to understand preceding generations of Christians in their historical contexts. We must neither rush to excuse them nor condemn them solely based on the tools of our own contexts, even as we admit that certain absolutes transcend contexts. Whether aloud or in writing, some kinds of statements, like some actions, have always been and will always be morally wrong, no matter how normalized they may be in their sociocultural contexts. In fact, the distance of time often obscures the original divisiveness of certain developments, such as the Spanish Inquisition. The recent work of early modern religious historian Fernando Cervantes illustrates this. Spain's Christian rulers had opposed the forced conversions of their Jewish and Muslim subjects, but eventually succumbed to pressure from aggrieved Gentiles, jealous and suspicious of their neighbors' perceived success.[34]

Some sins, it seems, are sins of context, toward which those alive at the time might be especially prone, depending on their social position. Sociocultural peer pressure is what it is—and perhaps always has been. But a saint should be a rebel, at least in part, against such contextual sin. They might even evidence some significant self-awareness and humility in the face of its gravitational pull. We theologians need to expand our definitions of sin to account for that, even if it means modifying our expectations of saints and of "perfection." Someone who is pretty close to perfect in some ways might be found wanting in numerous others.

Juan's words alone are enough to necessitate a radical reevaluation of his foundational assumptions, not least of which is just how much "perfection" any human might possibly attain in this life, even by the grace of God. To be human is to be human. We Christians must abandon the use of "perfection," except in properly contextualized quotations.[35] It is one thing for a gathering of Catholic and Lutheran church leaders to agree with Luther that "every saint is simultaneously a sinner," as in the *Joint Declaration on the Doctrine of Justification*—which takes pains to emphasize

---

[34]Cervantes, *Conquistadores*, 19–20.
[35]*The Oxford Dictionary of the Christian Church*, 3rd ed., s.v. "perfection."

the fundamental differences between the traditional Catholic and Lutheran approaches to human sinfulness.[36] It is another to make such an admission a dominant part of Christian (viz., Catholic) identity writ large.

Saint Juan and other saints are worthy of veneration. But a recalibration is in order, at least in terms of what might realistically be expected of their earthly lives. That may make our perception of what they did prior to glorification more complicated, but no less meaningful. In our own stumbling, we have as much to learn from their real mistakes as from any mythos of perpetual victory. Such a lowering of expectations for our fellow humans has the potential to elevate our appreciation for the love of God. Not that this is anything to receive passively. Another hard-won lesson from Lutheranism is Bonhoeffer's reminder that those who truly embrace God's forgiveness should demonstrate it in the whole of their lives, however imperfectly.[37]

Our handling of mystical theology, too, must demonstrate an awareness of human limitations. Juan claimed to attain the highest heights attainable by any mortal, traversing arid lands in the silence of his spirit, enduring long seasons of shadow before passing into the bright consolation of union with God that lay beyond. And then, in action and in word, aloud and in print, Juan deigned to guide others to make that ascent. A certain number of missteps are inevitable in describing the indescribable within the limits of human language. The minute a mystic expresses their experience in verbiage, they risk inaccuracy. As Juan pointed out, his written teachings exist "only to impart instruction and guide the soul through them to divine union," for "what [naked truths] in themselves are for the soul is beyond words."[38]

Let us theologians grapple with hard facts, even if it means wearing scars. But let us not yield when confronted with the rac-

---

[36]Pontifical Council for Promoting Christian Unity and the Lutheran World Federation. Heinrich Denzinger, *Enchiridion symbolorum [. . .]: Compendium of Creeds, Definitions, and Declarations on Matters of Faith and Morals,* 43rd ed. (San Francisco: Ignatius, 2012), 1136. See *Joint Declaration on the Doctrine of Justification* #29-30, www.lutheranworld.org.

[37]Dietrich Bonhoeffer, *Discipleship* (Minneapolis: Fortress, 2003), 43–45.

[38]*Ascent of Mount Carmel* II.26.1. in *The Collected Works of Saint John of the Cross,* trans. Kavanaugh and Rodriguez, 245.

ism, sexism, or other sins of any saint. Let us, too, train the next generations of theologians, who may someday need to pick a fight with some of us. And if we must lose sleep, let it be because of the as-yet nameless sins of today that will occasion that reckoning.

PART III

RACIAL JUSTICE

AND THE CHURCH

A Century of Catholics Addressing Racism in Their Church (circa 1922 to 2022)

Cecilia A. Moore

From the 1910s until the early 1950s, Dr. Thomas Wyatt Turner, a cradle Catholic born and raised in Southern Maryland, a botanist, and a civil rights activist, led a group of Black Catholics calling for the end of racism in the Catholic Church.[1] They called their organization the Committee Against the Extension of Race Prejudice in the Church. By 1924, their work to end racism in the church continued with a name change. Now, they called themselves the Federated Colored Catholics (FCC), and their focus was rooting out racism in Catholic seminaries, convents, churches, schools, hospitals, orphanages, etc. While the FCC welcomed all Catholics into membership, it believed that it should always have Black Catholic issues as the focus and should always be led by Black Catholics. Among the non-Black members were two prominent priests, Father John LaFarge, SJ, and Father William Markoe, SJ. For a while, their presence and contributions seemed beneficial, but by the early 1930s, it was clear that LaFarge and Markoe wished to have prominent leadership roles in the FCC when they began agitating to remove Dr. Turner as the FCC president and to shift the focus to "interracial" concerns. In a nasty

---

[1]See Marilyn Nickels, "Thomas Wyatt Turner and the Federated Colored Catholics," *U.S. Catholic Historian* 7, no. 2/3 (Spring–Summer 1988): 215–232; and Thomas Wyatt Turner and Marilyn Nickels, *From Sharecropper to Scientist: The Memoir of Thomas Wyatt Turner, Ph.D. (1877–1978)*, independently published, 2018.

power struggle in which the priests charged Dr. Turner of "Jim Crowing" the organization, they managed to unseat him.[2] Yet instead of bringing all FCC members under their leadership, the movement was fractured, with part of the members remaining in the FCC under the leadership of Dr. Turner and the rest going with LaFarge and Markoe to create what would ultimately become the Catholic Interracial Council (CIC). The first CIC was established in New York City, but soon other major US cities would establish them as well. Mostly led by priests and with greater numbers of white members than Black members, the CICs would become the leading national Catholic organization addressing issues of race in the United States until the late 1960s.

Between 1940 and 1965, the number of Black Catholics in the United States more than doubled from around 300,000 in 1940 to more than 700,000 by 1965. A good deal of this growth came from the success of a variety of "Negro apostolates," special evangelization efforts directed at Blacks. Among the most prominent Black Catholic voices that addressed racism in the Catholic Church and in American society were those of converts. Ellen Tarry was among the most eloquent and well-published of this group. She used her position as a Black Catholic writer and convert to try to raise American Catholic consciousness about the injustices and indignities Blacks faced on a daily basis.

In 1942, Tarry published "Know Thyself, America," in *Catholic World*.[3] Two things prompted her to do so. First, it was her effort to awaken American Catholics to the fact that racism, rather than the "other forces" (i.e., communism and socialism), was the greatest problem they faced. Second, she wished to point out gross racial injustices in the American legal and penal system by making Catholic readers aware of the impending execution of Odell Waller.[4] Mr. Waller was a Black farmer from Virginia who was found guilty of shooting to death a white man. Though Waller

---

[2]Cecilia A. Moore, "Black Catholics," in *The Cambridge Companion to American Catholicism*, ed. Margaret M. McGuinness and Thomas F. Rzeznik (New York: Cambridge University Press, 2021), 281.

[3]Ellen Tarry, "Know Thyself, America," *Catholic World*, June 1942, 298–303.

[4]Ibid., 299. See also Richard B. Sherman, *The Case of Odell Waller and Virginia Justice, 1940–1942* (Knoxville: University of Tennessee Press, 1992).

did shoot the man, the medical evidence presented in the trial showed that the man died not of gunshot wounds but instead of a collapsed lung. This case compelled Tarry to call the attention of American Catholics to the racist underpinnings and applications of American law and to the disproportionate application of the death penalty to Blacks.

Tarry declared that Black Americans had reached their limits and were starting to stand up resolutely for their rights. She wrote,

> A million black men who are tired of being bullied, tired of running away from their self-respect. You can see them all over the country—if you wish to. No doubt, there was one in your kitchen today. Perhaps he handed you the morning paper, shined your shoes or washed the windows in your office. You frowned and said: "My! That's a sullen looking Negro." But you were wrong. He was a discontented Negro.[5]

Tarry counted herself among the discontented. "If America is not blind, she must be asleep. Wake up, America! Give your black children a fair share to enjoy a full life as guaranteed by the Constitution. . . . Make this a Democracy without stain. And, in God's name, hear us before it is too late."[6] A month later, Mr. Waller was dead by execution, but the passion and urgency of Tarry's exhortation returned twenty years later in the rhetoric and action of the civil rights movement. Turner and Tarry dared to speak and act on their convictions; in so doing, they helped set the stage for some racial progress in the US Catholic Church in the 1950s and 1960s, and for Black Catholics to exercise their agency in amazing ways in the 1970s, '80s, and '90s.

The range of religious, social, and political concerns and experiences that African American Catholic converts shared on the pages of Catholic journals from the 1930s to the 1960s is impressive and provocative. Black Catholics had a lot on their minds; they believed that it was their responsibility to engage Catholics in joining in the work for civil rights, and they were confident that they would be heard. The fact that they succeeded

---

[5]Tarry, "Know Thyself, America," 300.
[6]Ibid., 303.

in publishing on issues of race, justice, and faith in mainstream Catholic journals reveals that there was a willingness to listen at this time. Here, Black Catholic converts set the foundation for a Black Catholic activism that would flower in the late 1960s with the commencement of the Black Catholic movement led by clerical, religious, and lay leaders who came from the ranks of Blacks who chose Catholicism between 1930 and 1960.[7]

Young Black and white Catholics worked for the integration of Catholic institutions and for civil rights. Through efforts like their "Manhattanville Resolutions" from 1933, Catholic women at Manhattanville College asserted that because they were receiving a Catholic education, they were obligated to work for "the full measure of social justice" for Blacks.[8] In the 1940s and 1950s, Black and white students from Xavier University of Louisiana, Loyola University of the South, St. Mary's Dominican College, the College of the Sacred Heart, and Ursuline College united to dismantle racism in Catholic institutions such as their own colleges and parishes by informing their actions with prayer, study, discussion, and reflection in the Southeastern Regional Interracial Commission.[9] Young people also formed the nucleus of the Omaha DePorres Club, which was led by Father John Markoe, SJ, in the 1940s and 1950s in Nebraska. Though not formally associated with any Catholic institution, most members were Catholic, and they used Catholic social teaching as the foundation for their activism, which included boycotting, picketing, and arbitration to end racial segregation and discrimination in public accommodations, schools, housing, and employment. Though they did not win every battle they launched, they did achieve

---

[7]See Cecilia A. Moore, "Catholics, Communism, and African Americans," in *Roman Catholicism in the United States: A Thematic History*, ed. Margaret M. McGuinness and James T. Fisher (New York: Fordham University Press, 2019), 240–263; Cecilia A. Moore, "Writing Black Catholic Lives: Black Catholic Biographies and Autobiographies," *U.S. Catholic Historian* 29, no. 3 (Summer 2011): 43–58; and Cecilia A. Moore, "Conversion Narratives: The Dual Experiences and Voices of African American Catholic Converts," *U.S. Catholic Historian* 28, no. 1 (Winter 2010): 27–40.

[8]Moore, "Black Catholics," 282.

[9]See R. Bentley Anderson, *Black, White, and Catholic: New Orleans Interracialism, 1947–1956* (Nashville: Vanderbilt University Press, 2006).

some meaningful victories for racial justice in the Midwest.[10] Also during this time, key US bishops integrated Catholic institutions in their dioceses, such as Cardinal Joseph Ritter, who integrated the schools of the Archdiocese of Indianapolis in the 1930s and in the Archdiocese of St. Louis in the 1940s, and Bishop Vincent Waters, who integrated the Diocese of Raleigh, North Carolina, in 1953, a year ahead of the *Brown v. Board of Education Topeka* US Supreme Court decision that declared racial segregation laws to be unconstitutional. Black civil rights organizations recognized these as significant contributions to the cause of civil rights. In the 1960s, the Decree on Ecumenism from the Second Vatican Council gave license to Catholics to get involved in interreligious work for justice. Although there had always been Catholic supporters in the long civil rights movement, especially Black Catholics, they would become most visible in the 1965 Selma Campaign.[11] However, by the late 1960s, white Catholic attention to questions of racism, particularly in the Church, started to fade as some of the most important civil rights victories were won, as the Black Power movement began to ascend, and as they turned their attention to other quests for social justice.[12]

From the 1970s through the 1990s, Black Catholics who were intent on Black liberation as well as remaining part of the Catholic Church dedicated themselves to what they called the "Black Catholic Movement." Turning to the experiences, accomplishments, failures, and struggles of their Black Catholic forebears, they returned to values and strategies they had employed and created new ones to make the Catholic Church a place of hope for Black people. They established new organizations such as

---

[10]See Matt Holland, *Ahead of Their Time: The Story of the Omaha De-Porres Club* (North Charleston, SC: CreateSpace Independent Publishing Platform, 2014).

[11]See Cyprian Davis, O.S.B., "Black Catholics in the Civil Rights Movement in the Southern United States: A.–P. Tureaud, Thomas Wyatt Turner, and Earl Johnson," *U.S. Catholic Historian* 24, no. 4 (Fall 2006): 69-81; Shannen Dee Williams, *Subversive Habits: Black Catholic Nuns in the Long American Freedom Struggle* (Durham, NC: Duke University Press, 2022); and *Sisters of Selma*, directed by Jayasri Majumdar Hart, 2007, documentary.

[12]See Matthew Cressler, *Authentically Black and Truly Catholic: The Rise of Black Catholicism in the Great Migration* (New York: New York University Press, 2017).

the National Black Catholic Clergy Caucus, the National Black Catholic Sisters Conference, the National Black Catholic Lay Caucus, and the National Office of Black Catholics, to name a few.

Black Catholic musicians and liturgists such as Father Clarence Rivers, Mary Lou Williams, Rawn Harbor, and many others embraced the Second Vatican Council's promotion of inculturated liturgies and brought the spirituals, gospel, and jazz into Catholic worship.[13] Black Catholic scholars founded the Black Catholic Theological Symposium to nurture and advance Black Catholic scholarship. They also created the Institute for Black Catholic Studies to aid in the formation of excellent and culturally competent ministers (lay, religious, and clerical) for Black communities. Although they did not solve the problems of race in the Catholic Church, they did equip Black Catholics with resources and relationships they could turn to in order to survive, celebrate, and grow in the Catholic Church and also the strength to continue to fight new battles.

The decision of the College Theology Society to focus its annual meeting and volume on racism and the Catholic Church is important. In this brief set of remarks, I offered historical examples of Catholics in the twentieth century who took up this work with varying degrees of success and failure. They, like us, recognized the utterly destructive and anti-Christian nature of racism and the ways it is woven into American Catholic practices, positions, and perspectives as US Catholics capitulated over and against their theological teachings endemic to American racism. We are not the first to work to dismantle it and to endeavor to create new or renewed Catholic institutions, churches, schools,

---

[13]Father Clarence Rivers was the first Black priest ordained for the Archdiocese of Cincinnati. He brought together Gregorian chant and the Black Spirituals in the music he created for Catholics in the second half of the twentieth century. He is most well known for his *American Mass Program,* which he debuted in 1963. Father Rivers advocated for all Catholics to engage in what he called "soulful worship." Mary Lou Williams was a renowned jazz composer and pianist. After converting to Catholicism in the 1950s, she decided to use her gifts as a jazz artist to create music for Catholic worship. She wrote several jazz masses. Rawn Harbor is a liturgist, composer, and musician. Mentored by Father Rivers, today he creates beautiful music, particularly psalm settings, for Catholic worship. I think it important to note that they all converted to Catholicism.

attitudes, practices, and, most importantly, hearts that are free of it. I hope these examples of Catholics grappling with racism in church and society will help us today. It is time that we expand our understanding of who is adversely affected by racism in the US Catholic Church and wider society to include Native Americans, Asian and Pacific Islander Americans, Latinx Americans, and more recently arrived persons of color from around the globe. I hope history and historical context might help us recognize and avert some of the most dangerous problems, traps, blind spots, and power struggles that have made it possible for racism to continue to shape us. My final hope is that knowing and understanding some of the ways that Black Catholics, beset by the evils of racism in the Church, addressed it historically and also made places for themselves within the Catholic Church—where they exercised agency, experienced safety and happiness, put their creativity to work, and accrued power and authority—will become a starting point for this new work.

Bishop Gumbleton and the Episcopacy of the Future

Daniel Cosacchi

In a November 4, 2021, address delivered to the Congress for Catholics and Public Life, Archbishop José Gomez of Los Angeles stated, "I believe the best way for the Church to understand the new social justice movements is to understand them as pseudo-religions, and even replacements and rivals to traditional Christian beliefs."[1] Many Christians who have been involved in social justice movements were aghast at such a statement. In particular, because this address was delivered in the wake of Black Lives Matter protests throughout the United States, Black Catholics and their allies were especially "appalled" at Gomez's words.[2] In a manner of speaking, Gomez was proposing the opposite of the 2022 College Theology Society's conference theme and this annual volume. Indeed, Gomez seemed to call for waiting in responding to social injustice. This outlook has been part of an approach utilized by a growing number of US bishops in recent decades, who decry in words or actions the work of social justice movements. It is a troubling trend that is in opposition to an earlier generation of bishops, the model of which is Bishop Tom Gumbleton, who saw such movements not as pseudo-religions but as part and parcel of their Catholic faith.

---

[1] José Gomez, "Reflections on the Church and America's New Religions," November 4, 2021, https://archbishopgomez.org.

[2] See Brian Fraga, "Black Catholics Respond with Dismay as Gomez Calls Protests Pseudo-Religions," *National Catholic Reporter,* November 5, 2021, www.ncronline.org.

When Bishop Tom Gumbleton was removed as pastor of Saint Leo Church in Detroit, Cardinal Adam Maida claimed that it was due to canon law, which required the bishop's resignation at age seventy-five. Never mind that auxiliary bishops are not required to submit such resignation letters or that Maida was equally free to keep Gumbleton on as pastor of the parish. The news made national headlines in both the ecclesial and secular press, having been picked up by the *New York Times*, among other outlets. It is only fair to put my cards on the table right at the outset. In a truly just Catholic Church, Bishop Tom Gumbleton would be the norm, rather than a noteworthy exception. Popes, cardinals, and bishops would look an awful lot like him: they would demonstrate on the front lines against warfare, campaign for women's ordination to the priesthood (and let's face it, in the church I am describing, women would already be members of the clerical state), stand up for survivors of sexual abuse by priests, work for just and fair treatment of those in the LGBTQ+ community, work for actual racial justice, and on and on. What I aim to do in this essay is to grapple with the reality that Gumbleton is, in fact an outlier, and look toward the future. In what follows, I try to draw a blueprint for what episcopal ministry might look like in the twenty-first century, according to a Gumbletonian model. I do this, like Gumbleton, as a white man, yet also like Gumbleton, aware of the necessity of a constant conversion toward a church that is antiracist.[3]

The aforementioned forced retirement of Gumbleton was an occasion of great consternation for his entire parish community. In this case, Gumbleton's "crime" was his giving testimony at a January 2006 case on the statute of limitations for survivors of sexual abuse by the clergy in Ohio. Gumbleton's offense was his taking a different position from the one that the Ohio bishops had

---

[3]In proposing Gumbleton as a model, I take seriously a call that M. Shawn Copeland and others have made: white Catholic bishops, pastors, and theologians need not invite Black Catholic theologians to make an antiracist ecclesiological argument for them; they have the tools to do so themselves. See M. Shawn Copeland, "An Imperative to Act," in *CTSA Proceedings* 75 (2021): 31. Throughout this essay, I capitalize the word "Black" unless it was not capitalized in a text that I am citing directly. I will not capitalize "white." For more on this thinking, see Nancy Coleman, "Why We're Capitalizing Black," *New York Times,* July 2, 2020, www.nytimes.com.

already taken, violating the communion of bishops. But what is the communion of bishops? Speaking of episcopal communion, the fathers of Vatican II write:

> But each of them, as a member of the episcopal college and legitimate successor of the apostles, is obliged by Christ's institution and command to be solicitous for the whole Church and this solicitude, though it is not exercised by an act of jurisdiction, contributes greatly to the advantage of the universal Church.[4]

As Amanda Osheim's analysis of the Congregation for Bishops' document *Apostolorum Successores* helpfully lays out, "In an apostolic communion, due to the bishops' mutual reception of one another, the church has a communion through its hierarchy."[5] In Gumbleton's estimation, however, episcopal communion has more to do with loyalty than anything else:

> So you begin to get a structure where everything comes from the top and works its way down, so you don't get people who have initiative, who have imagination, who are creative, who are the type of people you need as a leader. Leaders are not people who simply conform to what somebody else tells them.[6]

Gumbleton has worked for the good of both the local and universal church by looking at what is best for the world at large. He has taken to heart the first lines of *Gaudium et Spes*: "The joys and the hopes, the griefs and the anxieties of the men of this age, especially those who are poor or in any way afflicted, these are the joys and hopes, the griefs and anxieties of the followers of Christ."[7] Gumbleton's episcopal ministry has been preoccupied

---

[4]Dogmatic Constitution on the Church, *Lumen Gentium* (Vatican City: November 21, 1964), no. 23, vatican.va.

[5]Amanda C. Osheim, *A Ministry of Discernment: The Bishop and the Sense of the Faithful* (Collegeville, MN: Liturgical Press, 2016), 67.

[6]Joe Feuerherd, "Gumbleton Decries Lack of Leaders," *National Catholic Reporter*, March 16, 2007, 10.

[7]Pastoral Constitution on the Church in the Modern World, *Gaudium et*

with creating a reality of peace and justice, especially for those individuals and groups who have been historically marginalized by the institutional church. As Thomas Reese notes in his study of episcopal life in the United States, "A characteristic of episcopal governance is that it is primarily reactive and not proactive."[8] Although Gumbleton's episcopal ministry has certainly been reactive, it has also been proactive in the sense that he has gone to great lengths to respond to the key evils in the world around him with solutions that go beyond those of his brother bishops. The primary cause to which Gumbleton has reacted in his episcopal ministry has been the violence of warfare.

Gumbleton's time as a bishop coincided with a destructive time in global affairs. He was consecrated a bishop in 1968, and so the Cold War was looming large for his first years as a bishop. Even then, he was convinced by a pacifism which meant that violence was never justified. Unlike some other absolute pacifists, however, Gumbleton was committed to the primacy of conscience, as were the Council fathers. As he told his biographer, Peter Feuerherd, "I can never say because I am a pacifist, everybody else must be a pacifist."[9] This differs from some other pacifists, both Christian and not, who are convinced that everyone else ought to take on their own way of thinking.[10] Feuerherd notes, "Personal conscience was his creed. Gumbleton was willing to grant others a wide array of viewpoints, as long as they followed an informed conscience."[11] But Gumbleton's own informed conscience compelled him to take stances that were not popular either among the US bishops or the American public at large. Gumbletonian pacifism, in addition to its openness toward conscience, is informed by three main factors that can pave the way for episcopal communion on the issue of racism: nonviolent civil disobedience, simple living combined with rigorous analysis, and a spirituality of listening.

Spes (Vatican City: December 7, 1965), no. 1, vatican.va.

[8]Thomas J. Reese, *Archbishop: Inside the Power Structure of the American Catholic Church* (San Francisco: Harper and Row, 1989), 349.

[9]Peter Feuerherd, *The Radical Gospel of Bishop Thomas Gumbleton* (Maryknoll, NY: Orbis Books, 2019), 76.

[10]This same particular ideology is also on display in the "pro-life" movement, wherein many involved believe that it is impossible to be a Christian without voting for a certain political candidate.

[11]Feuerherd, *The Radical Gospel.*, 76.

Gumbleton was almost unique among the bishops of our time in his willingness to stand up for nonviolence through acts of civil disobedience, including those that resulted in his arrest. In the early 1970s, while Gumbleton was among the most active bishops in working to end the Vietnam War and in supporting conscientious objectors to military service, he wrote, "In light of all these efforts and this much involvement, I was stunned and hurt when I got a handwritten letter from Dan Berrigan in which he expressed anger and frustration that I had not joined in any actions of civil disobedience."[12] Shortly after receiving this letter, Gumbleton overcame his disappointment at Berrigan's forthrightness and decided that he ought to act in such a way after all. His first of many actions of civil disobedience took place when he joined "war protestors [who] trespassed at Oscoda Michigan Air Force Base, where pilots were trained for missions in Vietnam. . . . Gumbleton was the first American bishop to undertake such an action."[13] Likewise, Gumbleton is likely the only auxiliary bishop in American church history to join in a protest outside of his archbishop's home, to voice his opposition to Cardinal Edmund Szoka's closing of parishes in Detroit.[14]

Gumbleton was among a small number of bishops who took seriously the call to live simply along with the responsibility to teach. Even though bishops do not take vows or promises of poverty, and even bishops from religious orders are released from their vow of poverty, Gumbleton has made it part and parcel of his episcopal life. As his biographer notes,

Gumbleton was legendary for simple living . . . [having] made one move putting all his possessions in the back of a hatchback car. When [his] apartment was invaded by a burglar, the thief left empty-handed, finding little of value to take, other than the photos of Dorothy Day, Oscar Romero, and other Catholic social justice heroes that lined the walls.[15]

---

[12]Thomas Gumbleton, "Courage in Abundance," in *Apostle of Peace: Essays in Honor of Daniel Berrigan,* ed. John Dear (Maryknoll, NY: Orbis Books, 1996), 34.

[13]Feuerherd, *The Radical Gospel,* 48.

[14]See ibid., 62.

[15]Ibid., 107.

Like Day and Romero, though, Gumbleton has taken on the role not only as an activist committed to a simple way of life, but as an important thinker in the life of the church. His role in the drafting of the pastoral letter *The Challenge of Peace* is a lasting part of his legacy.[16] Moreover, as Jim Castelli writes in his definitive report on the drafting of that pastoral letter, "It was Gumbleton who ultimately got the U.S. bishops to oppose the Vietnam War."[17] More than two decades after leading the way for the bishops' conversion on Vietnam, and more than a decade after drafting large sections of *The Challenge of Peace*, Gumbleton was asked by his mother if his brother Dan would be going to hell on account of his being gay. This question occasioned another turning point for Gumbleton, who felt sure that his mother wasn't the only parent dealing with such a concern: "Gumbleton suggested that the bishops put out a pastoral letter directed to parents of gay children."[18]

In many ways, Gumbleton is a traditional Catholic. He serves the people of God in Michigan parishes; like many of his brother bishops, he prays the Rosary on a daily basis. In other ways, some of which I have already noted, he is different from his brothers in the episcopacy. In addition to participating in civil disobedience and being an ally to the LGBTQ+ community, Gumbleton takes seriously his role as a listener. In 1994, at the time during which Gumbleton was pushing for the pastoral letter to parents of gay children, he was also holding listening sessions for these families. As the *National Catholic Reporter* summed up the sessions, "The three days and five forums during which a bishop listened and talked appear to be unprecedented in this nation or any other."[19] Gumbleton was a bishop moving toward a synodal church long before Pope Francis reenergized this ancient ecclesial practice. Gumbleton has long been about journeying with the people of

---

[16]See Patricia McNeal, *Harder Than War: Catholic Peacemaking in Twentieth-Century America* (New Brunswick, NJ: Rutgers University Press, 1992), 251–58.

[17]Jim Castelli, *The Bishops and the Bomb: Waging Peace in a Nuclear Age* (Garden City, NY: Image Books, 1983), 69.

[18]Feuerherd, *The Radical Gospel*, 91.

[19]Dawn Gibeau, "Gumbleton Hears Gay Stories, Some Angry," *National Catholic Reporter*, November 11, 1994, 4.

God rather than simply leading them on the way, assuming that he knew the answers ahead of time. In spring 2022, I was honored to be a representative at my former institution for the Synod on Synodality. As I was compiling the comments from our students, faculty, and staff, the one that I kept encountering was, "This was the first time the church has ever listened to me." The Gumbletonian model for bishops privileges the lives and experiences of the entire community and believes they can teach the bishops.

Ignorance of racism, it must be noted, is Gumbleton's greatest regret from his early years of parish ministry, before he became a bishop. As he recounts of the general lack of response to racism during his years of ministry in Dearborn, Michigan, "Nobody talked about it. I never thought about how wrong that was. I never preached about it, I never thought about the sin of racism."[20] As Feuerherd notes, Gumbleton could see the personal but not social sin of racism in his early priestly years in Dearborn.[21] And nevertheless, we can look at Gumbleton's life now and see that this regret prompted a conversion experience for him. As early as 1967, Gumbleton was involved in civil rights activism in Detroit, and by 1996, Gumbleton was invited to be a keynote speaker at a conference on racism in the church. Looking back to his earlier years, Gumbleton "realized that the parish, by omission, had silently taken the side of those white ethnic Catholics who, having fled Detroit, wanted nothing to do with its black residents. The parish, lively and vibrant in the swirl of school and parish activities, had confronted no social criticism of the situation."[22] This would be a conversion experience that would behoove the US Catholic bishops as a whole to address, since they are slow to recognize the structural sin of racism as it has permeated society and become part of the general culture, as well as the ecclesial culture.

Kristin Heyer writes, "In his address at PCUSA's (Pax Christi USA) annual meeting in 2002, Bishop Gumbleton juxtaposed the pax Americana with the pax Christi, highlighting the inevitable tensions inherent in the organization's efforts to advocate for values that might contradict those prioritized by the American

---

[20]Feuerherd, *The Radical Gospel*, 34.
[21]Ibid.
[22]Ibid., 38.

way or a particular administration."[23] Perhaps on no issue do the pax Americana and the pax Christi differ so egregiously as on the issue of race. As M. Shawn Copeland contends, "We Christian theologians in the United States live and work in a house haunted by the ghost of chattel slavery."[24] She continues:

> [I]ts specter lingers in the continual shape-shifting of white racist supremacy: from the enslavement of Africans and their descendants to lynching's barbarous intimidation, from segregation to institutionalized racism, from intentional deprivation of poor white and minority communities to the world's highest rate of incarceration of black and brown members of those communities, from cultural denigration of the black body to the brutal treatment, even death, of black youth, women, and men at the hands of law enforcement officers or their agents. In the current national dispensation, ordinary (white) citizens feel empowered and justified to monitor, insult, harass, attack, even murder children, women, and men who are black, brown, Jewish, Muslim, immigrants, and refugees.[25]

To do theology today, especially alongside our undergraduates at our colleges and universities, means to deal with the church's racism in a forthright manner. Every introductory course we teach in our theology and religious studies departments must deal with the legacy of chattel slavery that hangs over our nation.

Bishops of today and tomorrow, then, can learn from the three areas of Gumbleton's own episcopal ministry in reacting to the social injustices of our time. In a particular way, the bishops can become an antiracist episcopacy if they take Gumbleton's approach seriously and implement it in their lives. First, the actions of civil disobedience. Gumbleton has ceased participating in these actions over the last decade or more, concluding that they are less effective than they once were, and concludes, "we

---

[23]Kristin E. Heyer, *Prophetic and Public: The Social Witness of US Catholicism* (Washington, DC: Georgetown University Press, 2006), 133.

[24]M. Shawn Copeland, *Knowing Christ Crucified: The Witness of African American Religious Experience* (Maryknoll, NY: Orbis Books, 2018), 81.

[25]Ibid., 82.

have to come out with a new strategy."[26] I am not as convinced as Gumbleton that the tactic has lost its luster. More likely is it that civil disobedience against war garners less attention because war is not on the forefront of most Americans' minds. But with the deaths of so many Black Americans at the hands of police officers, especially, structural racism is clearly part of our daily reality in the United States. Therefore, I remain convinced that civil disobedience has tremendous value, especially if the community carefully discerns the issue to which they must respond. The civil disobedience must be marked, however, by a clear commitment to nonviolence and a holistic movement toward peace, which is the only option for the Christian.

Echoing Pope Francis years before that pontificate began, Gumbleton notes the interconnectedness of peacemaking:

> Whether it is the interpersonal peacemaking implied in the command to leave our gifts at the altar until we have reconciled with those we may have wronged and even, perhaps *especially*, those who have wronged us, or working on the peaceful resolution of the group antagonisms and hatreds which are reflected in the strife between races and classes and nations, our lives and actions should reflect the total commitment to love displayed by Jesus, ultimately, on the cross at Calvary.[27]

Participation of Catholic bishops in civil disobedience against racism is a first step in responding to what James Keenan, SJ, refers to as hierarchicalism, which he notes, "is different from [a culture] that promotes servant bishops."[28] Gumbleton's episcopal ministry has always been interested in a model of service to the People of God. In today's reality in the United States, such service needs to be seen on the ground, especially in direct response to the realities of police killings of Black people. One of the most

---

[26]Feuerherd, *The Radical Gospel*, 105.

[27]Thomas J. Gumbleton, "Peacemaking as a Way of Life," in *One Hundred Years of Catholic Social Thought*, ed. John A. Coleman (Maryknoll, NY: Orbis Books, 1991), 303.

[28]James F. Keenan, SJ, "Hierarchicalism," *Theological Studies* 83, no. 1 (2022): 94.

compelling parts of Gumbleton's legacy is that he has refused to separate the many issues that plague our society, rather seeing the integration that Pope Francis has so prophetically written about in *Laudato Si'*. One of the key steps of being an antiracist, according to Ibram X. Kendi, is that one "struggles to remain at the antiracist intersections where racism is mixed with other bigotries."[29] This involves more than simply thinking that a given belief is right or wrong; it involves putting one's body and liberty on the line. Such is the fate of the bishop in this Gumbletonian model.

In the second case, Gumbleton has been a teacher, both through his spoken word and in the way he lives his life. Along with sanctifying and governing, teaching is one of the three principal functions of the bishop. As Saint Paul VI correctly observed, "Modern man listens more willingly to witnesses than to teachers, and if he does listen to teachers, it is because they are witnesses."[30] Who is really listening to their bishop when it comes to key questions in their lives right now? They are not ignoring the bishop because he has nothing valuable to say, but rather because the college of bishops has acted in such a manner that has silenced the voice of the congregation over the last decades. That is the definition of corruption. If these bishops were up for tenure in an institution—like the academy—that values teaching, many would surely be denied on account of moral turpitude. And yet the majority of bishops blame the media, rather than their own failings, for their inability to teach effectively. In an incredible 2016 study carried out by the Center of Applied Research for the Apostolate (CARA), bishops in the United States were presented with the following statement: "Media coverage of clergy sexual abuse has made it challenging to present or defend Church teaching in my diocese." In response to that statement, some 63 percent of bishops either answered "agree strongly" or "agree somewhat."[31] What these bishops do not seem to grasp is that the media is accurately covering their

---

[29]Ibram X. Kendi, *How to Be an Antiracist* (New York: One World, 2019), 226.

[30]Paul VI, *Evangelii Nuntiandi* (Vatican City: December 8, 1975), no. 41, vatican.va.

[31]Stephen J. Fichter, Thomas P. Gaunt, SJ, Catherine Hoegeman, CSJ, and Paul M. Perl, *Catholic Bishops in the United States: Church Leadership in the Third Millennium* (Oxford: Oxford University Press, 2019), 148.

own misdeeds. So who is truly at fault for the bishops' inability to teach? The bishops themselves. Teaching the faith today needs to include teaching with prophetic documents, as opposed to what the bishops offered in their 2018 pastoral letter on racism, *Open Wide Our Hearts*. In fact, their strongest condemnation in this letter was reserved for "violent attacks against police."[32] I urge the bishops of this country to take Gumbleton's analytical legacy to heart. As someone who was a driving force behind two of the bishops' most important documents, Gumbleton leads the way in how bishops can be a force for good through an intellectual lens.

The bishop of the future, then, will continue to teach, govern, and sanctify, but if their ministry is to have any effectiveness at all, it must carry out these essential tasks in a new way that better serves the people. Bishops have an important role in passing on the church's message. As Pope Francis realizes, "The language that young people understand is spoken by those who radiate life, by those that are there for them and with them. And those who, for all their limitations and weaknesses, try to live their faith with integrity."[33] These people are not just bishops and priests; and men who have been nominated for the episcopacy would do well to seek them out and learn from them how best to proclaim the words of everlasting life. In some circumstances, bishops may even cede some of their homilies to especially gifted preachers, both lay and ordained. All teaching in the church must be antiracist, or it will not be faithful to its gospel mandate. All of the bishops' sanctifying and governing should emerge from this teaching. Gumbleton has become a model in how to carry this out faithfully.

Finally, I must note how sincerely Gumbleton has listened. Today, if bishops are going to live as authentically antiracist stewards of the Gospel, they must listen in three areas. First, crucially, they must listen to the voices whose blood calls from the ground. They must listen to the litany of names of Black persons murdered in the United States: Jason Walker, Lindani Myeni, Daunte Wright, Andre Hill, George Floyd, Breonna Taylor, Freddie Gray, Michael Brown, all you holy women and men, pray for us. And also, they must listen to their families, friends, communities, and Black

---

[32]United States Conference of Catholic Bishops, *Open Wide Our Hearts* (2018), 5.

[33]Francis, *Christus Vivit* (March 25, 2019), no. 211.

theologians. In the second place, and this is much more difficult to justify, they must listen to those who are part of the system of racism—namely all of us—and even those who are guilty of overtly racist behavior. Listen to these words of Gumbleton:

> Clearly it is the role of the peacemaker to try and look not for the evil of those threatening the world with violence, with oppression, with nuclear annihilation, but to look for their goodness, their capability, and to begin working with them. Clearly the attitude of the nonviolent peacemaker ought to grow more receptive to possibilities of reconciliation within our own national community.[34]

Most importantly, the bishops who follow in Gumbleton's footsteps will listen to Jesus. Then, as Shawn Copeland writes, "Immersed in the heart of Christ, the disciple is nourished for a praxis of solidarity and compassion."[35]

I return finally to the relationship of being reactive and proactive. Bishops who live and serve like Gumbleton has done will certainly react to the realities of human life, especially those who are suffering the most. But, unlike Archbishop Gomez, they will not stop there. Whereas Gomez critiqued the work of social justice movements, the Catholic bishop of the future should embrace these movements and be on the front lines of their protests and activism. The 2022 College Theology Society Annual Convention took as its theme "'Why We Can't Wait': Racism and the Church." Or, as the author of the Letter of Saint James put it, "But be doers of the word, and not merely hearers who deceive themselves. . . . If any think they are religious, and do not bridle their tongues but deceive their hearts, their religion is worthless. Religion that is pure and undefiled before God, the Father, is this: to care for orphans and widows in their distress, and to keep oneself unstained by the world" (James 1:22, 26–27). When Gumbleton adopted the beginning of this passage as his episcopal motto more than a half century ago, he never would have imagined that someone

---

[34]Thomas J. Gumbleton, "The Role of the Peacemaker," in *War or Peace?: The Search for New Answers,* ed. Thomas A. Shannon (Maryknoll, NY: Orbis Books, 1980), 228.

[35]Copeland, *Knowing Christ Crucified,* 120.

would use him as a model for future bishops today. And yet his reflection on that motto is instructive for all Christians: "Being a doer of the word means taking all of the Scriptures, everything in these Scriptures, very seriously. You make them a part of your life—doers of the word, not hearers. It also means not only the scriptures, but Jesus."[36] To follow Jesus today means working toward an antiracist church. I am most grateful that Bishop Gumbleton has paved such a path for us these five decades, and I pray that Jesus' example of nonviolent love, forgiveness, care for the marginalized, and unconditional inclusion will lead our bishops to work for a future church that fulfills his dying wish: that they may all be one (John 17:22).

---

[36]Feuerherd, *The Radical Gospel*, 59.

Fratelli Tutti at the Intersection of Interfaith Studies and Whiteness

John N. Sheveland

One of the remarkable elements of the 2020 encyclical letter *Fratelli Tutti* of Pope Francis is the imprint upon it of Muslim-Catholic dialogue (§285).[1] The encyclical quotes from a collaborative statement issued one year prior by Pope Francis and the Grand Imam of Al-Azhar University in Cairo, Ahmad al-Tayyeb. Calling for "reconciliation and fraternity among all believers," *A Document on Human Fraternity for World Peace and Living Together* can also be noted for the effects upon the pope of dialogue with Muslims, and for the presence of Islamic teachings and Quranic themes. Through this co-authored document and the subsequent encyclical letter, Islamic teachings and Quranic themes now hold space in the papal magisterium.[2] How will this be received over time by American Catholics, and by white American Catholics in particular? Will the interreligious friendship and the presence of distinctively Islamic teachings in his writings be celebrated, greeted with indifference, or perhaps interpreted and dismissed through the distorting lens of polarization in the US context?[3] This chap-

---

[1] Pope Francis, Encyclical Letter *Fratelli Tutti* (On Fraternity and Social Friendship), October 3, 2020, www.vatican.va.

[2] Pope Francis and the Grand Imam of Al-Azhar Ahmad al-Tayyeb, *A Document on Human Fraternity and World Peace for Living Together*, February 3, 2019, www.vatican.va.

[3] See Asheley R. Landrum, "Polarized U.S. Publics, Pope Francis, and Climate Change: Reviewing the Studies and Data Collected around the 2015

ter argues that whiteness may be a limiting factor in the church's reception of these papal teachings and example (§§41, 44–46, 97, 220, 232) and that strategies for interruption will be needed in order for the encyclical letter to be received and implemented.

The encounters and friendship between the Pope and the Grand Imam represent a meaningful growth in the tradition which, only a few years prior, included Pope Benedict XVI's widely criticized treatment of Islam in a lecture at the University of Regensburg (2006).[4] While one should note the influence of dialogue on Pope Francis and the presence of the Quran in papal magisterium (not verbatim but in content and echo), one may wonder about the church's reception of *Fratelli Tutti* among leadership and laity. *Fratelli Tutti* gives eloquent expression to the Christian vocation to open wide one's heart to the world in love and solidarity, especially, in these years, to the migrant, the refugee, those displaced by war.[5] *Fratelli Tutti* captures the Christian response to such persons in a series of imperatives to "welcome, protect, promote, and integrate" (§129). The pope writes of a gratuitous openness to others precisely in the context of nationalisms which Francis identifies as narrow and oppositional to the gratuitous openness he defines as "the ability to do some things simply because they are good in themselves" (§130).

Fratelli Tutti offers a model of interreligious bridge-building and friendship to develop this gratuitous openness. Just as he did previously in the 2015 encyclical letter *Laudato Si'* (On Care for Our Common Home), Francis the pope calls to mind his namesake Francis the saint, from the thirteenth century, as inspiration for *Fratelli Tutti*.

> Unconcerned with the hardships and dangers involved, Francis went to meet the Sultan with the same attitude he instilled in his disciples: if they found themselves "among

---

Papal Encyclical," *WIREs Climate Change* 11 (2020): 1–13.

[4]Edmund Chia, "Regensburg and Dialogue," *Studies in Interreligious Dialogue* 17, no. 1 (2007): 70–82.

[5]"Open Wide Our Hearts" is the title of the U.S. Bishops' 2018 pastoral letter against racism. The text of the letter was voted upon and passed overwhelmingly at the November 2018 plenary assembly of bishops. See www.usccb.org.

the Saracens and other non-believers," without renouncing their own identity they were not to "engage in arguments or disputes, but to be subject to every human creature for God's sake." In the context of the times, it was an extraordinary recommendation.[6]

It was St. Francis's call for Christians to be "subject to every human creature for God's sake" that inspired Pope Francis's manner of encounter with Islam and the Grand Imam al-Tayyeb; it was less a formal intellectual dialogue than an informal, unscripted encounter around which a friendship and partnership subsequently developed. Indeed, the pope calls for a spirituality of interpersonal encounter somewhat more than a formal interreligious dialogue. As the Grand Imam and Pope Francis say in their *Document on Human Fraternity*, "we declare the adoption of a culture of dialogue as the path, mutual cooperation as the code of conduct, reciprocal understanding as the method and standard." Not included in the introduction of *Fratelli Tutti* are St. Francis's other words of counsel, to "announce" the Word of God in order that unbelievers might come to believe in the triune God. This omission, however, has less to do with Pope Francis's putatively denying evangelization and more to do with his gleaning particular wisdom from the tradition to implement today a Catholic identity predicated on *encounter*. Pope Francis calls on Saint Francis to support the call to love beyond borders by being subject to every human creature for God's sake. His intentional act of interpretation and meaning making around the St. Francis tradition finds support in contemporary author Eboo Patel, who invites interfaith leaders to construct their own identity on the basis of moments or persons of inspiration they purposefully retrieve from their home tradition for constructive application in the present.[7]

Similarly, Pope Francis reports on his own encounter and friendship with the Grand Imam of Al Azhar University in Cairo, Ahmad al-Tayyeb, since 2016. At the behest of the Grand Imam's assistant, Judge Mohamed Abdel Salam, they set out to co-author,

---

[6] *Fratelli Tutti* §3.
[7] Eboo Patel, *Interfaith Leadership: A Primer* (Boston: Beacon Press, 2016), 36.

in secret, a very plain-sense *Document on Human Fraternity*, released in Abu Dhabi during the pope's apostolic journey to the United Arab Emirates in February 2019. The intended audience is broad and popular, and the message includes content and echoes from the Quran.

Consider *Fratelli Tutti*, which quotes directly from that *Document on Human Fraternity*. Francis approves of the originally co-authored statement sufficiently to cite it at length in his own voice in *Fratelli Tutti* §285. While the language is not a direct quotation of Quran 5:32, it is very close; the content and the echo are unmistakable.

> In the name of innocent human life that God has forbidden to kill, affirming that whoever kills is like one who kills the whole of humanity and that whoever saves a person is like one who saves the whole of humanity. (*Fratelli Tutti* §285; *Human Fraternity*, 2)
>
> We decreed to the children of Israel that if anyone kills a person—unless in retribution for murder or spreading corruption in the land—it is as if he kills all mankind, while if any saves a life it is as if he saves the lives of all mankind. (Quran 5:32)

It is significant that both the *Document on Human Fraternity* and *Fratelli Tutti* include this echo from Sura 5 of the Quran. Not only is the echo unmistakable, but what is discovered as binding and worthy of repetition in the present context is the Quran's own making sense of itself as inherently connected to the people of the Book—Jews and Christians—here identified as the children of Israel. To receive this teaching into Catholic social teaching is thus not merely to embrace the irrevocable dignity of the human person, crucial and always prophetic as that is ("whoever saves a person is like one who saves the whole of humanity"). It is also to acknowledge, respect, and reiterate the Quran's own bridge-building techniques with the people to whom, according to the Quran's own understanding, God previously sent messengers and teachings and with whom the Quran understands itself to be in fraternal relationship.

Quran 5:32 is not the only example from the *Document on Human Fraternity* that, in effect, places echoes of the Quran into the mouths of the Grand Imam and Pope Francis. At least one other example can be found, which echoes the Quran's injunctions to protect places of worship, principally Jewish synagogues, Christian churches, and mosques.

> The protection of places of worship—synagogues, churches and mosques—is a duty guaranteed by religions, human values, laws and international agreements. Every attempt to attack places of worship or threaten them by violent assaults, bombings, or destruction is a deviation from the teachings of religions as well as a clear violation of international law. (*Human Fraternity*, 5)
>
> Those who have been attacked are permitted to take up arms because they have been wronged—God has the power to help them—those who have been driven unjustly from their homes only for saying, "Our Lord is God." If God did not repel some people by means of others, many monasteries, churches, synagogues, and mosques, where God's name is much invoked, would have been destroyed. (Quran 22:39–40)

It is worth a moment of pause to contemplate the force of the encounter and friendship of Pope Francis and the Grand Imam, how it contributes new language and theological angles into Catholic social teaching, and how that friendship has become the source of the Quran not verbatim but in content and echo having a place—holding space—in Catholic social teaching. Two observations may follow.

First, in a climate of widespread and often unacknowledged anti-Muslim sentiment, *drawing closer to that which is Islamic* (namely, Muslim people, leaders, the text of the Quran itself, joint struggle for shared justice imperatives and defense of the other, minorities, and houses of worship) is itself a way of undoing anti-Muslim sentiment, whereas the Islamophobia "industry" seeks to trigger in persons a desire for distance or space from the constructed other, the target of exaggerations or even untruths. Consider, for example, the exhaustive work of Georgetown's Bridge Initiative to track a wide range of current issues, organizations, and individuals related to Islamophobia, or the British government's 1997 Runnymede Report, which defined Islamophobia as "unfounded hostility towards Islam," and mentions eight stigmatizing characteristics frequently observed and adapted to local conditions, including that Islam is monolithic and static, that it's separate and does not share the values of other cultures, that it's primitive relative to the West, that it's aggressive and prone to a clash of civilizations, that it's an ideology not a religion, that it is intolerant to Western critique, that exclusion of Muslims is deserving, and that anti-Muslim hostility follows as a normal response.[8] Anti-Muslim sentiment, or what Amir Hussain may refer to more aptly as "misoislamia," is driven not only by fear of religious difference but by hatred of it, one that may couple racialized otherness and religious otherness in its objectifying gaze.[9]

Social psychologist and former president of the American Psychological Association Robert Sternberg has contributed a theory for the development of hate which allows us to appreciate how the emotions and cognitive states of hate are actually diverse, pluriform, and themselves bundled: (1) hate can take hold as a disgust response that seeks distancing from the target; (2) hate can arise quickly when a threat, real or perceived, is recognized and a subsequent anger or fear response takes hold, potentially with addictive associations; (3) often the fruit of educational systems, leadership, and propaganda impacting populations from a young age, hate can become cemented as a durable, nearly impossible to change cognitive commitment to the devaluation of the target group in a manner that individual members of the group are seen not as individuals but stereotyped representatives of the whole, perceived from within the in-group as uniform and negative. So too, these three root forms of hating can combine into complex and potent forms of hating.[10] For Sternberg, we

---

[8]Raymond Taras, "'Islamophobia Never Stands Still': Race, Religion, and Culture," *Ethnic and Racial Studies* 36, no. 3 (2013): 418. See also Eboo Patel, *Out of Many Faiths: Religious Diversity and the American Promise* (Princeton, NJ: Princeton University Press, 2018), 33–77.

[9]On "misoislamia" as a neologism, see Amir Hussain, "Confronting Misoislamia: Teaching Religion and Violence in Courses on Islam," in *Teaching Religion and Violence,* ed. Brian K. Pennington (New York: Oxford University Press, 2012), 118–148.

[10]Robert J. Sternberg, "The Duplex Theory of Hate: Development and Application to Terrorism, Massacres, and Genocide," *Review of General Psychology* 7, no. 3 (2003): 299–328.

develop anger or fear responses in connection to particular triggers, and in this case the triggers could be a headscarf, news coverage of a war zone or terrorism, the sound of Arabic spoken or recited, and others.[11]

What the pope has done in both the co-authored *Document* and his own encyclical letter is to help people of good will to undo those unfounded responses of disgust and distancing by replacing them with intimacy and what social justice scholar-activist Bryan Stevenson calls "proximity."[12] When theologians, pastors, and bishops teach *Fratelli Tutti*, they should lean into these dynamics of proximity and intimacy, go straight to the Muslim-Christian impetus of this encyclical and to its unmistakable Quranic themes and echoes, not only because these are ingredients to the teaching of Catholic social teaching but because, as honesty requires one to recognize, our minds have become colonized by cultural flows of anti-Muslim sentiment, and it is through encounter and intimacy that such malformation can be undone.

A second observation has to do with the church's reception of *Fratelli Tutti* as a community. Given the significance of the encounter of the Pope and the Grand Imam and what this encounter produced by way of teaching, the church and its educational institutions do well to revisit relationships at the local level and, in particular, parish interfaith activities for children. Francis went first not to ideas and formal dialogues, but to tenderness and kindness in relationships, and then produced something more formal by way of texts and teachings. Becoming more deliberate about opportunities for our children to engage other children across boundaries of difference would express leadership and a willingness to receive and implement the teachings of *Fratelli Tutti* on the part of adults, and would cultivate the leadership capacities and social capital on the part of children. Children often intuit that

---

[11]For a perceptive study of the stigmatization of Muslim women's head coverings, see Martha Nussbaum, *The New Religious Intolerance: Overcoming the Politics of Fear in an Anxious Age* (Cambridge, MA: The Belknap Press of Harvard University Press, 2012).

[12]See Bryan Stevenson, *Just Mercy: A Story of Justice and Redemption*, reprint ed. (New York: Spiegel and Grau, 2014); Khyati Y. Joshi, *White Christian Privilege: The Illusion of Religious Equality in America* (New York: NYU Press, 2021).

human difference is natural, regular. Perhaps if the church can receive and build Catholic identity as inclusive of such interfaith activities for children, where they simply share space and grow to love across boundaries, they can become teachers of adults in turn and help to remodel both church and society according to the vision of *Fratelli Tutti* as exemplars of encounter.

The formation of children in particular is crucial because, as Raymond Taras describes, Islamophobia "bundles" religious, ethnic, and cultural prejudices together,[13] which means the church needs to approach its own environment *ad intra* and *ad extra* with a critical willingness to recognize and deconstruct anti-Muslim sentiment with its attending racialization of Muslims. It means the church's proper work includes the untangling of bundled religious, racial, ethnic, and cultural prejudices early, often, and in developmentally appropriate ways. Similar to antisemitism, Taras shows, Islamophobia displays a variety of prejudices alongside mere religious prejudice, such that antisemitism is a larger bundling of prejudice than anti-Judaism, as Islamophobia contains a larger bundling of prejudices than unfounded animus against Islam as a religion. Islamophobia deserves intersectional analysis. In particular, Islamophobia racializes Muslim subjects by offering a "cryptic articulation of the concepts of race and racism," even if presenting only as a religious prejudice.[14] Overlaying cryptic articulations of race are additional contextual factors in Europe and North America, like anti-immigration, anti-minority, and anti-terrorism narratives, all frequently cited in *Fratelli Tutti* as a diminishment of a common humanity and a vocational task of Christians to undo and heal, through fraternity and social friendship.

Francis offers some diagnosis of the social situation relevant to anti-Muslim sentiment and the racialization of Muslims, though he does not use those terms. The following two examples from *Fratelli Tutti* §41 and §97 are indicative of how racism is mentioned in a variety of paragraphs, including §§20, 41, 86, 97, and 141.

---

[13]Taras, "'Islamophobia Never Stands Still,'" 425.
[14]Ibid., 422.

I realize that some people are hesitant and fearful with regard to migrants. I consider this part of our natural instinct of self-defense. Yet it is also true that an individual and a people are only fruitful and productive if they are able to develop a creative openness to others. I ask everyone to move beyond those primal reactions because there is a problem when doubts and fears condition our ways of thinking and acting to the point of making us intolerant, closed and perhaps even—without realizing it—racist. In this way, fear deprives us of the desire and ability to encounter the other. (§41)

Some peripheries are close to us, in city centers or within families. Hence there is an aspect of universal openness in love that is more existential than geographical. It has to do with our daily efforts to expand our circle of friends, to reach those who, even though they are close to me, I do not naturally consider a part of my circle of interests. Every brother or sister in need, when abandoned or ignored by the society in which I live, becomes an existential foreigner. They may be citizens with full rights, yet they are treated like foreigners in their own country. Racism is a virus that quickly mutates and, instead of disappearing, goes into hiding, and lurks in waiting. (§97)

Throughout these paragraphs, the mention of racism, while critically important and productive, is not fleshed out with studies about race, racialization, or whiteness. The references to racism instead appear more occasional, in connection with the treatment of the elderly or migrants, or the length of time it took for the church to condemn slavery, or narrow forms of nationalism. The force of the meaning of the term "racism" in the context of its use appears presumed. The good news is that the encyclical letter invites readers to think and feel differently about the impact of racism upon a range of social issues, implying a grasp of intersectionality or bundling. The bad news is that these references are not yet accompanied by a practice to help readers undo their own racism, unconscious and otherwise. In §41 it is very helpful that the text conscientizes readers of these primal reactions which, from a hate studies perspective, are associated with the amygdala and how propaganda can manipulate one's fight/flight (anger/fear) responses. But §41 makes no specific requests and offers no practical guide for undoing one's spontaneous racialized reactions. Those teaching the encyclical letter will need to strategize accordingly.

Likewise, §97 contains a valuable observation about the historical adaptability and durability of supremacy.[15] It is instructive to inventory the ways white supremacy has been a shapeshifter in the historical past and present, how it has adapted to new cultural factors, how some racialized persons can and have played its game and gained power and privilege, and that it has been predicated on being hidden in plain sight as Willie James Jennings has argued.[16] As Pope Francis implies, it is important to recognize how racism—specifically, whiteness—holds an attractive lure for many (i.e., it "lurks in waiting"). The encyclical employs not the more analytically precise language of white supremacy or whiteness but opts instead for "racism," a term even notorious white supremacists dodge and disavow. In the teaching and preaching of this encyclical letter, more precise language will be needed to confront the reader, disrupt their comfort, and facilitate their own painful reckoning with and deconstruction of racialized identity and privilege. Sections 41 and 97 (and also §§20, 86, and 141) do little to confront the reader or provide practices for the conversion of hearts. This being so, will the document be read by contempo-

---

[15]Kelly Brown Douglas, *Stand Your Ground: Black Bodies and the Justice of God* (Maryknoll, NY: Orbis Books, 2015), 3–46.

[16]Willie James Jennings, "Teaching and Living toward a Revolutionary Intimacy," in *"You Say You Want a Revolution?": 1968–2018 in Theological Perspective*, ed. Susie Paulik Babka, Elena Procario-Foley, and Sandra Yocum (Maryknoll, NY: Orbis Books, 2019), 12–14. One example of the adaptation of white supremacy by its exponents is the manufacture of neologisms like ethnopluralism, a theory of racial difference common among advocates of the European New Right and among identitarian and alt-right advocates. Ethnopluralism projects a racialization of others in which humanity is recognized as a mosaic of varieties of race, each with inherited essence and features, and each linked with a space or home in which it belongs, and where they are regarded as pure to the degree they stay in their space. Moving from their own space into the spaces of others, however, renders them a threat to the purity of others. Disharmony results from mixing. See Mattias Gardell, *Lone Wolf Race Warriors and White Genocide* (Cambridge: Cambridge University Press, 2021), 10–11.

rary white Catholics through the lens of whiteness, which is to say, through the lens of comfort protected, rectitude presumed, and in spaces, mostly homogenous, where our bundled or intersecting biases remain protected and invisible to our untrained eyes? Or will it be read—and taught—with a sharper angle of attack and willingness to confess cultural sin, our participation in it, and the historical shaping or inheritance of the same?

I borrow this line of questioning from Jeannine Hill Fletcher, who wrote about the manner in which *Nostra Aetate* (Declaration on the Relation of the Church to Non-Christian Religions) may have been received in the racialized climate of the US in 1965. She expressed concern that *Nostra Aetate* may not have done enough in its own time to disentangle notions of religious supremacy from racialized supremacy, neither in the authorship of the declaration nor in the community's reception of it, and that in our time it does not do enough.[17] One can pose similar questions for the reception of *Fratelli Tutti*: given the rise in ethno-religious nationalisms globally; given the thriving and violent white supremacy visible in our public and ecclesial lives; given the entanglement of anti-Muslim sentiment with the racialization of Muslims from a presumptive center of whiteness, can we honestly say that *Fratelli Tutti* does enough to interrupt the religio-racial project on display in the North Atlantic? The encyclical repeatedly repudiates racism and its role in our disowning of refugees and migrants, for example. But will its words, in our hearing, shade too close to the comfort of our domestication? Will the church's reception of the encyclical itself be domesticated, blunted by a whiteness to be protected above all else? An obvious action facing the church is to enter into conversation with a developed inventory of whiteness so as to perceive its bundled features in our lives, feelings, and public spaces.[18] Karen Teel models such an inventory in her contribution to this volume. The productive reader should not expect the encyclical to do the work of the reader for himself or herself, but rather be summoned by the text into new and authentic forms

---

[17]Jeannine Hill Fletcher, "Foreign to the Mind of Christ: Nostra Aetate in America's Religio-Racial Project," in *The Future of Interreligious Dialogue: A Multireligious Conversation on* Nostra Aetate, ed. Charles L. Cohen, Paul F. Knitter, and Ulrich Rosenhagen (Maryknoll, NY: Orbis Books, 2017), 61–76.

[18]Jennings, "Teaching and Living toward a Revolutionary Intimacy," 9.

of responsibility for one's own formation and conditioning, and preparation for conversion.

Yale theologian and pastor Willie James Jennings analyzes whiteness through how it thinks, feels, and hides—and attaches to each an action step for the renunciation of it. In response he calls for a "revolutionary intimacy" and specifies it as "an intentionality of intimacy of life together."[19] Pope Francis and Grand Imam Ahmad al-Tayyeb embody one direction such revolutionary intimacy might take.

According to Jennings, we must forget about whiteness as phenotype or even as European heritage. Instead,

> Whiteness was never a person or a people, whiteness was never an aspect of creation, and whiteness has certainly never been a state of grace. Whiteness was and is a way of being in the world and a way of perceiving the world at the same time. Whiteness was and is a way of imagining oneself as the central facilitating reality of the world, the reality that makes sense of the world; whiteness is a frame of reference that interprets, organizes, and narrates the world, and whiteness is having the power to realize and sustain that imagination. Whiteness was and is a form of life built upon imperial possibilities.[20]

In the teaching and in the reception of this powerful encyclical letter, we will need to take ownership of the ways in which whiteness thinks, feels, and hides, and then to renounce the same. We will need, according to Jennings, to enter freshly into the life of Jesus as a learner in order to renounce the disputational and masculinist form of how whiteness thinks (referenced in this volume by Simon-Mary Aihiokhai); we will need to renounce the ways whiteness feels by recognizing *that* whiteness feels, that it has an affective structure that feels normal and positive but which stands in need of conversion; and we will need to renounce the ways whiteness hides by denying whiteness the invisibility it seeks, by renouncing the need to control space and to shape communities according to

---

[19]Ibid., 14.
[20]Ibid., 5.

geographic whiteness, which Jennings describes as forming "lives lived in parallel," and the false comfort of what he describes as a "suburbia of mind if not of place."[21] *Fratelli Tutti* can take us far along this path on the strength of its Muslim-Christian encounter and its open, repetitive disavowal of racisms with their bundled features and shapeshifting ways. But it falls to the responsibility of white Catholics to conduct our own inventories of whiteness and to set aside our bundled biases for the encyclical's prophetic summons to human encounter and intimacy to gain a fuller reception within and beyond the church.[22]

---

[21]Ibid., 12–13. See note 15, above, on ethnopluralism.

[22]I am grateful to anonymous reviewers who offered generous and critical feedback on an earlier draft of this chapter, to the volume editors who did the same, and to my colleagues Dr. Gloria Chien and Rabbi Elizabeth Goldstein for our earlier collaborative work on *Fratelli Tutti* at Gonzaga University.

The Church, Urban Violence, and Racial-Spatial Inequity in Baltimore

Reading Acts through Liberation Theology

Vincent Lui

If God so loved the world, then, asks Gustavo Gutiérrez, "How is it possible to tell the poor, who are forced to live in conditions that embody a denial of love, that God loves them?"[1] Gutiérrez's incisive question raises further questions: Who exactly is forcing the poor to live in such dehumanizing conditions? What if it is Christians and churches that have been guilty of such sin? These questions can be applied to many situations around the world today. However, in order to be as relevant as possible to my local context, I shall focus on urban violence and racial-spatial inequity in Baltimore City, Maryland. Many cities across the United States grapple with urban violence and racial-spatial inequity.[2] A discussion of Baltimore applies to cities facing similar issues because Baltimore was the birthplace of the public policies of racial-spatial inequity.[3] I ask: What does it mean to be a Christian

---

[1]Gustavo Gutiérrez, *A Theology of Liberation: History, Politics, and Salvation*, rev. ed. (Maryknoll, NY: Orbis Books, 1988), xxxiv.

[2]See, e.g., Educational Fund to Stop Gun Violence, "Community Gun Violence," efsgv.org.

[3]Lawrence Brown, *The Black Butterfly: The Harmful Politics of Race and Space in America* (Baltimore: Johns Hopkins University Press, 2021), 63. Brown lists city ordinances, real estate practices, mortgage lending, code enforcement, municipal budgets, zoning laws, urban planning, urban renewal, and urban development.

and what does it mean to be the "church" within the "White L" of Baltimore City's "Black Butterfly,"[4] as Baltimore City faces the seemingly intractable problem of high rates of deadly violence and its systemic and structural causes?

Why do I ask these questions? Simply put, Black[5] lives are being lost to urban violence at appallingly high rates. In Baltimore, the homicide rates have been extremely high,[6] averaging over 333 murders each year since 2015 and 230 murders each year from 2007 to 2014.[7] I have asked several churches in Baltimore's White L how they are responding to the problem, but I received no satisfactory answers. This is perhaps unsurprising if one considers the fact that the neighborhoods of the White L—the geographic center of Baltimore that runs mostly north-to-south—are predominantly White and much wealthier than the surrounding neighborhoods.[8]

Full disclosure: In my nine years in Baltimore, I have attended various churches within the White L and lived in the White L for six years; three years ago, my wife and I chose to live in the Black Butterfly. As violence has spiked during the COVID-19 pandemic, my wife and I have heard gunshots at the next block from our window. As we pray for our neighbors, this essay is also a search for ways to make a difference in our community and the lives of

---

[4]See ibid., 9, 14.

[5]I follow Eve Ewing (cited by the MacArthur Foundation), who capitalizes the word White, as well as the phrases Whiteness and White supremacist. As Ewing explains, we ought to not render the identifiable and measurable social benefits of Whiteness invisible, "while the rest of us are saddled with this unpleasant business of being racialized." Eve L. Ewing, "I'm a Black Scholar Who Studies Race. Here's Why I Capitalize 'White,' " *ZORA*, July 2, 2020, https://zora.medium.com; Kristen Mack and John Palfrey, "Capitalizing Black and White: Grammatical Justice and Equity," *MacArthur Foundation*, August 26, 2020, www.macfound.org.

[6]In 2013, for example, Baltimore City had the fifth highest homicide rate in the nation, at 37.4 per 100,000 people. Justin Fenton, "New FBI Statistics: Baltimore No. 5 in Murder Rate," *Baltimore Sun*, November 10, 2014, www. baltimoresun.com. As context, the national homicide rate in 2013 was 4.5 per 100,000 people, meaning that Baltimore's homicide rate has been extremely high and seemingly intractable. See FBI, "Crime in the United States 2013," https://ucr.fbi.gov.

[7]*Baltimore Sun*, "Baltimore Homicides," Baltimore Sun Media Group, https://homicides.news.baltimoresun.com.

[8]See Brown, *The Black Butterfly*, 14. One need only walk north from Johns Hopkins University to Loyola University Maryland to see the wealth.

our neighbors. Neither my wife nor I are White or Black, but I bring my standpoint as an American-born Asian male of lower-middle-class immigrants, who have had their shares of struggles in the US. Also, notably, I am writing this essay as a student of Loyola University Maryland, which is situated in the northern region of the White L. Again, my questions arise from within the White L, and they apply to the churches and Christians within the White L, including myself. While attending various churches in Baltimore's White L, I found it increasingly untenable to sing of God's love every Sunday without addressing the conditions in the Black Butterfly that embody a denial of love. Given the dearth of answers from churches in the White L during the recent period of heightened violence, I embarked on my own research. This essay captures part of my ongoing effort to synthesize public policy analysis and theological analysis of the problems facing Baltimore.

White L and Black Butterfly:
The Historical and Theological Depth of Sin in Baltimore

If churches and Christians in the White L seem largely unmoved by the violence in Baltimore, then it will be useful to examine some of the major differences between the White L and the rest of Baltimore. Here, the conditions that embody a denial of love—when plotted on a map—form the shape of a butterfly. The Black Butterfly is a term coined by Lawrence Brown to describe the overlap between racial segregation and political, economic, and sociocultural inequity.[9] Maps of homicides, poverty rate, and concentration of Blacks or African Americans by census tract all share a similar butterfly pattern.[10] In the middle of the Black Butterfly is the White L, which is characterized by relative safety, wealth, and concentration of Whites.

The basic geographical analysis above begins to problematize notions of "senseless violence," a phrase that the author sometimes

---

[9]Ibid., 9.

[10]Regarding violence, see the *Baltimore Sun*, "Baltimore Homicides." Regarding race, see United States Census Bureau, "2020 Census Demographic Data Map Viewer," https://mtgis-portal.geo.census.gov. Regarding poverty, see United States Census Bureau, "Census Poverty Status Viewer (ACS19)," https://mtgis-portal.geo.census.gov.

encounters in personal conversations and media reports. Much more sophisticated geographical analysis could be done. However, for the sake of brevity, consider Brown's sharp explanation for the violence:

> [W]hat appears to be senseless begins to make more sense once the downward cycle of Black neighborhood destruc-tion is taken into account. . . . A homicide epidemic erupts when the effects of invisible and slow violence accumulate over time and the cycle of Black community destruction reaches a critical stage. . . . When Black neighborhoods are *systemically deprived* of resources due to regimes of urban apartheid, crime and violence often escalate. Structural violence slowly becomes manifest through fast and visible street violence.[11]

Furthermore, Black communities have suffered ongoing histori-cal trauma from multiple waves of uprootings, disruptions, dis-possessions, and displacements[12]—trauma that has never been adequately repaired or allowed to heal, as White supremacist institutions, systems, policies, practices, and budgetary decisions continue to inflict harm.[13]

Here, Brown takes a structural perspective when naming the guilty parties that are forcing the poor to live in conditions that embody a denial of love. Elsewhere Brown is more direct, arguing that, from the structural violence of segregationist policymaking to the physical violence of enslavement and lynchings, violence has been—and continues to be—the "central organizing principle of white supremacy in America."[14]

White supremacists are indeed guilty of creating conditions that embody a denial of love. Nonetheless, I would be remiss in omitting the culpability of Christians and the church throughout history, given that the White Europeans who colonized the world identified themselves as Christians. What is more, however, is the fact that racialized—and therefore, racist—thinking arose from

---

[11]Brown, *The Black Butterfly*, 166, emphasis added.
[12]Ibid., 55. (See also Appendix A therein.)
[13]Ibid., 106.
[14]Ibid., 62.

Christian historical theology, as Willie Jennings documents in detail.[15] This means that not only are White supremacists culpable, but also the White privileged. However, what is emphasized here is that there is both a historical and a theological depth to the sin committed by Christians in creating conditions that embody a denial of love. Such depth warrants deeper consideration. A reflection in light of the Word of God will help draw out the implications.

Saul in Acts and St. Paul Street in Baltimore: Jesus Calls the Violent Faithful to Deep Repentance

Going back to the beginning of the church in Acts 2, Pentecost was the event when the Spirit revealed God's desire and will to join peoples to God and to one another, and God Godself began enacting it, as Jennings comments.[16] However, the religious elites were unwilling to understand God's new revelation.[17] Instead, within their deep religiosity, the elite were comfortable using violence to maintain their own power and execute their own vision of justice.[18] The most dramatic example was Saul, prior to his conversion and identity as Paul.[19]

From the White European Christian colonialists, to White supremacists, to the White privileged, to Christians and churches in the White L[20] surrounded by high homicide rates in the Black Butterfly, such Christians—including myself—have problematically resembled Saul rather than Paul, and are therefore called to deep repentance by Jesus Christ.

As Jennings retells it, the Christians in Acts are opposed not by

---

[15]Willie James Jennings, *The Christian Imagination: Theology and the Origins of Race* (New Haven, CT: Yale University Press, 2010).

[16]Willie James Jennings, *Acts, Belief: A Theological Commentary on the Bible* (Louisville, KY: Presbyterian Publishing Corporation, 2017), Proquest e-book, 23.

[17]Acts 4–9:2. Unless otherwise stated, biblical references are from NRS-VUE.

[18]Ibid., especially Acts 7–9:2.

[19]Acts 9–13.

[20]Coincidentally, St. Paul Street in Baltimore runs north-to-south straight through the heart of the White L.

evil God-haters but by faithful people.[21] Saul, thus, approved of their killing of Stephen, and he participated in the wider persecution of the church, violently seizing and imprisoning believers (Acts 8:1–3). However, Jennings emphatically reminds the reader that Saul is a killer, elaborating upon his character:

> No one is more dangerous than one with the power to take life and who already has mind and sight set on those who are a threat to a safe future. Such a person is a closed circle relying on the inner coherence of their logic. . . . Violence, in order to be smooth, elegant, and seemingly natural, needs people who are closed circles. . . . His rationality demands his vision of justice.[22]

Similarly, violence in Baltimore is seemingly smooth, elegant, and natural. With machine-like consistency, it has produced approximately 300 to 350 homicides annually from 2015 to 2021, and—before then—approximately 200 to 240 homicides from 2008 to 2014.[23] In a pretty disturbing way, plotting the data on a graph reveals relatively stable lines as if displaying a natural experiment. It is reminiscent of the Latin phrase from the field of economic analysis, *ceteris paribus*.

The violence in Baltimore also seems natural (or normal) in how various institutions and individuals in the city address it (or do not). For example, although various churches in the White L have acknowledged the spike in homicides over the past seven years or put up "Black Lives Matter" banners, any significant changes to their *modi operandi* have been slow to reveal themselves. And aside from broad remarks about the causes of the violence, the general sentiment of my various neighbors around the city is that much of the situation is "beyond our control." Some of the more apparently educated elites in the White L churches continue to echo old arguments, such as asking why people in the Black Butterfly do not work harder or that Black culture can be a negative influence. The implication is that the suffering of people

---

[21]Jennings, *Acts*, 61.

[22]Ibid., 76.

[23]*Baltimore Sun*, "Baltimore Homicides." Use the time frame filter to see data for each year. Also recall the statistics cited earlier.

in the Black Butterfly is a natural consequence of their choices. However, once I ask what types of opportunities are available to those in the Black Butterfly or why—for example—Baltimore County suffers far less than Baltimore City, I rarely receive satisfying answers.

To break open the closed-circle logic in the examples above, one need only consider the deep history of violence in cities such as Baltimore. White European Christian colonialists were closed circles, having appropriated the power to take life, and those descendants who have marked other peoples as a threat to their safe future (that is, White supremacists and those subscribing to Whiteness—the White privileged) have been dangerous and deadly to those other peoples. Although some have attempted to resolve the hypocrisy of claiming God-given liberty while oppressing certain groups of people (e.g., in the Civil War or the civil rights movement), backlash follows each effort.[24]

Lest any churches and Christians in the White L of Baltimore (including non-White Christians such as myself) believe they are guiltless, it is crucial to recall the interconnectedness between racial inequity and spatial inequity in Baltimore. Thus, in the White L, Christian identity inescapably overlaps with Whiteness. Further, as racialized and racist thinking has its roots in Christian theology, Christians of the present face the consequences of the deep historical and theological sin of their forebears, the sociostructural effects of which must be corrected in tangible ways. That is the task set before the Christians and churches in the White L, and not to undertake the task is a sin of omission.

In other words, Christians such as myself who are situated in churches within the privileged White L—surrounded as they are by the suffering of the Black Butterfly of Baltimore—are called to satisfactorily answer Gutiérrez's question, which bears repeating: "How is it possible to tell the poor, who are forced to live in conditions that embody a denial of love, that God loves them?"[25] The most fundamental answer to this question as applied to Baltimore? Striving to help others save their own lives. The words of Paul in Colossians 1:28–29 are fitting here: "It is [Christ]

---

[24]Brown, *The Black Butterfly*, 32–63.
[25]Gutiérrez, *A Theology of Liberation*, xxxiv.

whom we proclaim, warning everyone and teaching everyone in all wisdom, so that we may present everyone mature in Christ. For this I toil and strive with all the energy that he powerfully inspires within me."

The Good News—Christ Set Us Free:
Integral Liberation and the Preferential Option for the Poor

How would the gospel of Jesus Christ be good news to those who are suffering in the harsh and unjust conditions in Baltimore? The good news would entail release to those who are captive within this status quo of violence, release of all who are involved—the potential victims, the would-be perpetrators, and those with wealth, power, or privilege who maintain the status quo.[26] That is, salvation should lead to liberation.

Importantly, per Gutiérrez, liberation is not an end in itself; rather, "the fullness of liberation—a free gift from Christ—is communion with God and with other human beings."[27] Such communion—enabled by the freedom *to* love—is the telos of freedom *from* sin.[28] The sin of social injustice is comprehensively addressed in the concept of "integral liberation."[29]

Liberation is integral in that there are three approaches to it, each pertaining to distinct yet "reciprocally interpenetrating" levels of human life.[30] The three levels of integral liberation, reflecting three dimensions of human reality, are (1) the economic, social, and political, (2) the psychological and cultural consciousness of human self-determination, and (3) the theological.[31] Theologian Daniel Castillo names these as the socio-structural, cultural/psychological, and theological levels.[32] The socio-structural level pertains to social, political, and economic arrangements.[33] In con-

---

[26]See Luke 4:18.

[27]Gutiérrez, *A Theology of Liberation*, 24.

[28]Ibid., 23–24. Gutiérrez cites Galatians 5:1: "'For freedom Christ has set us free.'"

[29]Ibid., 44–46.

[30]Ibid., 24.

[31]Ibid., 17–20, 24.

[32]Daniel P. Castillo, *An Ecological Theology of Liberation* (Maryknoll, NY: Orbis Books, 2019), 40.

[33]Gutiérrez, *A Theology of Liberation*, 17–20, 24.

trast, the cultural/psychological level pertains to the interior of the person.[34] Examples include neutralizing racism and self-racism. At the theological level, liberation is salvation.[35] An important implication follows: Although the theological dimension can be seen as encompassing the socio-structural and the cultural/psychological dimensions, as well as underlying both, it is not free from error, and correctives from outside of theology and within it should be utilized to correct errors whenever they arise.[36]

Gutiérrez's integral view critiques the idealist or spiritualist approaches to liberation.[37] Instead, through Jesus' incarnation, salvation history and broader human history are now one.[38] As such, Christ has also assumed the role of our neighbor,[39] which serves as a basis for what Gutiérrez calls the "preferential option for the poor."[40] In considering the parable of the final judgment in Matthew 25, Gutiérrez finds that not only is the love of God inseparable from the love of one's neighbor but "love for God is unavoidably expressed through love of one's neighbor."[41] Therefore, translating theology into action is critical. The task of liberation theology, after all, is "critical reflection on Christian *praxis* in light of the word of God."[42]

"Why Are You Hurting Me?": Saul's Preferential Option for the Poor Jesus and the Depth of His Repentance

Reading Acts 9 through Gutiérrez's preferential option for the poor, Jesus' question to Saul can be seen as an invitation into liberation at the theological level. He is afflicted with physical blindness, which perhaps reflects his theological blindness (Acts

---

[34]Ibid., 21, 24.
[35]Ibid., 25.
[36]See Castillo, *An Ecological Theology of Liberation*, 48.
[37]Gutiérrez, *A Theology of Liberation*, 25.
[38]Ibid., 84–91, 86.
[39]Ibid., 112–116.
[40]Ibid., xxv–xxvi. For an explanation of the connection between "history is one" and the preferential option for the poor, see Castillo, *An Ecological Theology of Liberation*, 22.
[41]Gutiérrez, *A Theology of Liberation*, 114–115.
[42]Ibid., xxix.

9:3–9). Thereby, Saul, "the closed circle, is broken open by God. . . . Yes, a killer was confronted and stopped in his tracks, but equally powerful, the rationality for his murderous actions was shattered. There is no rationale for killing that remains intact in the presence of God," Jennings argues.[43] This is because of the intimate question that Jesus asks Saul: "'Why are you hurting me?'" (Jennings's translation).[44] Jennings continues: "[T]his genre of question flows most often out of the mouths of the poor and women and children. The question casts light on the currencies of death that we incessantly traffic in, and it has no good answer. The only good answer is to stop."[45] Jesus' question arises from what he has accomplished, and now the question "belongs to God. It belongs with God. Hurt and pain and suffering have reached their final destination, the body of Jesus."[46] Christ is our neighbor.

"Who are you, Lord?" (Acts 9:5). The reply: "I am Jesus, whom you are persecuting." Then immediately, Jesus gives Saul a task to demonstrate his liberation: "Now get up and go into the city, and you will be told what you must do" (v. 6). In short, Saul complies. That is, Saul repents by obeying the voice of Jesus; Saul now "knows" Christ, and immediately acts.

Ananias's reception of Saul in Acts 9:10–19 is pivotal, and more could be said, but there are two highlights. First, perhaps in a preview of the socio-structural effect of Saul's liberation and the *depth* of his repentance, the Lord tells Ananias: "I myself will show [Saul] how much he must suffer for my name" (9:16). Second is Ananias's obedience to receive him as "Brother Saul." It is after this establishment of kinship that Saul redirects his use of power and privilege as an elite—that is, his resources at the socio-structural level—beginning in Acts 9:20–22.

Saul's story will come full circle. Per Jennings: "Saul, who was once a closed circle of violence, is now encircled in hatred" as one who now serves God in the midst of violence, and "Saul will in fact later see himself as a slave."[47] In Christ's usual manner

---

[43]Jennings, *Acts*, 77.
[44]Ibid.
[45]Ibid.
[46]Ibid.
[47]Ibid., 81.

of turning over the world order, slavery to the righteousness of Christ means liberation.[48]

The early church is thus liberated from Saul's persecution, and—assuming the name Paul—he works to liberate others, suffering state-sanctioned torture and ultimately—according to tradition—martyrdom.[49] In terms of Paul's work for socio-structural liberation, he helped to build and strengthen the early church, which ultimately brought about a new religious, political, and social institution (with considerable economic power). This has no doubt, in turn, led to problems in history, but the universal church is nevertheless the "sacrament of salvation."[50]

In sum, repentance must move from the spiritual (i.e., the theological) dimension of reality outward to the other dimensions of reality (i.e., the cultural/psychological and socio-structural), for Christians are called to "bear fruit worthy of repentance" (Matthew 3:8). Socio-structural liberation of oneself entails tangible action and use of resources for the socio-structural liberation of the oppressed, with the ultimate goal of liberation that enables the oppressed to freely choose communion with the God of Jesus Christ. The depth of Paul's repentance is the depth that is called for by integral liberation.

Toward Praxis: Spiritual Preparation, Repentance, Reparations, and Racial Equity Work

To end, it will be useful to discuss preparation for a praxis of integral liberation. The following applies to Christians and churches in the White L of Baltimore City who are not yet engaged in a robust racial equity strategy. It is beyond the scope of this essay to present a substantial proposal. Furthermore, due to the political sensitivity of nascent efforts to create significant socio-structural change in Baltimore, detailed examples will not be provided herein. However, the following may be helpful in framing ideas for action. In addition, an example of a concrete

---

[48]See Romans 6:19.

[49]See e.g., Benedict XVI, "General Audience: Saint Paul (20): St. Paul's Martyrdom and Heritage," The Holy See, February 4, 2009, https://www.vatican.va.

[50]See Gutiérrez, *A Theology of Liberation*, 143.

step taken in preparation for creating socio-structural change will be discussed.

To reiterate, the telos of liberation is communion; that is: "the fullness of liberation—a free gift from Christ—is communion with God and with other human beings."[51] This entails at least two core spiritual disciplines by which to prepare for the work of socio-structural change: (1) celebration and (2) prayer. Gutiérrez puts it eloquently, explaining that "the first task of the Church is to celebrate with joy the gift of the salvific action of God in humanity, accomplished through the death and resurrection of Christ."[52] With regard to prayer, Gutiérrez emphasizes depth when he writes: "Prayer is a privileged way of being in communion with Christ. . . . [D]uring his final prayer . . . he was 'in an agony' as he struggled for his life, so that his sweat 'became like great drops of blood' ([Luke] 22:44–45). Our communion with the prayer of Jesus must reach this point of 'agony'—that is, of combat."[53] Thus, the practices of celebration and prayer represent praxis at the theological and cultural/psychological levels of integral liberation.

After spiritual preparation, there are two considerations for framing repentance that lead to socio-structural change. The first is the historical guilt of the Christian church in enacting White, European Christian colonialism. To adequately address the problem, repentance ought to lead to reparations at a workable institutional level. The Christian ethicist Jennifer Harvey has argued for reparations in light of the failures of a "reconciliation paradigm" practiced by White Protestants to address racial injustice.[54] Here in Baltimore, the Episcopal Diocese of Maryland (located within the White L) implemented its reparations policy, accepting grant applications in March 2022 to their $1 million reparations fund, which was created in September 2020.[55] Therefore, by its example, the Episcopal Diocese of Maryland represents

---

[51]Ibid., 24.

[52]Ibid., 148.

[53]Ibid., xxxi–xxxii.

[54]Jennifer Harvey, "Which Way to Justice? Reconciliation, Reparations, and the Problem of Whiteness in US Protestantism," *Journal of the Society of Christian Ethics* 31, no. 1 (2011).

[55]The Episcopal Diocese of Maryland, "Reparations in the Diocese of Maryland," https://episcopalmaryland.org.

a notable local, Christian example of reparations. Policies of reparations have been found to be politically feasible at the local level in various cities.[56]

The second consideration is the depth to which repentance must go. Given the depth of injustice in Baltimore, work for justice must be equally deep. To not do so is a sin of omission, as mentioned earlier. Repentance would mean deep engagement in working for justice. As Gutiérrez points out, the integral view of liberation avoids the pitfall of "shallow analyses and programs of short-term effect initiated under the pretext of meeting immediate needs."[57]

A Step Forward in Celebration and Prayer

As a Christian who aspires to move away from being like the murderous and self-righteous Saul and toward being like St. Paul, I can no longer wait for current leaders to change the status quo. The following example is merely a start to working for justice at the socio-structural level, but a start which is in line with Gutiérrez's call for celebration and prayer.

On Saturday, July 30, 2022, my wife and I—as recommended by a church within the White L—participated in a "prayer caravan" held by Act Now Baltimore, The Multi-Cultural Prayer Movement, and the Baltimore City Police Department.[58] Police Commissioner Michael Harrison was in attendance. (While the author acknowledges the controversy in police-community relations, it seems that the goal of socio-structural change is to help create just institutions, not to antagonize institutions.) There were celebratory acts of worship and earnest prayer throughout the day.

---

[56]Thai Jones, "Slavery Reparations Seem Impossible. In Many Places, They're Already Happening," *Washington Post*, January 31, 2020, https://www.washingtonpost.com; Breeanna Hare and Doug Criss, "Six Questions about Slavery Reparations, Answered," CNN, August 15, 2020, https://www.cnn.com. For promising research into reparations programs within specific professional fields, such as the Reparations in Education Collective in Howard County, Maryland, see Aminah Jahad Raysor, "Reparations in Education: The RIE Collective" (MA capstone, Loyola University Maryland, 2022), poster.

[57]Gutiérrez, *A Theology of Liberation*, 25.

[58]Sinéad Hawkins, "Religious Leaders Team Up with Police for Prayer Motorcade across Baltimore City," Fox News, July 31, 2022, https://foxbaltimore.com.

As it happened, the author and several other participants were present when a person overdosed on the street. The person was about to fall, but I myself and others held the person up, perhaps preventing serious injuries to the person. While we prayed, others brought a chair and alerted the police officers on the scene, and the officers were able to reverse the overdose and call the paramedics quickly. Remarkably, the person got up, declined medical treatment, and walked away.

I do not claim this as my St. Paul moment, in which Paul healed a man in Lystra, who then sprang up and walked (see Acts 14:8–19). Further, my anecdote above is not an example of socio-structural change, but it can nonetheless be read as a metaphor of it: Amid celebration and prayer, hold up those who are suffering to keep them from falling, protect them while calling for more help, then giving them the freedom to go where they wish to go.

The Jesus within those who suffer in places such as Baltimore's Black Butterfly beckons Christians to bring the love of God outside of their privileged bubbles in places such as the White L. Let us not wait.

PART IV

FROM "I CAN'T BREATHE" TO THE BREATH OF LIFE: REIMAGINING OUR THEOLOGY AND PRACTICE

Fear of the Lord
Includes Faith and Works

Adverse Childhood Experiences, Law Enforcement Officers, Domestic Terrorists, and Fear in Implicit Racial Bias

Shawnee Daniels-Sykes

In this essay, I offer that even law enforcement officers who are trained methodologically to fear are not spared from their own adverse childhood experiences (or ACEs) and their categories. Furthermore, domestic terrorists, some of whom are driven by fear as it relates to racial or white replacement theory, are not spared from adverse childhood experiences. Neither are Church leaders and members spared from this phenomenon.

I believe that the issue of fear within implicit racial bias plays a critical role within the confines of ACEs and their categories. When parents and/or significant others instill racist ideologies or teach racism to a child, this, too, causes mental and physical harms.[1] Notably, racism is not something a child inherits; it is taught and learned. My main contention, then, is that Church leaders and members must not only engage in moments of prayer and reflection, but must also be public agents, protesting the fear driving implicit racial bias in the context of ACEs categories, as these problems are manifested in adulthood. Research studies show

---

[1] See Brooke Emery, "The Upbringing of a Creature: The Scope of a Parent's Right to Teach Children to Hate," *Modern American* 4, no. 2 (Fall 2008): 60.

that socialization and internalization processes instill unfounded fears of people of color when done at very young ages, perhaps by significant others, social media, and various environments, among others; they are then manifested in adulthood.

To further develop my argument, I will briefly (1) discuss ACEs and relate them to the notion of fear in implicit racial bias by law enforcement and domestic terrorists, (2) comment on the USCCB Pastoral Letter *Open Wide Our Hearts* and relate it to law enforcement officers, domestic terrorists, and social justice movements, and (3) present the phrase "fear of the Lord" as one concrete action for the Church in addressing the fear response within implicit racial bias as it points to law enforcement officers and domestic terrorists.

ACEs and Fear in Implicit Racial Bias

The CDC-Kaiser Permanente's ACEs Study is one of the largest investigations of childhood abuse and neglect and household challenges for later-life health and well-being. Essentially, abuse in early childhood can lead to a propensity toward future violence, victimization, perpetration, and life-long mental, physical, emotional, and spiritual health problems.

The 1995–1997 ACEs study reveals a powerful relationship between our emotional experiences as children and our adult emotional health, physical health, and major causes of mortality in the United States.[2] ACEs and their categories are common.

About 61% of adults surveyed across 25 states reported that they had experienced at least one type of ACE category: [e.g., physical, sexual, and emotional abuse; childhood physical and emotional neglect; witnessing domestic violence as a child; and living with a substance abusing, mentally ill, and/ or incarcerated household member as a child]. Nearly 1 in 6 reported that they had experienced four or more types of ACEs, which, in turn, can have lasting, negative effects on health and well-being.[3]

---

[2]Vincent J. Felitti, "The Relation between Adverse Childhood Experiences and Adult Health: Turning Gold into Lead," *Permanent Journal* 6, no. 1 (Winter 2002): 44.

[3]"Preventing Adverse Childhood Experiences," *Center for Disease Control and Prevention*, www.cdc.gov.org.

What happens in childhood—like a child's footprint in wet cement—commonly lasts throughout life. Time does not necessarily heal; time conceals ACEs and their categories.

ACEs with fear in implicit racial bias in tandem with firearms use and misuse by law enforcement officers and domestic terrorists threaten the human family of God. Even though a growing number of articles explores the impact of ACEs on law enforcement officers and domestic terrorists, ACEs still remain understudied. While gaps in the research persist, Catholic Church teaching, which champions the health and safety of all human beings, remains "a best kept secret." We all deserve to continue to inhale and exhale rhythmically the breath of life and not fear that law enforcement officers and domestic terrorists have left untreated or have not attended to their ACEs categories, including fear in implicit racial bias.

Over the past four decades, social psychology research repeatedly demonstrates that most individuals of all races and ethnicities have fear that drives implicit racial bias, linking, for instance, Black and Brown bodies to criminality and white bodies with innocence. Fear in implicit racial bias can negatively and unconsciously influence judgments and behaviors in ways that people are unaware of and thus largely unable to control.

It is important to note that fear is a natural, powerful, unpleasant, and primitive human emotion. It involves universal biochemical responses (fight or flight reactions), as well as high individual emotional responses. Fear alerts us to the presence of danger or the threat of harm, whether that danger is physical or psychological. However, it is all right to have fear or to be afraid, but one must not let fear take over the driver's seat in one's life. Rather, when fearful, one must remain anchored. When unanchored, fear can cause law enforcement officers to engage in increased scrutiny or racial profiling, biased evaluations of ambiguous behaviors, interactions that promote racial anxiety, acting on racial hunches, the fostering of negative interactions and constructing reasonable suspicions, and so on.[4] To further illustrate this, Larry Smith notes in an essay titled "Police Are Trained to Fear":

---

[4]See L. Song Richardson, "Implicit Racial Bias and Racial Anxiety: Implications for Stop and Frisks," *NYU Law*, www.law.nyu.edu.

In all the training I had, officers were trained to fear even the average citizen—to be aware that someone will take your gun and use it on you, to be alert for ambushes, to be ready to fix yourself up if shot so you can keep going. But the flip side of this over-defensiveness is that citizens are afraid of the police, and their fear is what gets them killed in many cases. I chased plenty of people who, when caught, said they were scared of us.[5]

The aforementioned categories of ACEs have embedded in them the notion of fear, including fear that promotes implicit racial bias. Fear affects all persons. Arguably, when law enforcement officers' backgrounds include any unattended to or untreated categories of ACEs and fear in implicit racial bias in tandem with the training that they have that includes ways "to keep law enforcement officers afraid or fearful,"[6] one will most likely agree that fear kills. Fear kills the body, mind, and spirit.

In their own study of ACEs in ninety-one former white supremacists, Steven Windisch, Pete Simi, Kathleen Blee, and Matthew DeMichele found that there were "elevated rates of childhood risk factors with 63% of participants having experienced four or more adverse experiences during the first eighteen years of their lives (as compared to 55% of a comparison "high risk" sample and 16% of the U.S. general population sample)."[7] Research shows a connection between ACEs, their categories, and domestic terrorists. The vast majority have experienced physical, mental, and emotional trauma at a young age.[8] I add fear in implicit bias, especially if the domestic terrorist is focused specifically on eliminating/killing people of certain racial, ethnic, and/or religious backgrounds.

[5]Larry Smith, "Police Are Trained to Fear," *Medium,* November 26, 2018, gen.medium.com.

[6]Ibid.

[7]Steven Windisch, Pete Simi, Kathleen Blee, and Matthew DeMichele, "Measuring the Extent and Nature of Adverse Childhood Experiences (ACE) among Former White Supremacists," *Terrorism and Political Violence* 34, no. 6 (2020): 1207–1228, https://doi.org/10.1080/09546553.2020.1767604.

[8]Emily Pyrek, "Experts Note Connection between Adverse Childhood Experiences, Mass Shooters," *La Crosse Tribune* (WI), August 9, 2019.

USCCB, *Open Wide Our Hearts*

The US Conference of Catholic Bishops is aware of racism in policing and among domestic terrorists.[9] However, what more must be done by the Church to counter this evil? James 2:14–17 (NRSV) says: "What good is it, my brothers and sisters, if you say you have faith but do not have works? Can faith save you? . . . Faith by itself, if it has no works, is dead." *Open Wide Our Hearts* is replete with faith-based statements along with narrative depictions of the problems driving racism in this country.

Open Wide Our Hearts claims that "[r]acism can often be found in our hearts—in many cases placed there unwillingly or unknowingly by our upbringing and culture."[10] In particular, we witness repeatedly the stubborn tenacity of the fear within implicit racial bias in adults in the shooting of the unarmed by law enforcement officers/vigilantes and in mass shootings by domestic terrorists.

Furthermore, *Open Wide Our Hearts* acknowledges that "too often racism comes in the form of the sin of omission, when individuals, communities, and even churches remain silent and fail to act against racial injustice when it is encountered."[11] The president of the USCCB, Archbishop José Gomez, characterized contemporary social movements such as the Black Lives Matter (BLM) movement as "pseudo-religions based on profoundly atheistic ideologies that are hostile to Catholic belief."[12] At least those who are actively engaged in BLM are doing something concrete and visible to address the problem of the senseless deaths of innocent human beings in a manner that is unconditionally pro-life and not strictly pro-birth focused. To be unconditionally pro-life, in this instance, would involve social justice movements that speak to the need to address ACEs and their categories, along with the

---

[9]See the June 24, 2020, letter to US Senators from the United States Conference of Catholic Bishops.

[10]United States Conference of Catholic Bishops, *Open Wide Our Hearts: The Enduring Call to Love: A Pastoral Letter Against Racism*, 2018, 5.

[11]Ibid., 4.

[12]José Gomez, "Reflections on the Church and America's New Religions" (November 4, 2021), https://archbishopgomez.org.

negative effects on law enforcement officers and domestic terrorists, including implicit racial bias.

Furthermore, if the fear driving implicit racial bias in light of
ACEs prevents the Church from getting involved in social justice
movements, then it might be helpful to push for faith and works
perspectives through the lens of fear of the Lord. When one fears
the Lord, one is awe-inspired by the faith and works of God.

Fear of the Lord

Indeed, countless people/saints have stood up for social justice
and have been assassinated, marginalized, despised, and discred-
ited by the Church and society. The Church standing up and
publicly protesting the unethical behaviors of law enforcement
officers and domestic terrorists to mitigate and stop these behaviors requires fear of the Lord, including faith and works. This
means that Church leaders and Church members must view the
adverse effects of these behaviors as perpetuating a severe public
health crisis and not a political debate where particular social
movements are sparked but subsequently denigrated by Church
leaders. Constructively, Church leaders and Church members
might heed, for example, the thirteen bipartisan recommendations
proposed by the American College of Surgeons in 2018.[13] These
recommendations could ignite social movements by Church leaders that uphold human dignity and human flourishing.

---

[13]ACS-COT Firearm Strategy Team (FAST), "13 Recommendations Based
on Public Safety Principles," *American College of Surgeons,* facs.org.

From Monstrous to Critical Relational Intimacy

Challenging the Deadening of Our Moral Compass

Melissa Pagán

> *The starting-point of critical elaboration is the con-*
> *sciousness of what one really is, and is "knowing*
> *thyself" as a product of the historical processes to*
> *date, which has deposited in you an infinity of traces,*
> *without leaving an inventory . . . therefore it is impera-*
> *tive at the outset to compile such an inventory.*
> —Antonio Gramsci, *Prison Notebooks*
> *(1929–1935)*

In her work on Caribbean Canadian poet Dionne Brand, Diana Brydon notes how Brand continuously challenged us to execute such a Gramscian inventory of the traces, some might say the ghosts, of oppressive historical processes that continue to form and inform our present and orient our future. Brydon notes that Brand, in her poem "Inventory,"[1] highlights a type of intimacy that adheres in and through time as she writes in such a way as to reveal how "the past inhabits the present," and how the *enactment of intimacies* has the power to change everything on

---

[1]Dionne Brand, *Inventory* (Toronto: McClelland & Stewart, 2006).

small and large scales, and for better or worse.² Indeed, the subject in Brand's poem is one who observes the incessant accounts of violence in the world—those related to racism, heterosexism, ecocide, etc.—on the evening news. The inventory she creates spotlights how too many have grown "perversely accustomed" to the violence surrounding us and entreats us to do as the poets do and refuse: refuse the deadening of our moral compass, refuse the shattering of our human connection. As the subject in her poem does, she calls for us to bear witness to and "gather the nerve endings spilled on the streets . . . count them like rice grains . . . (and) keep them for when they're needed."³

Such poetry enacts and summons the prophetic in word and action as it challenges us to relinquish our rituals of indifference to intimate experiences of interminable violence meted out against Black, Indigenous, and other racialized persons in the United States. My understanding of the concept of "intimacy" is indebted to Lauren Berlant, a theorist of queer and affect theories. Berlant claims that "intimacy names the enigma of . . . a range of attachments . . . and it poses a question of scale that links the instability of individual lives to the trajectories of the collective."⁴ In this sense, intimacy "builds worlds" and "creates spaces."⁵ While relationality imagined as a form of intimacy is often framed as a wholesome reflection upon familial, romantic, or sexual relationships, feminist and queer theorists of color warn us against such romanticization. Christina Sharpe, in her text *Monstrous Intimacies: Making Post-Slavery Subjects*, argues that intimacies can be monstrous. Sharpe defines monstrous intimacies as "a set of known and unknown performances and inhabited horrors, desires and positions produced, reproduced, circulated and transmitted, that are breathed in the air and often unacknowledged to be monstrous."⁶

²Diana Brydon, "Dionne Brand's Global Intimacies: Practising Affective Citizenship," *University of Toronto Quarterly* 76, no. 3 (Summer 2007): 994, 998.
³Ibid., 992.
⁴Lauren Berlant, "Intimacy: A Special Issue," *Critical Inquiry* 24, no. 2 (Winter 1998): 283.
⁵Ibid., 282.
⁶Christina Sharpe, *Monstrous Intimacies: Making Post-Slavery Subjects* (Durham, NC: Duke University Press, 2010), 3.

Monstrous intimacies reflect an ongoing indifference to the ways that relations of power and domination associated with racism, sexism, and heterosexism persist under the logics of coloniality. Thus, if we desire social justice, we must begin to take an inventory of the monstrous intimacies of coloniality. In this essay, I utilize my twofold feminist decolonial method of analysis, provide a brief sketch of an inventory of monstrous intimacies forged under the logics of coloniality at the space of the colonial difference, and move to uplift decolonized intimacies that enable different modes of relating in the world. The first part of this method, which I term a hermeneutics of *el grito*, attempts to mark and illuminate the struggles of those who have been relegated to a ghostly, dehumanized form of existence under the monstrous intimacies of the colonial difference. The second part of my method, which I term a hermeneutics of *vincularidad*, enables the possibility of rethinking the concepts of solidarity and relationality, a possibility that can only come into being after the apocalypse of monstrous intimacies.

Monstrous Intimacies:
The Violence at Spaces of Colonial (In)Difference

The *hermeneutics of el grito* is an interpretative framework that privileges the *gritos* or cries, the gasps of lament, emanating from the resident bodies at the colonial difference. As I have noted before,[7] my development of this hermeneutic was inspired by what decolonial theorist Nelson Maldonado-Torres has termed Frantz Fanon's "phenomenology of the cry," especially as Fanon articulates it in his *Black Skin, White Masks*. This "cry," as he understands it, is "the first marker of an enslaved and suffering subjectivity . . . a sound uttered as a call for attention, as a demand for immediate action or remedy, or as an expression of pain that points to an injustice committed or something that is lacking."[8] These suffering subjects are those occupying the ghostly space of dehumanization, or the colonial difference. Maldonado-Torres

---

[7]See, for example, Melissa Pagán, "Cultivating a Hermeneutics of *El Grito* in the Eye of the Storm," *Perspectivas* 15 (2018): 68–73.

[8]Nelson Maldonado-Torres, *Against War: Views from the Underside of Modernity* (Durham, NC: Duke University Press, 2008), 133.

theorizes that this space was created, legitimized, and has been maintained since the time of the colonization of the Americas via processes that construct and then relegate persons to a subhuman/subontological status by virtue of their race, ethnicity, gender, and sexuality. This space enacts incessant and multifaceted violence that is ontological, phenomenological, epistemological, material, and spatial; the cries and testimonies of those occupying this space are what we must reckon with as monstrously intimate.

If we take an inventory of some of these monstrous intimacies, we must reckon with wailing echoes of "I can't breathe," "I love you, Mom," "I want my mom," and simply, "Mama!"—all cries of the Black victims of unbridled police violence, the continued annihilation and degradation of Black *being* in the United States. Murder and violence, coupled with the vulnerable intimacy of calling for one's mother out of distress, calling for mercy, attempting to beseech the humanity of those that are intent to destroy you are some of the most poignant examples of monstrous intimacy we might find. Consider, too, the monstrosity on display as we watch and circulate video after video of Black folks, Latinx folks, Indigenous folks, and trans folks being maimed, hunted, shot, and murdered. Indeed, these monstrous intimacies are reminiscent of what philosopher and Black studies scholar Calvin Warren terms an "ontometaphysical holocaust,"[9] wherein Black persons are treated as merely lowly "equipment," objects, used instrumentally to satisfy the demands and desires of white supremacist structures and continued workings of coloniality, rather than respected as human persons with dignity.[10] This space of the colonial difference has characterized the existence of colonial subjects with strong legacies of trauma and dispossession, of dislocation and exile, not only in society but also in the Church.

In my view, if theologians and ethicists seek to foster norms of justice and emancipation that sustain human dignity; defy the

---

[9]While Calvin Warren theorizes that the "ontometaphysical holocaust" is one that is particular to Black persons, I write with an eye to expanding this category to those occupying the colonial difference. This said, Warren is correct to indicate the prevalence and severity of anti-Blackness throughout the globe. Calvin Warren, *Ontological Terror: Blackness, Nihilism, and Emancipation* (Durham, NC: Duke University Press, 2018), 27.

[10]Ibid.

violence of the colonial difference; and undermine the violence, alienation, and apathy constitutive of monstrous intimacy current theo-ethical frameworks and basic core concepts need to be transformed and reconstructed in basic decolonial terms. For example, the concept of a hermeneutics of *el grito* provides us with a starting point as it helps us to begin reframing the "preferential option for the poor" as an option with and for those at the colonial difference, with those whom our intimacy is currently exercised only monstrously, those who are disposable and lacking in grievability.

Toward a Critical Relational Intimacy to Resist Monstrous Intimacy

The second part of my twofold decolonial feminist method is the hermeneutics of *vincularidad*. *Vincularidad* challenges us to rethink how we understand relationality and solidarity, and in so doing empowers us to awaken from the lulls of monstrous intimacy upheld via the logics of coloniality. Decolonial theorists Catherine Walsh and Walter Mignolo argue that the notion of *vincularidad* is a way to "reimagine relationality."[11] Indeed, the Spanish term *vincularidad* can be loosely translated as relating, bonding, being tied together, etc. I understand *vincularidad* as a way to express how we are planted and rooted together—our roots facilitate breathing and connection, and only under circumstances where all roots can breathe can the fullness of growth occur. Monstrous forms of intimate connection indeed lead to and sustain violence and death. Tragically, these forms of intimacy abound and are indicative of our complicity. Moreover, I would argue that all too often, popular notions of "solidarity" function toward complicity insofar as one's own solidaristic proximity to suffocating roots does not in itself enable resuscitation. Nominally, solidarity is supposed to suggest that one is interested in deconstructing structures of domination. Paradoxically, current modes of enacting solidarity seem to contribute to what Black feminists have called "spirit murder." As Jennifer Nash has noted,

---

[11] Walter Mignolo and Catherine Walsh, *On Decoloniality: Concepts, Analytics, Praxis* (Durham, NC: Duke University Press, 2018), 161–166, 239.

spirit murder is "a reality that wounds are left on the flesh, psyche, and even soul of those who experience violence *and* the wounds . . . that haunt perpetrators of violence, including a willingness to accept, and to render *unseen,* those who are dispossessed."[12] The paradox numbs the human spirit into an indifference around the workings of violence even as the human claims to be fighting for its end. This is to say that our moral sensibilities are muted, narrowing who we consider to be a part of our moral community of accountability and disregarding the humanity of others, all while diminishing our own humanity. This feeling of indifference maintains distance between us, numbs our consciences, and weakens any sense of responsibility, let alone response, we take. To justify grieving the lost lives or violence against vulnerable groups requires a collective struggle, a collective reminder that their lives do not mean less, but rather that we are rooted and intertwined with them and should seek forms of intimacy that reflect that fact. One might take a moment and consider that the Movement for Black Lives began with a love letter. Upon reflection on the murder of Trayvon Martin in 2013, Alicia Garza, one of the founders of the movement, posted on Facebook a "Love Letter to Black Folks," which stated, "We don't deserve to be killed with impunity. We need to love ourselves and fight for a world where Black lives matter. Black people, I love you. I love us. We matter. Our lives matter."

Intimacy at its core and in its non-alienating forms is sharing vulnerability with all of creation. Intimacy in *all* our relationships enables us to regard ourselves as deeply interconnected with others, to realize that our own well-being is connected to and reliant on the other. This type of intimacy allows us to be open to the possibility of being able to be "undone"[13] by others, and by the suffering of others. Encouraging critical relational intimacy can then be a way to build, repair, or restore relationships with others in ways that certain conceptions of solidarity cannot. It can be a pathway to resisting and healing from spirit murder, along with legacies of violence and the marred and monstrous intima-

---

    [12]Jennifer Nash, *Black Feminism Reimagined: After Intersectionality* (Durham, NC: Duke University Press, 2019), 123–124.

    [13]Judith Butler, *The Force of Non-Violence: An Ethico-Political Bind* (New York: Verso, 2021), 185–204.

cies maintained at the colonial difference, to become more fully human, more fully engaged in action that reflects the gospel.

While *vincularidad* as critical relational intimacy can enable resistance to the extractability and disposability of bodies and land, it must also always be driven by a desire to build and sustain ecologies of reparations. The hermeneutics of *el grito* enables a recognition of the racist and heterosexist violent structures of coloniality that manifest along the lines of the material, phenomenological, ontological, and epistemic. Thus, when we consider how we can mend our broken roots, denounce monstrous intimacy, and move toward *vincularidad*, we must begin by igniting our moral imaginations to envision ecologies of reparations that map along the same lines. The specific content of what such repair and healing requires must be placed in the hands of those communities of the colonial difference; however, those privileged within the logics of coloniality who wish to exercise critical relational intimacy must do the courageous work of challenging themselves, their cultures, and their traditions. Repair at the colonial difference, with its multitude traces and ghosts, cannot occur outside of such commitment. Thinking with the decolonial feminist interpretive construct—the hermeneutics of *el grito* and hermeneutics of *vincularidad*, I hope, promotes an apocalypse of the monstrous intimacies of coloniality and supports respective communities' struggles for re-existence.

In Defense of Latinx

A Theological Microintervention

Héctor M. Varela Rios

The identity descriptor "Latinx" has been discussed in popular culture quite often lately, as I will detail below.[1] Conversely, as a professor of Latinx theology in a US-based university, I have often wondered: What work is the word Latinx doing in my job title, and for whom? What do people assume and expect when they hear that? In other words, what is included and excluded about my research, teaching, and service with the adjective? Is it about me or about those I am accountable to?[2] As a Latinx man, I know

---

[1]From here forward, when I write Latinx (in the singular, without quotation marks, and by itself) I am referring to the word. When used in the plural (i.e., Latinxs), I am referring to the members of the US Latinx community. As an adjective, as in "Latinx community," it references a specific way of doing/living from and for that specific community. I will use Latinidad or Latinidades when referring to Latinx ontologically without forgetting or erasing its inherent diversity and complexity. The reader should note that all these are capitalized, as they are referring to shared identity and experiences among a specific group of people. The reader should also note that I do not italicize words in Spanish (such as Latinidad) as a measure of dignidad. I also have a close personal and professional connection to being Latinx: I am a Puerto Rican cis/het man who researches Latinx theology and popular religious beliefs and practices.

[2]I immediately think of one: on February 24, 2020, Alexa Negrón Luciano, a poor transgender woman of color, was shot and killed in the town of Toa Baja in Puerto Rico, my country of origin. Her murder occurred hours after she appeared on social media being interrogated by police regarding her use of the women's bathroom in a local fast-food establishment. The hate crime renewed widespread calls to address not only transphobia but also racism

the word Latinx is not value- or consequence-free.

This chapter intends to positively valorize Latinx using concepts from Christian theology and from psychology. Taking seriously discussions appearing recently in the news media, I will start with a short background on Latinx and briefly explore two news articles (which I criticize) that mostly portray its use negatively. Pushing back against that portrayal, I will first argue that Latinx is a linguistic form of the theological source mestizaje/mulatez and then emphasize its emancipatory work using theory around microaggression and microintervention. Putting both together, I suggest Latinx is theologically microinterventional (i.e., antiracist/antisexist due to its theological valences). I intend to evidence this claim by looking back at the two news articles and turning their microaggressions into theological microinterventions.[3]

Background on Latinx and Recent News Accounts[4]

Within the last few years, Latinxs have grown increasingly impatient with the "most recent iteration" of their assigned ra-

---

and homelessness on the island. Yet as I write, the murder has fallen from the public eye, mostly because Alexa was a poor trans woman, therefore, a non-person to normative cultural and religious sensibilities. But her story remains the spark for this article and my small and inadequate attempt to sincerely remain accountable to Alexa and so many others.

[3]A note on word choice: I will use Latinx descriptively to refer both to the individual and to communities living in the United States that have ancestry in Mexico and in the countries of Central America, South America, and the Caribbean—but only those that were colonized from the fifteenth century onward by Spain and Portugal. In other words, Latinx on this occasion excludes ancestry from English-speaking countries, French-speaking countries, and Dutch-speaking countries (and related local languages/dialects). Latinx also does not include Latin American people and non-colonized people, that is, those folks that originate and/or still live in the American countries named above. However, besides this colonizer baggage, Latinx ancestry includes Indigenous people (i.e., those present before colonization) and African people (i.e., those imported as slaves) to varying degrees. More on this when discussing mestizaje/mulatez.

[4]For further background on Latinx, see Frederick Luis Aldama and Christopher González, *Latinx Studies: The Key Concepts* (New York: Routledge, 2019); Claudia Milian, *LatinX* (Minneapolis: University of Minnesota Press, 2019).

cial and ethnic label, indeed with labeling itself.[5] The proximate historical background of that impatience is thus: as a response to the obvious presence and increasingly hard-fought agency of people from Mexico, Central and South American countries, and the Spanish-speaking Caribbean in the United States, the 1970 US Census included for the first time the category "Hispanic" as a racial descriptor. As racial/ethnic groups started to differentiate within US culture, by the 2000 US Census this category morphed to "Latino." Angered by the Spanish language's inherent andro-centrism, feminist activists and allies (including academics) almost immediately started using Latino/a, Latina/o, Latin@ (thereby including both binary genders) and, more recently, Latinx to signal the inclusion of non-binary genders. Even so, all these iterations are fiction, part of what Daisy Machado calls Anglo-America's "historical imaginary."[6] For one, as Edwin Aponte and Miguel De La Torre write, there is no single "Latinx homogeneous whole"; complex diversity and fragmentation are of the essence of Lati-nidad.[7] Within the Latinx community itself and their allies, the loanword Latine has arisen recently, mainly because it retains gender fluidity and is closer to normative Spanish. More on this neologism later.

Going by recent media articles, whether it is proper to use Latinx is still very much in question. Mid 2019, the online peri-odical *Mother Jones* published a piece that seems to "embrace" the word while acknowledging its problematic origins and the plethora of other concurrent descriptors, such as the gendered terms mentioned earlier and hyphenated identities.[8] In August 2020, the Pew Research Center published survey results that showed "only about a quarter of Hispanic or Latino adults had

[5]Ed Morales, *Latinx: The New Force in American Politics and Culture* (New York: Verso, 2018), 3.

[6]Daisy Machado, "History and Latino/a Identity," in *The Wiley Blackwell Companion to Latino/a Theology*, ed. Orlando O. Espín (Oxford: Wiley Blackwell, 2015), 37.

[7]Edwin David Aponte and Miguel A. De La Torre, *Introducing Latinx Theologies*, rev. ed. (Maryknoll, NY: Orbis Books, 2020), 15.

[8]John Paul Brammer, "Digging into the Messy History of 'Latinx' Helped Me Embrace My Complex Identity," *Mother Jones*, May/June 2019, www.motherjones.com. A hyphenated identity is one that emphasizes its multiple origins such as Cuban-American or Afro-Latinx.

even heard of Latinx . . . [and] only 3% used it."[9] This Pew Research is cited often to deride the term and, worse yet, emphasize its dangers as a racial and ethnic descriptor, including in the two articles I will describe next.

The first article is an NBC news piece that concentrates on "why" the word "offends or bothers [Latinxs]."[10] This author maintains Latinx is "pretentious" and "exclusionary."[11] First, Latinx was born in white elitist liberal-progressive academia and "doesn't follow the traditional structure of Spanish" because of the "x" at the end. Indeed, it also does not follow other Central and South American–based pronunciations of "x," where it can be pronounced as the "ch" in child and as the aspirated "h" in hotel. Second, along with the history and diversity of the terms Hispanic and Latino, Latinx erases their hard-won inclusion and agency within the term American, especially in the political arena. Third, the author affirms that "Pew polling over nearly two decades consistently shows" that Latinxs "want to be identified by our nationalities. . . . We are Mexican Americans, Colombians, Venezuelans, Salvadorans, Puerto Ricans, Brazilians, Hondurans, and so on."[12]

The second article is a *National Geographic* piece that cautions against widespread use of Latinx due to the essentializing nature of "pan-ethnic terms."[13] According to the author, pan-ethnic terms like Latinx "are used by [non-Latinxs] as shorthand for race—a social construct that has little to do with actual origin and everything to do with a person's appearance."[14] In the article, the author

---

[9]Luis Noe-Bustamante, Lauren Mora, and Mark Hugo López, "About One-in-Four U.S. Hispanics Have Heard of Latinx, but Just 3% Use It," *Pew Research Center*, August 11, 2020, https://www.pewresearch.org.

[10]Luisita López Torregrosa, "Many Latinos say 'Latinx' Offends or Bothers Them. Here's Why," *NBC News Online*, December 14, 2021, https://www.nbcnews.com.

[11]Ibid.

[12]Ibid.

[13]Erin Blakemore, "'Hispanic'? 'Latino?' Here's Where the Terms Come From," *National Geographic*, February 10, 2022, https://www.nationalgeographic.com.

[14]Ibid. I cannot develop this point further due to space, but it should be evident from the US Census questions around race and ethnicity. See "Hispanic Origin" at the US Census website, https://www.census.gov.

quotes sociologist Nancy López: "To pretend that every Latino occupies the same racial status is ignoring the lived realities of a pigmentocracy."[15] Afro-Latinx serves as an example of this; it is still routinely invisibilized even by other Latinxs. López's insight is helpful to think about essence yet also about the intersectionality of race and gender within Latinx. The article ends: "We have to try to create bridges of understanding and empathy for people who are different from ourselves."[16]

Latinx as Mestizaje/Mulatez

The concerns in both articles are understandable. On one level, Latinx could be perceived as condescending and erasing, the most obvious among many past (and ongoing) colonizations. Yet Latinxs have in recent times developed concepts that engage and defuse such concerns—mestizaje/mulatez is one example. For Latinx theologians, this concept is a theological source, and I suggest Latinx is a linguistic expression of this source. Mestizaje/mulatez refers to the miscegenation of Indigenous, African, and/or Spanish peoples during the violent conquest and genocide of what we now call Latin America and its subsequent reception and ongoing critiques by Latin American and Latinx scholars. Jorge Aquino identifies "three stages of development" for mestizaje/mulatez as a concept.[17] In the first stage, Latinx scholars from the 1980s to the early 2000s, most of them Christian, appropriated mestizaje/mulatez as a primary theological locus, that is, claimed that it stands at the core of what Christianity is.[18] In the second stage, scholars from the 2000s onward critique this collapse

[15]As quoted in Blakemore, "'Hispanic'? 'Latino?' Here's Where the Terms Come From."

[16]Ibid.

[17]Jorge A. Aquino, "*Mestizaje:* The Latina/o Religious Imaginary in the North American Racial Crucible," in *The Wiley Blackwell Companion to Latino/a Theology*, ed. Orlando O. Espín (Malden: Wiley Blackwell, 2015), 286–302.

[18]See, for example, the work of Virgilio Elizondo, *Our Hispanic Pilgrimage* (San Antonio: Mexican American Cultural Center, 1980); Justo González, *Mañana: Christian Theology from a Hispanic Perspective* (Nashville: Abingdon, 1990); and Ada María Isasi-Díaz, *La Lucha Continues: Mujerista Theology* (Maryknoll, NY: Orbis Books, 2004).

of race, class, and gender into a singular mestizaje/mulatez via decontextualization and what could be considered theological "sugarcoating."[19] The current yet concomitant third stage implies a theoretical "rethinking" of mestizaje, especially from remarkable Chicana and queer scholars.[20] Of this last stage, Aquino writes: "[T]hese approaches . . . portend formidable critical challenges around future *anti-racist* political activism on behalf of Latin@ communities in the United States."[21] In other words, we are living the moment when mestizaje/mulatez not only considers sexuality alongside race and ethnicity but is analytically useful toward antiracism—toward the proximate empowerment and eventual emancipation of those folks minoritized.

Standing within this tradition, Latinx exemplifies mestizaje/ mulatez. The word gestures beyond a specific racial, ethnic, and sexual category toward a polyvalent theological source, that is, an emergent expression of intersected identity that works to affirm disparate struggles while still sharing humanity and hope for a better future. Said otherwise, Latinx is linguistic mestizaje/ mulatez, a multivocal representation of a lived ethic of eyes-wide-open justice that extends beyond the words' racial/ethnic/sexual content into human dignity, worker rights, civil participation, solidarity, and so on. What difference does it make that Latinx is linguistic? As a form of speech, it creates a discursive space prone to both harmony and conflict with impactful consequences.[22] Be-

---

[19]See the work of Néstor Medina, *Mestizaje: Remapping Race, Culture, and Faith in Latina/o Catholicism* (Maryknoll, NY: Orbis Books, 2009) and Rubén Rosario-Rodríguez, *Racism and God-talk: A Latina/o Perspective* (New York: NYU Press, 2008). The critique emerges in light of the plethora of distinct Latin American and Latinx experiences with colonialism and imperialism both at home and abroad, the vast differences between mestizxs/ mulatxs (phenotypically, for one; economically, for another), and the equally wide-ranging reception by power, the immense influence upon mestizaje/ mulatez by non-Christians and/or non-mestizxs/mulatxs, and, most importantly, the erasing of the violence behind the terms.

[20]See the work of Gloria Anzaldúa, *Borderlands/La Frontera: The New Mestiza* (San Francisco: Aunt Lute Books, 1987); Ana Castillo, ed., *Goddess of the Americas* (New York: Riverhead Books, 1997); and Robyn Henderson-Espinoza, *Activist Theology* (Minneapolis: Fortress, 2015).

[21]Aquino, *"Mestizaje,"* 284, my emphasis.

[22]While a detailed analysis goes well beyond the scope of this article, my background for speech is indebted to speech-act theory (cf. J. L. Austin, John

ing so, speech as microaggressive or microinterventional can help elucidate this polyvalence.

Latinx as Microintervention and Its Theological Valences

The history and experiences behind Hispanic, Latino, Latino/a, Latina/o, Latin@, and now Latinx and Latine are certainly rooted in life-negating structural/systemic oppression, what psychologist Derald W. Sue and others call macroaggression.[23] In the articles above, we see that the everyday use of Latinx is construed as microaggressive by some Latinxs—perhaps more individual and subtler, yet no less hurtful. However, I suggest that if one sees Latinx as linguistic mestizaje/mulatez, this allegedly microaggressive essence is transformed into one that encourages human flourishing. In other words, Latinx changes to an antiracist/antisexist microintervention with theological grounding.

Part of a fairly recent scholarly framework in psychology, the term microaggression was first coined to elucidate racist interactions in the aftermath of the civil rights movement in the late 1960s. In the mid-2000s, Sue widened its purchase to include other power asymmetries, such as sexism, especially among minoritized folks such as women and people of color. For instance, microaggressions are "everyday slights, insults, putdowns, invalidations, and offensive behaviors that people of color experience in daily interactions with generally well-intentioned White Americans who may be unaware that they have engaged in racially demeaning ways toward target groups."[24] On the contrary, microinterventions are:

Searle, Barry Smith). For me, Latinx is a perlocutionary speech act.

[23]Derald Wing Sue, *Microaggressions in Everyday Life: Race, Gender, and Sexual Orientation* (Hoboken, NJ: Wiley, 2010); Derald Wing Sue, Cassandra Z. Calle, Narolyn Méndez, Sarah Alsaidi, and Elizabeth Glaeser, *Microintervention Strategies: What You Can Do to Disarm and Dismantle Individual and Systemic Racism and Bias* (Hoboken, NJ: John Wiley and Sons, 2021).

[24]Derald Wing Sue, Sarah Alsaidi, Michael N. Awad, Elizabeth Glaeser, Cassandra Z. Calle, and Narolyn Méndez, "Disarming Racial Microaggressions: Microintervention Strategies for Targets, White Allies, and Bystanders," *American Psychologist* 74, no. 1 (2019): 129. There are three main "forms" of racial microaggression: microassault ("racism at the individual level," e.g., commenting on a Latinx's lack of accented English), microinsult ("subtle

> [T]he everyday words or deeds, whether intentional or unintentional, that communicate to targets . . . (a) validation of the experiential reality, (b) value as a person, (c) affirmation of the racial or group identity, (d) support and encouragement, and (e) reassurance that they are not alone. . . . [Microinterventions] serve to enhance psychological well-being, and provide targets, allies [i.e., parents, significant others, and others], and bystanders, with a sense of control and self-efficacy . . . [and] provide a repertoire of responses that can be used to directly disarm and counteract the effects of microaggressions by challenging perpetrators.[25]

I want to highlight three aspects of this definition that shape Latinx as microinterventional and theological coincidentally.

First, Sue and others affirm that microinterventions, just like microaggressions, exist not only as "deeds" but also as "words" and, therefore, operate within the realm of speech and action, just like theology. This insight is not as self-evident as it seems. All of us know aggression well—it is a very human act, be it individual or societal.[26] But the beauty of focusing on the "micro" level is that the widespread, markedly human act of speech also becomes the origin of the aggression and the intervention.[27] In other words, both microinterventions and theology are driven by speech communication (or lack thereof), just like Latinx is. As a

---

snubs," e.g., assuming a Latinx is uneducated or unskilled about a certain subject), and microinvalidation ("communications that exclude, negate, or nullify" individual experiences, e.g., tokenizing Latinxs). Racial microaggressions are "constant and continual," "cumulative," "continuous reminders," and "symbolic" of past macroaggressions. For more, see Sue, Calle, Méndez, Alsaidi, and Glaeser, *Microintervention Strategies*, 8.

[25]Sue, Alsaidi, Awad, Glaeser, Calle, and Méndez, "Disarming Racial Microaggressions," 134.

[26]We also might know something about intervention, be they body-based (e.g., physically preventing escalating violence) or structural (e.g., the 1973 *Roe v. Wade* decision, overturned 6/25/2022).

[27]In other words, it is very hard to think of a speech-driven macroaggression or macrointervention—for an obvious one, slavery in the US did not solely appear through words (it also took violent actions) or did not disappear with the Emancipation Proclamation (it took decades of grassroots, life-affirming actions; indeed, it has been argued slavery has not gone away and just remains hidden through white supremacist strategies).

Latinx theologian, I am reminded of the discursive nature of en conjunto and the disconnect that happens when collaboration and accountability are not foundational values of theological discourse.[28]

Second, microaggressions and microinterventions are opposed not in terms of intent but of impact. A microaggression can originate from good intentions or can be initiated by friend or foe. The only way to distinguish them is via their consequences. For instance, a well-intended word of validation is life-negating if it reduces the target's dignidad.[29] The opposite, however, is untrue: no microintervention starts as microaggression. A misguided intervention can be "unintentionally" aggressive, but aggressions can never, in Sue's words, "validate" or "value" the target's painfully obtained slice of full humanity within an already aggressive shared reality.

Third, and perhaps most important, microinterventions are praxical by nature. While often originating at the level of word, they have materiality and intend to effect palpable improvement

---

[28]José David Rodríguez and Loida I. Martell-Otero, *Teología en Conjunto* (Louisville, KY: Westminster John Knox Press, 1997). Representing the united-yet-different nature of mestizaje/mulatez, Latinx indexes the en conjunto nature of the community, that is, the life-affirming collaboration and internal accountability that makes Latinxs a diverse and self-sustaining group. Latinx is not a melting pot but a sancocho being "human"—a community of distinct flavors working side-by-side toward a fulfillment that transcends the mixing itself, that is, an evolving and future-facing discursive space of latinidades that remains tied to its past and grounded in the present. Cf. Héctor M. Varela Rios, "Sancochando Theological Anthropology: One Puerto Rican Heavy Soup as a Heuristic," *Perspectivas* 15 (Summer 2018), https://perspectivasonline.com.

[29]Dignidad remains in Spanish because it grows from specific Latinx experiences. Relatedly, while Latinx signifies a tumultuous history and problematic self-identity, it still exhibits tremendous ethical promise within Latinx experience. As well as it can be done using a single word, Latinx seeks to maintain dignidad for each Latinx imago Dei out there. Cf. Ismael García, *Dignidad: Ethics through Hispanic Eyes* (Nashville: Abingdon Press, 1997). Latinx lives matter, whether cis/het or LGBTQ+, white-passing or Afro-, binary or non-binary, güere, indie, or negre. Latinx seeks to open doors, not close them. Even if awkwardly, Latinx engenders our own autochthonous solidarity, una solidaridad nuestra y auctóctona. Cf. Roberto S. Goizueta, *Caminemos con Jesús: Toward a Hispanic/Latino Theology of Accompaniment* (Maryknoll, NY: Orbis Books, 1995).

for those folks minoritized's daily existence.[30] As Sue and others explain, wise microinterventions should allay anxiety, diminish situational danger/chaos, challenge aggressors, and others, and do so immediately.[31] Microinterventions "have teeth," in other words; they are embedded in lo cotidiano with temporal efficacy.[32] That makes them praxiological by nature—microinterventions that do not produce change for its intended targets are not microinterventional at all.[33]

Latinx as Theologically Microinterventional —Final Thoughts

How can the microinterventional be seen more specifically in the two articles explored above? On the first article, the author affirms the pretentious and exclusionary nature of Latinx, especially in light of its rejection by everyday Latinos and Latinas. This argument is not only elitist but also full of microaggressions. First, it is fact that Latinx comes from academia but that should not preclude its usage. The word Hispanic, dear to the League of United Latin American Citizens (LULAC) and many Latinxs, is an invention of the US government, an attempt to agglomerate and

---

[30]Materiality refers to real-life, near, tangible, and long-lasting presence and agency.

[31]For me, wise includes safety and bravery. Sue and others caution that microinterventions can increase danger to targets, allies, or bystanders; that is, it might be best to walk away from microaggression. Yet microinterventions need courage as well. For one example of countless others, there would have been no conviction in the George Floyd trial without Darnella Frazier and others (that is, the people who shot the video).

[32]That does not mean that everybody must, and can, respond in the same way—intervening also depends on individual and communal privilege. Said otherwise, not everybody risks equally during microinterventions. For one, privilege is revealed through allyship, and allyship is much easier for white folks in the US.

[33]Latinx also symbolizes how Latinxs want to be. Latinxs are "*mañana* people" (cf. González, *Mañana,* 1990). The aim is not to reduce all Latinxs to a racial/ethnic opaqueness but that their "queer" (strange, alien) cotidiano life in the US is something to be embraced if they are to have a tomorrow (cf. Henderson Espinosa, *Activist Theology,* 65–80). Latinxs are, in more ways than one, the "unexpected 'x' factor" in US society (Morales, *Latinx,* 4) and x-factors are deciding factors, harbingers of change and opportunity, catalysts, creative forces.

erase difference. Second, the assertion that Latinx is exclusionary is nonsensical: What exactly does it exclude Latinxs from? Latinx aims to include those who have been traditionally excluded while still signifying a complex history and identity. On the contrary, this claim is nothing more than explicit binary thinking and machismo (that is, Latinx toxic masculinity). And, third, as seen in the history behind the words themselves, Latinx is not more erasive than Hispanic, Latino/a, or Latina/o have been, especially among Latinxs themselves. For one, Hispanic erases all of Latinidad's pre-Conquest history in Abya Yala, the land renamed "North and South America" by colonizers.

The second article focuses even more on the erasive aspect. I agree that pan-ethnic terms tend to essentialize, just like Hispanic did for Afro-Latinxs, but do not necessarily reduce—the mestize/mulate nature of Latinx is inherently plural and visibilizes more than the all-encompassing Hispanic or the binary Latino/a ever could. Though all these words carry macroaggressions of racism and classism and can often feel like microinsults for machista Latinxs, it also names the identity chasms Latinxs, in general, need to publicly address.[34] Indeed, I would turn sociologist López's implications around: Latinx does "create bridges of understanding and empathy." Latinx, when conceptualized as antiracist/antisexist microintervention, is one such bridge, even if incomplete, ill-fitting, and imperfect.

How is Latinx's microinterventional nature theological as well? I suggest that Latinx is a theological microintervention by doubling back to Latinx as linguistic mestizaje/mulatez—that is, as an experientially grounded theological source of en conjunto collaboration and accountability, of individual and communal dignidad, and of lo cotidiano that should encourage ongoing mutuality between the normative and the queer as part of its telos. Mestizaje/mulatez is no disconnected idea; it impacts the lives of real people through their outlook and actions in this world. Latinx identity is expressed throughout mestize/mulate cultures, an accretion of histories, experiences, perspectives, bodies, affect, beliefs and practices, indigeneity, and so many others carried in a

---

[34]See Miguel A. De La Torre, "Beyond Machismo: A Cuban Case Study," *Annual of the Society of Christian Ethics* 19 (1999): 213–233.

united-yet-different flesh. As linguistic mestizaje/mulatez, Latinx
signifies who Latinxs are and want to be, yet always fluid and
contested.

Within the complex framework that mestizaje/mulatez provides, Latinx is not only ethical but also praxical. Latinx is effectively *doing something* for a specific group of people (Latinxs)
in a world that dehumanizes as one of its norms. When God said,
"Let us make them in my image," God was opening not only a
space for inclusion but also for equal participation (in God's case,
with divinity). In similar fashion, Latinx is a praxical linguistic
mechanism that allows Latinxs to work for and be accountable
to all Latinidades. Said otherwise, Latinx operationalizes en
conjunto. En conjunto literally means "in collaboration," yet it
also needs to remain praxically attached to its target communities. More specifically, Latinx transcends valid yet worn concerns
with diversity and inclusion toward the more valuable "real-life"
emancipation from everyday racist/sexist structures and actions.

I construe Latinx as a necessary condition of justice. In other
words, the ethical force of the word means that there can be no
justice without the diversity and inclusion Latinx provides. Using Latinx is close to a categorical imperative: to be validated
as Latinx, one needs to be constantly present; to be valued and
affirmed, one needs to continually count; to feel supported, one
needs to feel safe; to be empowered, one requires agency. The intersectionality of Latinx entails not only antiracist ways of speaking
and doing but also antisexist (and anticlassist, anti-ableist, and
so on). In other words, Latinxs cannot speak of justice without
speaking justly; therefore, it also operationalizes dignidad. Latinx
is an active self-awareness of our own dignidad, an autochthonous
dignity that springs from the tragedy of conquest yet also from
the victory of vibrant Latinidades in the US and elsewhere.

I allow that Latinx is a problematic word because of the history that produced and sustains it. But Latinxs in the past have
appropriated and transformed terms with arguably tense origin
into symbols of lucha and success within everyday life. Indeed,
some in the community have recently adopted another word in
this sense: Latine. The "e" ending is grammatically acceptable in
Spanish and also keeps the non-binary nature of Latinx (some
words are already gender-neutral, e.g., "estudiante" for male and
female students). This new iteration best expresses the localized

eschatological hope Latinx theologians talk about, a hope that creates the world Latinxs aspire to, the "not-yet-but-already-now" life. Latine's microinterventional nature and theological valence similarly affords harmonious life (or as close as one can get) to occur materially, that is, visibly and impactfully in lo cotidiano and other spheres of Latinx life.

Food Ethics, Race, and Integral Liberation

The Witness of Black Vegans

John Sniegocki

In this essay I explore the insights of the tradition of Black veganism.[1] Contrary to popular perceptions of veganism as being almost exclusively a movement of white people, a significantly higher percentage of Blacks in the United States identify as vegetarian or vegan than do whites. For example, a recent poll by the Pew Research Center found that 8 percent of Blacks in the US self-identify as vegetarian or vegan, more than double the 3 percent rate of the overall (mostly white) population.[2] I explore some of the reasons for the rapidly growing popularity of veganism in the Black community, examine some of its historical roots, and highlight several features that make Black veganism distinctive, particularly its holistic understanding of the nature of oppression. I also suggest several ways that insights from the Black vegan tradition could enhance understandings of integral liberation and integral ecology that have been developed in recent Catholic social teaching.

---

[1] In this essay I capitalize the descriptor "Black" while using lowercase for "white," following the guidelines of the Associated Press. For explanation of the reasons behind these guidelines, which center especially on greater shared Black cultural identity and history, see "AP Says It Will Capitalize Black but Not White," *Associated Press,* July 20, 2020, www.ap.org.

[2] "Why Black Americans Are More Likely to Be Vegan," *BBC News*, September 11, 2020, www.bbc.com.

Perceptions of Vegans
as White and Wealthy

A recent documentary on vegans of color in the US is titled *The Invisible Vegan*.[3] The title is meant to highlight the marginalization of people of color within the mainstream culture's portrayal of veganism. Similarly, there is a common perception of vegetarians/vegans as being primarily wealthy. This too is challenged by the statistical evidence. Recent polling shows that persons with lower incomes ($30,000/year and under) identify as vegetarian/vegan at a rate twice as high as those with higher annual incomes ($75,000 and above).[4] Overcoming these stereotypes is important so that the existence and contributions of all vegans are acknowledged. Also, the existence of these stereotypes can serve as a significant barrier to people considering vegan diets. For example, many vegans of color share that they were accused of "acting white" when they initially made a commitment to a vegan diet. And the myth that being a vegetarian/vegan requires being wealthy clearly can serve as a hindrance to dietary change.

History of Black Vegetarianism
and Veganism in the United States

One way to begin overcoming some of these stereotypes concerning veganism is to foster greater historical awareness. Plant-based diets in the Black community in the United States, for example, have strong historical roots in multiple religious traditions, including those of Seventh-day Adventists, African Hebrew Israelites of Jerusalem, Rastafarians, and the Nation of Islam.

Seventh-day Adventism has a membership that is about one-third Black. This tradition has strongly encouraged vegetarianism since 1863, when Ellen White received what she understood as a revelation from God discouraging the consumption of meat. The

---

[3]See theinvisiblevegan.com. Also see Khushbu Shah, "The Vegan Race Wars: How the Mainstream Ignores Vegans of Color," *Thrillist*, January 26, 2018, www.thrillist.com.

[4]See RJ Reinhart, "Snapshot: Few Americans Vegetarian or Vegan," *Gallup*, August 1, 2018, news.gallup.com.

main rationale for avoiding meat for White concerned the health benefits of a vegetarian diet.[5]

The second religious group, the African Hebrew Israelites of Jerusalem, is a tradition that understands Blacks to be descendants of the biblical Israelites. The core members of their community migrated to Israel from Chicago in the 1960s, but thousands of additional adherents live in the US and elsewhere. The majority of their members are strict vegans, and they run a chain of vegan restaurants in cities such as Chicago, Atlanta, St. Louis, Los Angeles, and Washington, DC. The founder of this tradition, Ben Ammi Ben-Israel (whose birth name was Ben Carter), understood veganism to be the healthiest diet for humans. He also viewed it as being the diet recommended by the Bible in Genesis 1:29, in which God is portrayed as saying: "I give you every seed-bearing plant on the face of the whole earth and every tree that has fruit with seed in it. They will be yours for food." A plant-based diet, Ben Ammi says, is "us going back to live in harmony with the will of the creator."[6]

A third religious tradition that has influenced Black veganism is Rastafarianism. This tradition, founded in Jamaica in the 1930s, stresses the importance of a vegetarian, organic, whole foods diet for human physical, mental, and spiritual well-being. It places emphasis on what it terms "ital" living (derived from the word "vital"), which is centered on the concept of "livity," an energy given by God that flows through all people and living things. Meat is considered to be "dead" food (which, of course, it is) and is understood to undermine "livity," thereby harming physical and spiritual health. More broadly, Rastafarians place a strong emphasis on love and compassion, which for many extends to animals.[7]

Last, a fourth main religious tradition that has influenced Black

---

[5]See Amirah Mercer, "A Homecoming: How I Found Empowerment in the Black History of Plant-Based Diets," *Eater*, January 14, 2021, www.eater.com.

[6]Michael Miller, "Ben Ammi's Adaptation of Veganism in the Theology of the African Hebrew Israelites of Jerusalem," *Interdisciplinary Journal for Religion and Transformation in Contemporary Society* (2021): 1–29, DOI: 10.30965/23642807-bja10019.

[7]Paige Curtis, "The Unsung Caribbean Roots of the Vegan Food Movement," *Yes!*, July 21, 2021, yesmagazine.org.

veganism is the Nation of Islam. Its most prominent leader, Elijah Muhammad, wrote a two-volume work on proper diet, *How to Eat to Live*, published in 1967 and 1972. Muhammad strongly discouraged the consumption of meat and of so-called soul food, which he described as a "slave diet." "These foods," he wrote, "destroy us. We are, by nature, vegetable- and fruit-eating people." A vegetarian diet, he argued, would foster better physical health and stronger mental power.[8]

Each of these traditions has focused primarily on the health benefits of a vegetarian or vegan diet. While the majority of Black vegans today are not members of these religious groups, and the reasons for adopting a vegan diet are now much broader, these traditions continue to play significant direct and indirect roles in Black veganism. For example, numerous prominent Black vegan cookbook authors were raised in families affiliated with one of these traditions, and these groups often run vegetarian or vegan restaurants or health food stores that foster plant-based diets in Black communities.

Along with these religious groups, other figures in the Black community have played a prominent role in encouraging plant-based diets. Perhaps the most well known and influential was the comedian and civil rights activist Dick Gregory, who became a strong proponent of a vegan diet in the 1960s. For Gregory, the rejection of meat was rooted primarily in a commitment to nonviolence: "Because I'm a civil rights activist, I am also an animal rights activist. Animals and humans suffer and die alike. Violence causes the same pain, the same spilling of blood, the same stench of death, the same arrogant, cruel and vicious taking of life. We shouldn't be a part of it."[9] Gregory would later also strongly emphasize the health benefits of a vegan diet, particularly a vegan diet focusing on raw foods, influenced especially by his friendship with the pioneering Black nutritionist/naturopath Dr. Alvenia Fulton. His book *Dick Gregory's Natural Diet for Folks Who Eat: Cookin' with Mother Nature*, published in 1974, heavily influenced by the teachings of Fulton, has had wide influence.[10]

---

[8]See Mercer, "Homecoming."

[9]Quoted in "Why Black Americans."

[10]Dick Gregory, *Dick Gregory's Natural Diet for Folks Who Eat: Cookin' with Mother Nature,* ed. James R. McGraw with Alvenia M. Fulton (New

Gregory, like Elijah Muhammad, saw the "soul food" diet (which contains an emphasis on meat, especially parts of animals that slave owners did not want, along with deep frying, high amounts of sugar, etc.) as being unhealthy and a product of slavery. He was critical of those in the Black community who ignored the negative health impacts of such a diet:

> I personally would say that the quickest way to wipe out a group of people is to put them on a soul food diet. One of the tragedies is that the very folks in the black community who are most sophisticated in terms of the political realities in this country are nonetheless advocates of "soul food." They will lay down a heavy rap on genocide in America with regard to black folks, then walk into a soul food restaurant and help the genocide along.[11]

For numerous decades Gregory and Fulton served as major voices in the Black plant-based movement. Some other very influential pioneering figures in this movement, particularly in the health realm, have included Queen Afua, author of *Heal Thyself for Life and Longevity;* Laila Afrika, author of several books on African holistic healing; and herbalist/healer Alfredo "Dr. Sebi" Bowman. Many contemporary Black vegans who prioritize health issues cite the influence of one or more of these pivotal figures.

A Closer Look at the Reasons for Black Veganism

The reasons given by contemporary Black vegans for their dietary choices are numerous. Some of these reasons overlap with reasons commonly given by non-Black vegans, such as concern for animals or concern for the environment. Some reasons, however, are more distinctive, and these are what has led to the creation of the very term "Black veganism" to designate a particular approach to the adoption of a vegan diet and lifestyle. In other words, Black veganism is not simply generic veganism practiced by Blacks, but rather it is a more specific and holistic way of understanding the

---

York: Harper and Row, 1974).

[11]Quoted in *Sistah Vegan*, ed. A. Breeze Harper (Brooklyn: Lantern Publishing, 2020), 21.

foundational reasons for being vegan. Aph Ko, creator of the website Black Vegans Rock (blackvegansrock.com) and co-author with her sister Syl of the book *Aphro-ism: Essays on Pop Culture, Feminism, and Black Veganism from Two Sisters*, states: "Black veganism is not just about Black people eating kale or whatever, it's talking about the world, talking about oppression in a totally different way, and re-envisioning a more liberatory world."[12] Some of the key features of this liberatory worldview include:

1. Health, Decolonizing of Diet

Health has consistently been a central focus of Black veganism. This concern for health, however, is seen in the broader context of systemic injustice. The forces of slavery, colonialism, racism, and capitalism are understood to have systematically undermined Black health. In the current context in the United States this manifests as higher rates of food insecurity and hunger, shorter life expectancy, and significantly higher rates of heart disease, diabetes, cancer, stroke, and other health problems than are experienced by the white population. The reclaiming of health through veganism is seen as an act of resistance against these powerful forces of oppression.[13]

The adoption of a vegan diet is also seen as a way of reconnecting with the traditional diets of West Africa, from where most slaves were taken. As physician Milton Mills states:

When we look at the traditional diets of our West African ancestors, we see they were based on a wide range of whole plant-based foods that were very low in fat, like whole grains, green leafy vegetables, and beans, nuts and peas. They contained no dairy foods and very little meat on a daily basis. Studies have shown that when African Americans eat a diet that is consistent with the traditional West African diets of our ancestors—that were primarily or entirely plant-based—we have very low rates of heart disease, diabetes,

---

[12]Quotation from "The Surprisingly Black History of Veganism," *ATTN:* on *YouTube*, February 19, 2020, www.youtube.com.

[13]See, for example, Danni Roseman, "How Black Veganism Is Revolutionary and Essential for Our Culture," *Blavity*, June 24, 2017, www.blavity.com.

high blood pressure, stroke and cancer. But when we eat the standard American diet, not only do we develop these chronic diseases, but we develop them to a greater degree than Caucasians do.[14]

Rather than equating Black culture with traditional forms of slavery-influenced "soul food," Black vegans such as Mills suggest reconnecting with earlier, predominantly plant-based African traditions.

> Unfortunately, after the *institution* of slavery ended, we kept the *culture* of slavery with us by continuing to eat a diet that is essentially a vestige of the plantation and oppression. The real tragedy of the Black experience in America when it comes to food is that a plant-based diet is our true heritage as people of color, not so-called Soul Food. Plantation food is not Soul Food and is not true to our cultural heritage. Study after study has shown that this food leads to excess disease and premature death in Black populations.[15]

Many Black vegans, it should be noted, suggest ways of reconceptualizing and re-creating healthier vegan forms of soul food so that the positive aspects of the soul food tradition (such as culinary creativity and the positive emotional connotations that people may have with certain foods/flavors) can be retained even while the problematic parts detrimental to health are left behind.[16]

Black vegans often speak of the need to "decolonize" diet. As Tinece Payne, founder of a nonprofit holistic health center in North Carolina, states: "We're returning to our natural selves and not being colonized. We're putting an end to the slave mentality."[17]

---

[14]Interview with Milton Mills, in Tracye McQuirter, *African American Vegan Starter Guide*, 5, www.byanygreensnecessary.com.

[15]Milton Mills, "A Sacred Obligation," in *Brotha Vegan*, ed. Omowale Adewale (Brooklyn: Lantern Publishing, 2021), 98.

[16]See Christopher Carter, *The Spirit of Soul Food: Race, Faith, and Food Justice* (Chicago: University of Illinois Press, 2021); Bryant Terry, *Vegan Soul Kitchen: Fresh, Healthy, and Creative African American Cuisine* (Cambridge, MA: Da Capo Press, 2009); Jenné Claiborne, *Sweet Potato Soul* (New York: Harmony Books, 2018).

[17]Quoted in Zakiyaa Taylor, "Deep Roots: Communities of Color and

Amirah Mercer speaks of her adoption of a vegan diet as a reclaiming of her cultural identity. "Plant-based eating," she says,
"is probably one of the Blackest things I could do. As a Black
woman in America, my veganism is, in fact, a homecoming."[18]

2. Challenging Interrelated Forms of Oppression

Another distinctive feature of Black veganism is the recognition
that various forms of injustice are profoundly interrelated and
share common roots. This includes seeing the connections between
the mistreatment of animals and racism. As Aph Ko states, "many
of us have come to the conclusion that our experiences of racial
oppression are deeply entangled with animal oppression on a
fundamental level."[19] Numerous Black vegans cite the influence
of books such as Marjorie Spiegel's *The Dreaded Comparison,*
which highlights similarities between the treatment of animals and
the treatment of slaves, and Charles Patterson's *Eternal Treblinka,*
which highlights parallels to the Holocaust. The latter book takes
its title from Jewish author and vegetarian Isaac Bashevis Singer's
famous quote: "In relation to them [i.e., animals], all people are
Nazis; for the animals it is an eternal Treblinka."[20] Those making
these comparisons, which can of course be controversial, stress
that they are not claiming that the mistreatment of a cow or pig
or chicken is morally equivalent to the mistreatment of a human
being, but rather that they are seeking to highlight that these
realities nonetheless share similar roots and features.

A common way that racism has often been justified has been
to describe Black people as less-than-human, as "animals," with
wealthy white heterosexual males understood as the standard
of the truly human (and this of course has implications with
regard to sexism, classism, homophobia, and other forms of

---

the Plant-Based Movement," *OMD for the Planet,* February 28, 2019, www.
omdfortheplanet.com.
    [18]Mercer, "Homecoming."
    [19]Aph Ko, "On Animal Liberation," in *Starter Guide,* 19.
    [20]Marjorie Spiegel, *The Dreaded Comparison: Human and Animal
Slavery* (Philadelphia: New Society Publishers, 1988); Charles Patterson,
Eternal Treblinka: Our Treatment of Animals and the Holocaust (New York:
Lantern Books, 2002).

discrimination as well). One response to such a hierarchical anthropology could simply be to assert one's own full humanity, without challenging the mistreatment of non-human animals. But in the view of many Black vegans, this would leave the root of the problem (i.e., oppressive mentalities based in hierarchical dualisms) insufficiently challenged. Black veganism understands itself as an attempt to fundamentally subvert and resist oppressive, hierarchical anthropologies entirely. Black theologian Christopher Carter states:

> In this way, I suggest that when people of color make the argument that we "are human, too," we are not critiquing the system of white supremacy; rather, we are making a claim that we should be included among the humans who are allowed to exploit other creatures—this is an argument for equality with the oppressor rather than the dismantling of the reasoning that morally justifies the oppression. This realization ultimately led me to reach a conclusion I never expected: veganism, specifically Black veganism.[21]

Carter emphasizes that Black veganism is not only for Blacks. Rather, it is an approach to veganism that recognizes the intersectionality of oppressions and seeks to challenge oppression in all of its forms. This worldview can be embraced by persons of any race:

> Black culture and the experiences of Black people are the starting point for my construction of Black veganism. However, the "Blackness" of Black veganism should be understood as an orienting disposition, meaning one does not have to be Black to practice Black veganism. Instead, the "Blackness" of Black veganism signifies a commitment to an anti-oppressive way of being in the world that signifies our commitment to being in solidarity with the exploited and dispossessed.[22]

---

[21]Christopher Carter, "How Black Veganism Can Decolonize Soul Food," *The Grio*, April 22, 2022, www.thegrio.com.
[22]Ibid.

As a Christian, Carter also relates Black veganism to his understanding of Jesus. He says, "Black veganism seeks to opt out of structures that normalize violence and suffering and live into ways of being in the world consistent with Jesus's spiritual path of radical compassion and his way of nonviolent social transformation."[23]

3. Reasons Shared with Veganism More Broadly

The above two features are at the core of what makes Black veganism distinctive. At the same time, many Black vegans embrace reasons for being vegan that are common among vegans in general while adding attention to how these issues especially affect people of color and stressing how the various issues interrelate.

(a) Animals: Concern for non-human animals has become a more central feature of Black veganism over the past couple of decades. Although earlier forms of Black vegetarianism and veganism mainly focused on a human health rationale, awareness of the horrific nature of factory-farm animal-raising and its extraordinary scope (over nine billion animals are killed for food each year in the United States alone) has led to deepened reflection on the plight of animals. But the issue of animals is not viewed in isolation. It is seen as part of an overarching system of oppression and domination that needs to be challenged, which includes, for example, the need to challenge core features of capitalism. For example, well-known radical Black activist and vegan Angela Davis states, "[Veganism] is I think a part of a revolutionary perspective. How can we not only discover more compassionate relations with human beings, but how can we develop compassionate relations with the other creatures with whom we share this planet? And that will mean challenging the whole industrial capitalist form of food production."[24] Among the realities to be challenged are food insecurity and so-called food deserts, or, as many prefer to call it, "food apartheid." Attention to these broader food justice issues is an integral part of Black veganism.

---

[23]Carter, *Spirit of Soul Food*, 14.

[24]Angela Davis, "On Revolution: A Conversation between Grace Lee Boggs and Angela Davis," *Radio Project*, March 2, 2012, transcript, www. radioproject.org.

(b) Exploited Workers: Workers in slaughterhouses experience the highest injury rates of any occupation in the United States, along with high rates of mental health problems. Slaughterhouse workers are often undocumented immigrants, who cannot challenge their oppressive working conditions. Similarly, workers in factory farms, often people of color, experience negative health impacts from exposure to urine, feces, and other toxins.[25] Concern for such exploited workers is an important component of Black veganism.

(c) Ecology: Another newer emphasis in Black veganism, shared with many other vegans, is concern about the ecological impacts of the production of meat and other animal products. Numerous authors, for example, cite a United Nations study that found that the livestock industry is responsible for more greenhouse gas emissions than the direct emissions of all forms of transportation combined. The report also cited the livestock industry as one of the main causes of deforestation, soil degradation, and water and air pollution—realities that disproportionately affect communities of color.[26]

(d) World Hunger: Raising animals for human consumption, especially when they are fed beans, grains, and other foods rather than simply grazing on pastures, is extremely inefficient. It takes, for example, about six pounds of grain/bean protein feed to livestock to get one pound of meat protein. Five-sixths of the protein and vast quantities of other nutrients are lost to human consumption in the process.[27] The world can feed many more people on plant-based diets than on meat-centered diets. Again, it is disproportionately people of color who experience the impacts of hunger.

(e) Nonviolence and Compassion: At the heart of embracing a vegan diet for many Black vegans are the spiritual implications of such a choice. These include an embrace of nonviolence and

---

[25]Carter, *Spirit of Soul Food*, 58–60, 83–84.

[26]Food and Agriculture Organization of the United Nations, *Livestock's Long Shadow: Environmental Issues and Options* (Rome: FAO, 2006), www.fao.org.

[27]David Pimentel and Marcia Pimentel, "Sustainability of Meat-Based and Plant-Based Diets and the Environment," *American Journal of Clinical Nutrition* 78 (2003): 661S.

resistance against forces of violence that have so often harmed people of color. "Veganism," says Dexter Scott King (son of Martin Luther King Jr. and Coretta Scott King), "has given me a higher level of awareness and spirituality."[28] Breeze Harper, editor of the pioneering volume *Sistah Vegan*, speaks of the importance of *ahimsa*-based veganism (drawing on a term from Hindu and Buddhist traditions), "a life of practicing noninjury or harmlessness to *all* living beings."[29] Many stress how embracing a vegan diet has helped them to feel a deeper sense of connection with the world. For example, Anthony Carr states:

> Veganism to me is a journey to connectedness: connections to myself, my Blackness, and Earth. It is a revolutionary rejection of violence and the violence that continues to happen to Black and Brown bodies. . . . Veganism is about living a life of peace and nonviolence with all creatures on Earth, of reconnecting to the earth. I believe that part of my Blackness and my maleness involves living with compassion in this world.[30]

Rapper Styles P states: "A plant-based diet kinda makes your soul lighter. I had a newfound respect for all life."[31]

What Catholic Social Teaching Could Learn from Black Veganism

There are a variety of similarities between the worldviews of Black veganism and Catholic social teaching (CST). In *Laudato Si'*, for example, Pope Francis develops the notion of "integral ecology," building on the concept of "integral development" that was articulated by Pope Paul VI and the notion of "integral liberation"

---

[28]Jill Howard Church, "Dexter Scott King, Son of Rev. Martin Luther King Jr., on Veganism as a Form of Non-Violence and Spiritual Growth," *Vegetarian Times*, January 14, 2022, www.vegetariantimes.com.

[29]Harper, *Sistah Vegan*, xxvi.

[30]Anthony Carr, "A Journey to Connectedness," in *Brotha Vegan*, 133, 135.

[31]Cited in Zachary Toliver, "These 47 Black Vegans Who Save Animals Inspire PETA," *PETA*, February 1, 2019 (updated February 3, 2022), www.peta.org.

developed by Pope John Paul II.[32] Integral ecology recognizes the deep interconnections between social justice issues and ecological issues. It calls us, as Francis puts it, to hear both "the cry of the earth" and the "cry of the poor"[33] and to recognize that the crises of economic inequality and ecological destruction are results of the same underlying problematic system and worldview. All of these teachings of Francis would be affirmed by the tradition of Black veganism.

In *Laudato Si'*, Francis asserts that all creatures have inherent value, "a value of their own in God's eyes."[34] This represents an important milestone in official papal teaching. Pope John Paul II, for example, had favorably quoted a Vatican II statement that "Man is the only creature that God willed for its own sake."[35] Francis clearly disagrees with this claim, and the tradition of Black veganism would join him in this disagreement.

Yet while Francis affirms the inherent value of all creatures, he never explicitly explores the implications of this affirmation for our dietary choices. This is an area where dialogue with Black veganism could be fruitful. Nor, with one recent important exception, does Francis explore how our dietary choices affect the environment, world hunger, or workers.[36] Black veganism, through its analysis of such issues, can help CST more deeply examine how our dietary choices are deeply interconnected with broader social and ecological realities. It can help us understand how truly hearing and responding to the cry of the poor and the cry of the earth (including the cries of non-human animals) may require significant dietary change for many, especially in First World contexts.

---

[32]See Pope Paul VI, *Populorum Progressio*, March 26, 1967, www.vatican.va; Pope John Paul II, *Centesimus Annus*, May 1, 1991, www.vatican.va.

[33]Pope Francis, *Laudato Si': On Care for Our Common Home*, May 25, 2015, no. 49, www.vatican.va.

[34]Ibid., no. 69.

[35]Pope John Paul II, *Centesimus Annus*, no. 53, citing the Vatican II document *Gaudium et Spes*, no. 24.

[36]The one recent exception is a statement by Francis that encourages reduced meat consumption for ecological reasons. In a July 6, 2022, letter to the EU Youth Conference, Francis wrote: "There is an urgent need to reduce the consumption not only of fossil fuels but also of so many superfluous things. In certain areas of the world, too, it would be appropriate to consume less meat: this too can help save the environment." Available at www.vatican.va.

When Francis speaks of a call to ecological conversion, infused with "a spirit of generous care, full of tenderness" and "a loving awareness that we are not disconnected from the rest of creatures,"[37] the tradition of Black veganism can help show how to live such a vision more deeply.

The tradition of Black veganism can also help CST better understand that addressing issues of structural racism in its many forms must be a central part of the quest for "integral liberation." While CST expresses opposition to racism, too often it does not explore in sufficient depth the many ways that structural racism is manifested. Black veganism devotes much attention to these structural issues, in relation to food ethics and beyond.

Overall, through its holistic approach to food ethics and its articulation of the interrelated nature of various forms of oppression and liberation, Black veganism has much to offer in conversation with CST. It is to be hoped that such a conversation flourishes.

---

[37]Pope Francis, *Laudato Si'*, no. 220.

From Spaces of Fracture
to Places of Flow

How "Urban Alchemy" Can Enliven Catholic Social Teaching and Transform Our Campuses

Maureen H. O'Connell

In May 2021, a twenty-two-member commission at La Salle University released a comprehensive report, "Begin Again: Truth and Transformation," identifying ruptures in our campus climate that preclude a culture of belonging and proposing recommendations to address them.[1] I was drawn to a recommendation about integrating into the campus master plan "a public arts program reflecting the cultural, ethnic, and religious diversity of the La Salle community."[2] I find myself wondering how we ought to go about this, especially in distinctively Catholic ways. How can we harness two of the traditions that set us apart in the landscape of higher education—the Catholic intellectual tradition (CIT) and the Catholic social tradition (CST)—in turning non-spaces across our campus footprints into chrysalis-like places for institutional, cultural, and social change on personal and collective levels?

I suggest that Dr. Mindy Thompson Fullilove can be a generative conversation partner. The daughter of civil rights community

---

[1]"Begin Again: Truth and Transformation," La Salle University's Joint Commission on Diversity, Equity, Inclusion and Justice, May 2021, https://www.lasalle.edu.
[2]Ibid., 14.

organizers in South Orange, New Jersey, Fullilove is a social psychiatrist, writer, and educator who focuses on displacement, urban mental health, and collective consciousness.[3] She offers tools for turning *spaces* we *pass through* on the way to somewhere else into *places* we *come to* in order to create and experience community. In what follows, I spell out Fullilove's framework and identify how we can use it to translate three central principles of CST into place-based aesthetic expressions that can help us create more places that build up our capabilities for life in community, capabilities that have been compromised by racism.[4] I highlight Catholic campus communities implicitly doing this aesthetic work.

From Fracture to Flow

At the heart of Fullilove's work is attention to the fundamental truth that "we make our social systems and our social systems make us"; and that symbiotic process happens in physical spaces in one of two ways: fracture or flow.[5] Our systems can either operate with a "divide and conquer" mentality that keeps people separated—from each other, from the goods we need to flourish, from our natural environment; or they can operate with a "mesh and prosper" approach that deepens our connection to each other, to the resources needed to live a good life, and to the environment around us. Fullilove insists that fracture happens to particular spaces and is a repetitive, iterative, downward spiraling phenomenon. As proof, she turns to America's long history of sort-

---

[3]See www.mindyfullilove.com and also the University of Orange, which she co-founded in 2008 in Orange, New Jersey: https://universityoforange.org.

[4]Throughout I capitalize the words "Black" and "Indigenous" in order to acknowledge the distinct ethnic realities and histories of peoples in these groups, and to honor ongoing attempts from within these populations to resist a culture of white supremacy that has attempted to erase them. I do not capitalize the term "white," since it is a far more socially constructed racial designation and doing so can decenter whiteness in order to make space for that cultural reclamation work, even among people in this racial category. I'm thankful to the editors of this annual volume for sharing a succinct resource to help unpack this further: Mike Laws, "Why We Capitalize 'Black' and Not 'White,'" *Columbia Journalism Review*, June 16, 2020, www.cjr.org.

[5]Mindy Thompson Fullilove, "The Ecology of Inequality," *TED Talks*, May 18, 2018, www.ted.com.

ing spaces, particularly urban spaces. She pays attention to spaces because spaces shape the collective consciousness of people who inhabit them. Social displacement leads to social disintegration because "spatial homogeneity" breeds toxicity.[6]

How? Borders, real or figurative, breed what she calls "invisibilization." When we don't see each other, we become strangers, and fantasies about people on the other side of borders supplant the realities of their lived experiences. This leads to social disintegration, which shreds our social networks and impedes our cognitive abilities for what she calls the "intergroup global workspace" or the generativity and ingenuity of "cognitive activity that takes place in a combined space."[7] In her study of the impact of fracture on health care organizations attempting to respond to the AIDS crisis, for example, Fullilove discovered that a lack of a "common platform for collective thinking" made problem solving more challenging. "[Responders] were caught in a profound paralysis, unable to recognize and respond to patterns of threat and opportunity. In that context, the AIDS epidemic made its merry way from person to person, unhampered by the multitude of impediments an aroused public might have thrown in its path."[8]

Social homogeneity also breeds toxicity because of the trauma sorting creates in our bodies. Fullilove explains how segregation creates experiences of grief which, when unprocessed, become unhealthy: "The experience of place is encoded in our muscles and our bones," Fullilove says.[9] As a result of sorting, much of what all people feel in their bodies is a sense of mourning. Black people are still mourning the literal displacement from or destruction of places to which they once belonged; and in some senses, white people are too: "White people, too, loved their neighborhoods and to this day mourn their lost homes. When they exchanged wonderful urban neighborhoods for cars, malls, and lawns, they

---

[6]Mindy Thompson Fullilove, *Urban Alchemy: Restoring Joy in America's Sorted-Out Cities* (New York: New Village Press, 2013), 108.

[7]Ibid., 29.

[8]Ibid., 32; referencing Rodrick Wallace and Mindy T. Fullilove, *Collective Consciousness and Its Discontents: Institutional Distributed Cognition, Racial Policy, and Public Health in the United States* (New York: Spring, 2008).

[9]Mindy Thompson Fullilove, *Root Shock: How Tearing Up City Neighborhoods Hurts America, and What We Can Do About It* (New York: New Village Press, 2016), 226.

abandoned not just the city but also the togetherness and socia-
bility of their heritage."[10] In short, fracture "drains the spirit."[11]

Why do I find Fullilove's concept of "fracture" helpful in terms
of thinking about racism, especially on campuses? Certainly, we
can track the history of our campus spaces onto much of the
downward spiral of sorting.[12] We can also recognize that even in
the midst of diverse campuses like mine, we still sort ourselves into
homogenous spaces: cafeteria tables, classroom spaces, academic
departments, residence halls, and sports fields. We know that this
homogeneity affects the intergroup global workspace that so
many of our universities desire to be. Sorting on our campuses
impedes our abilities to respond to the crises that many of us hope
to prepare students for, if not respond to ourselves.

To underscore my point here, in the quote from Fullilove that
follows, imagine replacing the word "city" with the phrase "university" or even "*Catholic* university":

> I became convinced that our cities were mired in a profound
> contradiction. Human beings create cities so they will have
> a site for social and cultural interaction and development.
> Cities fulfill this function because people connect with
> each other and exchange goods and ideas. The sorted-out
> American city cannot do what it is meant to do, as division
> is antithetical to connection, conquering to exchange. It is
> this deep contradiction that rumbles in the guts of our cit-
> ies: we feel the unease, suffer from the dysfunction, and act
> out the madness.[13]

There is good news. Fullilove unabashedly professes that we can
transform downward spirals into upward ones; we can replace
fracture with "flow" or "place-restorative behaviors" that "re-
integrate the city, restoring our ability to recognize and solve
problems, return our social sanity."[14] To facilitate flow, Fullilove

---

[10]Fullilove, *Root Shock*, 225.

[11]Fullilove, *Urban Alchemy*, 109.

[12]See my attempt to do this in three Catholic institutions of higher education with which I've been affiliated in *Undoing the Knots: Five Generations
of American Catholic Anti-Blackness* (Malden, MA: Beacon Press, 2021).

[13]Fullilove, *Urban Alchemy*, 33.

[14]Ibid., 40.

proposes nine elements of urban restoration, which she organizes into three movements that to my mind reflect the praxis of CST: align through keeping the whole city in mind, finding what you're for, and making a mark; create through unpuzzling the fractured space, unslumming all neighborhoods, creating meaningful spaces; and connect through strengthening the region, showing solidarity with all life, and celebrating your accomplishments.[15]

Although articulated from the perspective of and for audiences in the social sciences and public health, Fullilove's framework has an explicit justice ethic, and a feminist one at that. Her aim is human flourishing, which she understands not only in terms of material goods delivered through equitable systems but also, and even more important, relational goods arising from networks of connection and belonging. Other-oriented, collective creativity—particularly when intentional about physical space and its impacts on embodied experiences of people within them—can be a conduit for both material and relational goods. To that end, when rooted in Catholic aesthetics and ethics, we can harness a few of these elements to transform our campuses from fractured spaces into places of flow and build the individual and collective muscle to reverse the downward spiral of racism.

Unpuzzling Fractured Spaces
and the Preferential Option for Those Made Poor

For Fullilove, the element called "unpuzzle the fractured space" is all about perspective. Unpuzzling helps us get clear about the external forces putting pressure on our communities that "leave us confused about how to live together" in sorted spaces.[16] In other words, it's about unraveling the tangled mess in which our histories of segregation, classism, and sexism continue to ensnare us, especially in the sorted-out spaces where we live most of our lives. "Unpuzzling," Fullilove says, "opens the space and frees us

---

[15]For full description and application of each to a variety of urban contexts, see Fullilove, *Urban Alchemy*. I have also used *The Urban Alchemy Workbook: A Reading Companion* in my place-based courses: https://static1. squarespace.com/static/57224b002fe131c3a731755c/t/59cdc4f7cd0f68167 8b48e00/1506657536874/Urban-Alchemy-Workbook-1.pdf.

[16]Fullilove, *Urban Alchemy*, 38.

to get to know each other."[17] In our campus contexts, unpuzzling
fractured spaces helps us not only to perceive the fracture but
also to recognize the ways that *our institutions themselves* have
been and continue to be a source of that fracture. I think the
preferential option for those made poor is the CST corollary to
Fullilove's unpuzzling fractured spaces. The preferential option
is not simply about modeling God's special love for those who
are marginalized. It is also about perceiving marginalizing forces
more accurately through their eyes or from what community organizers dub the perspective of those "closest to the pain." Those
who know fracture *in their bones* are often those who know to
unpuzzle the spaces where that fracture happens.

M. Shawn Copeland's theological aesthetics provides a compelling link between unpuzzling and preferring. Copeland herself
made a turn to aesthetics in her political theology in order to "[see]
in the dark" or to plunge into the darkness of the still unfolding
afterlife of the middle passage.[18] In her words, she has spent her
theological career "down at the crossroads" of racism and sexism in Catholic theology in the US, a puzzled and fractured space
no doubt, in order to diagnose the symptoms of social suffering
and then to share the resources of "survivance" within the Black
Catholic tradition.[19] When placed in dialogue with Fullilove's
notion of the pain of being sorted into spatial homogeneity, Copeland's aesthetics can help us see in the dark on our campuses in
order to perceive more accurately the crossroads where the sorting
and fracturing forces of today's empires mark space and bodies

---

[17]Ibid.

[18]M. Shawn Copeland, "Theology at the Crossroads: A Meditation on
the Blues," in *Uncommon Faithfulness: The Black Catholic Experience*,
ed. M. Shawn Copeland, with LaReine-Marie Mosely, SND, and Albert J.
Raboteau (Maryknoll, NY: Orbis Books, 2009), 103–105. See my engagement with Copeland's aesthetics as a resource for racial justice in "Disturbing
the Aesthetics of Race: M. Shawn Copeland and the Justice of Beauty," in
*Enfleshing Theology: Embodiment, Discipleship, and Politics in the Work
of M. Shawn Copeland*, ed. Robert Rivera and Michele Saracino (Lanham,
MD: Lexington Books, 2008), 233–248.

[19]Copeland, "Theology at the Crossroads," 98. Sharon Welch notes that
the word "survivance" originates among Indigenous Americans to "capture
the dynamic play of survival and transformation" within their traditions. See
After Empire: The Art and Ethos of Enduring Peace (Minneapolis: Fortress
Press, 2004), 43.

for dehumanization. Copeland can also help bring a theological dimension to Fullilove's verb to "unpuzzle." As "junctures of deliberation, turning, crossroads signify a place or moment of deep imposing mystery, of access to dense and opaque power," she says.[20] She claims this is a similar power we remember in the anamnestic moment of Eucharist. "Do this in remembrance of me" is about eating the flesh of Jesus in order to recall that Jesus did not erase the various forms of difference on the marked bodies with which he came in contact in the empire of his time, but rather encountered those differences in order to liberate people from the unfreedoms that came with them. It is about recalling that Jesus used his marked body to unpuzzle fractured people, to unpuzzle fractured space.

So what does this have to do with unpuzzling fractured spaces on campus? Initiatives to rename campus buildings in order to address racist histories provide opportunities to identify and then to linger, like Copeland, at the crossroads of the fractures in our communities. Copeland's ideas about beauty suggest that these renaming efforts can be more than just the preferential option for those who stand at crossroads, but rather the preferential option to create spaces where we can learn how to "see in the dark" by remembering people whose experiences can illuminate ways to align ourselves with the memory of Jesus.

Consider Loyola University of Maryland's decision to remove Flannery O'Connor's name from one of its residence halls in the summer of 2020 after the release of a cache of personal letters revealed O'Connor's anti-Blackness. Tia Noelle Pratt implicitly wonders if the space, now named for Thea Bowman, has been sufficiently unpuzzled. Pratt sees a missed opportunity to grapple with ways in which the Church and the Catholic culture to which Flannery O'Connor belonged—and which shaped her prized imagination—were thoroughly racist. While not disputing the significance of Bowman, Pratt implicitly invites further unpuzzling of this space via the preferential option for those made poor, in this case, those made poor in the same Catholic literary tradition in which O'Connor stands. She points out two Catholic women of color writers—Toni Morrison and Louise Erdrich—who interrupt

---

[20]Copeland, "Theology at the Crossroads," 98.

the whiteness of the Catholic imagination, as well as the apathy about racism within the Church. "Could *that* be why they're not readily identified with the Catholic literary imagination?" Pratt wonders. "Yet, this is exactly what we need the broader Church to be—an institution that is willing to fully acknowledge and articulate the ways it has hurt its members. And we have to be *imaginative* enough to embrace the possibility of that."[21] Unpuzzling requires creativity.

Similarly, for the past three years, Gonzaga University has attempted to stand at the crossroads of white supremacy and clericalism in the process of institutionally acknowledging a named abuser of Indigenous children who hailed from the Jesuit's former Oregon Province and resided in a Jesuit residence attached to the campus. Perhaps what's most notable about this is how Gonzaga went about unpuzzling this fracture, tapping the multi-perspectivalism and empathy offered by the restorative practice of circle conversations.[22] The community discerned five recommended areas of engagement, one of which involves creating memorials and liturgies. Gonzaga plans to create a labyrinth to honor victims and a permanent display in their main building to detail Gonzaga's history with Native communities.

These examples of unpuzzling the fractured space, when rooted in the preferential option for people made poor, help us see that decisions to rename spaces or to create spaces of candor do not foster uncritical cancel cultures, but rather intentional crossroads cultures where we move across thresholds of apathetic, fearful, and homogenous spaces into multi-everything places of empathy, curiosity, imagination.

"Find What You're For" and Solidarity

With "find what you're for" Fullilove encourages restoration oriented around shared values, visions, and latent assets within communities. This is the fundamental first step in her approach to

---

[21]Tia Noelle Pratt, "'I Bring My Black Self': Sr. Thea Bowman's Challenge to the Church," *Commonweal Magazine,* November 2, 2020, www.commonwealmagazine.org.

[22]"The University Commission on Gonzaga's Response to the Catholic Sexual Abuse Crisis to the President of Gonzaga University," September 1, 2021, https://gonzaga.azureedge.net.

strategic planning since figuring out what you're for—what you stand for, your shared dreams—can lead to meaningful action, particularly when people take the time to figure out "What does this group *mean* when they say that?"[23] In her experience, this clarifying process requires artistic expression—visual note taking, poetic reflection on communal memories, guided movement through spaces. To this extent, "find what you're for" is political as it calls people together to "achieve in space what they imagine in relationships" so as to resist top-down strategies that often foster fracture and displacement.[24] She calls this "empowered collaboration."[25]

Nichole Flores's *Aesthetic Solidarity: Our Lady of Guadalupe and American Democracy* can help unpack this element's connection to the Catholic principle of solidarity, when that experience of shared purpose and belonging includes otherwise minoritized populations.[26] Just as Fullilove cautions against orienting strategic plans around *assumptions* of shared goods, Flores contends that paying attention to the ways Latine communities continue to participate in the unfolding power of the Guadalupan story, with all of its narrative, sensorial, and emotive details, provides a touchstone for communities who insist that they and their visions of the good life matter in the face of powers that tell them otherwise. Flores reminds us that "the little story" of Juan Diego, particularly as it continues to be told and performed in communities marginalized from the common good, contributes to the bigger story of God's work to liberate the oppressed by amplifying what these communities—sorted by forces of fracture to use Fullilove's language—stand for. "Aesthetic solidarity . . . [asserts] that aesthetic experience can promote communal encounters that affirm human dignity both within and across broader society."[27]

So where can we find examples of aesthetic expression of institutional commitments? At Villanova University in 1998, Peggy

---

[23]Fullilove, *Urban Alchemy*, 115.
[24]Ibid.
[25]Mindy Thompson Fullilove, "Psychiatric Implications of Displacement: Contributions from the Psychology of Place," *American Journal of Psychiatry* 153 (December 1996): 1521.
[26]Nichole M. Flores, *Aesthetic Solidarity: Our Lady of Guadalupe and American Democracy* (Washington, DC: Georgetown University Press, 2021).
[27]Ibid., 141.

Mach sculpted a bronze statue, *St. Augustine the Teacher*, which stands at the intersection of crisscrossing pathways that connect several academic buildings.[28] In 2001, the university commissioned her to add a female student and again in 2014 to add a Black student. Here we see an evolving commitment to expressing what the university is for by including the perspectives and assets of those beyond those who have embodied the campus' dominant culture. We see a physical representation of a tradition that continues to unfold in an ever-expanding capacity for leaning into and learning from and with difference.

A second example comes from an April 2022 listening session as part of the global synod on synodality involving students and campus leaders from fourteen Catholic campuses and Newman Centers in the Archdiocese of Philadelphia, led by Archbishop Nelson Perez.[29] To amplify students' engagement with the synodal experience of bold speech and deep listening, artist Becky McIntyre, an alum of Saint Joseph's University, created an interactive art installation that visually captured four hundred students' joys and obstacles of journeying with the Church. Students offered their ideas on translucent colored paper in the shape of footprints, which they added to a life-sized sketch of the official synod logo that McIntyre painted on a large window in the gathering space, creating a stained-glass window. The installation, *A Window in the Future of the Church: Journeying Together in Celebration and Accountability* points to the power of the arts in this global process that in many ways is about collective discernment to "find what we are for" as a Catholic faith community and paying attention to ways we can turn those spaces of listening into sacramental places of encounter.

---

[28]See images in Villanova's digital collection: https://digital.library.villanova.edu/Collection/vudl:172455.

[29]See Synodality in Catholic Higher Education in Philadelphia website: https://synodalityinphillyhighered.wordpress.com/. See also Maureen H. O'Connell, "On 14 College Campuses, Young Adults Are Heard via Synod," *Catholicphilly.com*, March 30, 2022, https://catholicphilly.com. Finally, for potential application of the Philadelphia synod experiment to an approach to evangelization rooted in the solidarity to which synodality calls us, see Ernest Miller, FSC, "Pope Francis' Synod Could Be Key to Reaching Young Catholics," *National Catholic Reporter*, June 21, 2022, https://www.ncronline.org.

Create Meaningful Places
and Human Dignity

When it comes to the element she calls "create meaningful spaces," Fullilove means converting *spaces* people *pass through*, the non-places so to speak, into *places* that people *come to* by tapping memory. For a space to become a place, Fullilove says it needs to be meaningful for all who come to it for all of the different reasons that bring them there. It requires being attentive to ways in which our spaces either pull people together, inviting them in, which she calls sociopetal spaces that promote social interaction and social capital; or how our spaces end up pushing people apart or what Fullilove calls sociofugal spaces that keep a divided and conquered status quo in place.[30]

Since so many of our campus spaces reflect the dominant culture of our Catholic institutions, many are, by default, white spaces and as such experienced as sociofugal by peoples of color. Urban sociologist Elijah Anderson explores the felt phenomena of racialized spaces.[31] Anderson's antidote to spaces of domination, surveillance, and forced assimilation is to create cosmopolitan spaces in which no one single culture dominates or where all can feel at ease, where all tacitly know that they belong. To be Catholic about it, cosmopolitan places of belonging affirm the dignity of all human beings in such a way that everyone can be and become who they are with confidence. But to create these kinds of places requires recognizing the inherent whiteness in so many of our spaces that makes our invocations of human dignity ring hypocritical at best and dangerous at worst. If the adage that asking white people to describe whiteness is like asking fish to describe water is apt, then clearly our ineptitude stems in large part from the whiteness of our physical habitats. So how can the arts play a role here?

Christopher Pramuk's theological aesthetics can be of assis-

---

[30]Fullilove, *Urban Alchemy*, 203.

[31]Elijah Anderson, *Black in White Space: The Enduring Impact of Color in Everyday Daily Life* (Chicago: University of Chicago Press, 2021); and *The Cosmopolitan Canopy: Race and Civility in Everyday Spaces* (New York: W. W. Norton, 2012).

tance, especially for those of us who identify as white, in trying to figure out what makes spaces white. His most recent book, *The Artist Alive*, centers on classroom spaces where he uses the arts as a way of initiating the lifelong process of self-discovery and self-expression. This is especially true when the arts create dissonance in our experiences.[32] "The most powerful art is that which holds opposite or seemingly irreconcilable aspects of human experience in a single field of vision," Pramuk says.[33] For example, he recounts how a sudden awareness of the physical and figurative distance between him and other white suburban fans of Stevie Wonder's *Songs in the Key of Life*, awakened him to his racial identity as a young person. In short, in paying attention to experiences other than his own, Pramuk sees himself more clearly, especially the racial dimensions of his identity that homogenous spaces render invisible. When we see ourselves more clearly, possibilities for better loving ourselves arise, which in turn unleash our capability for creating meaningful spaces with and for others.

Pramuk shared an example from his own campus, Regis University, which in 1998 acquired a sculpture of a distinctively African crucified Christ by a Denver artist. In 2010 Regis installed it on campus in the middle of a meditation garden on the west side of the campus, surrounded by native plants.[34] The sculpture in that space provides what Pramuk described to me, just days after the mass shooting of ten Black Americans in the Tops supermarket in Buffalo, as a "powerful counterpoint" to the "resurrection Jesus" in the university's chapel. In visually linking the Crucified with Black maleness, the cross connects the irreconcilable elements of the central mystery of Christianity—a God who suffers and dies a violent death at the hand of religious, economic, and military authorities—with irreconcilable experiences of Black men with similar forces in the US. That dissonance, displayed outside the traditional sacred campus space in a previously unmarked space, invites deeper reflection about central mysteries of the faith, about what it means to love as God loves, about who belongs in and to

---

[32]Christopher Pramuk, *The Artist Alive: Explorations in Music, Art and Theology* (Winona, MN: Anselm Academic, 2018), 18.

[33]Ibid., 264.

[34]See file:///Users/Maureen/Downloads/Art+at+Regis+University.pdf.

that campus community. It is now a place where people come in moments of irreconcilability.

Conclusion—Agitate, in Spaces, for Your Beloved

To be sure, many Catholic communities currently face challenges when it comes to using public art around campus, which point to the power of the arts in facilitating either fracture or flow in campus communities. Still, Fullilove's impulses about aligning, creating, and connecting can provide important guardrails or signposts for wading into these troubled waters; and the elements themselves are in fact practices that can help us do so with the hope of turning the fracture they illuminate into flow. With so much emphasis on our campuses around belonging, we would do well to pay attention to ideas she articulated about the relationship between belonging and space, long before belonging was *en vogue*: "The sense of belonging, which is necessary for psychological well-being," she said in 1996, "depends on strong, well-developed relationships with nurturing places."[35]

---

[35]Fullilove, *Urban Alchemy*, 43.

CALL TO ACTION

College Theology Society
President's Award

NETWORK Lobby for Catholic Social Justice

Joan F. Neal

Receiving this distinction as NETWORK celebrates our fiftieth anniversary is an extra special experience.[1] As you may know, we were founded by Catholic women religious in 1972, in the progressive spirit of Vatican II, as a contemporary expression of the mission of Jesus Christ. Our founders were pioneers in the ministry of political advocacy, and when they opened our doors in April 1972, we became the first registered Catholic lobby in the United States. While our ministry has grown over the years, we are still that feisty, little group of advocates that pursue federal legislators and their staffs, virtually now, knocking on their doors over and over again until they hear us out, on behalf of those who are negatively affected by the policies *they* make, the laws *they* pass, the systems and structures *they* authorize, re-authorize and/or fund, *and* by all the actions *they fail to take* on behalf of the common good. There were only a few sisters on staff in the beginning, but today we have nearly twenty-five persons on staff

---

[1]For more on the College Theology Society's President's Award, please see the CTS's website at www.collegetheology.org.

in Washington, DC, four of whom are women religious, and over 100,000 members and supporters around the country—priests, sisters, and laypeople. Through the gift of the Holy Spirit, our voice just keeps getting amplified louder and louder, and God keeps bringing wonderful new organizations to us, like you, with whom we can work and partner and change the country for the better.

As we began our fiftieth year in January 2022, we also undertook a strategic planning process to help us articulate a vision for the next six years and chart a course toward realizing that vision. We have just completed the process and articulated our vision in this way:

> Responding to the signs of the times as a recognized moral leader and a trusted Catholic voice, by 2028 NETWORK will advance a diverse national movement of justice-seekers—a beloved community—who will consistently exercise their power to influence federal policies that dismantle systemic racism, center equity and reparatory justice, secure our democracy, and protect our common home.

This is clearly not a vision we can realize on our own. Political ministry requires many and varied partners as well as participants in the mission. As a Catholic ministry or a faith-based ministry, it requires a certain level of understanding of and commitment to the Christian mission—the orientation and dedication to the common good and to a radical option for those who are pushed to the margins. At the heart of our advocacy is the dignity of every person stemming from our relationship to and in God—a bedrock principle of our faith and the Catholic social tradition. This is precisely where, from my perspective, there is an intersection between us as advocates, and you in the College Theology Society. We cannot advocate effectively without the formation your scholarship provides that enables us to make the moral case for just and equitable public policies.

Indeed, at this particular time in US history, when our democracy is at risk, when the institutional Church seems to be both impotent and compromised, we need your diverse voices, your scholarship emanating from the experience of people on the margins of society, your wisdom informed by a historical-critical perspective. We need you at this critical time in human history to interpret, to articulate, to circulate, to form, to guide, to model, and to constantly renew what and how we understand God, ourselves, our neighbor, and all of creation.

You have an awesome calling and responsibility. And because many of you teach young adults, you also have an important opportunity now—to shape a new generation, to form their minds and their understanding in such a way that the sin of racism might someday cease to exist. You have an opportunity to shape a group of adults in this country and around the world, who can and will be the advocates for a just and equitable society once and for all—one where the sins of racism, sexism, classism, ableism, and every other "ism" are things of the past. I think you hear that calling right now. I think you realize the *kairos* moment we are experiencing. I think you know what to do. And I pray you do it.

From the perspective of an advocate, let me say that without your analysis, reflection, scholarship and framework, without your deep discernment, we, NETWORK, would be just another special interest or partisan voice calling for change. Your work provides us the deep foundation and the resonant language to articulate the moral argument for a just and equitable society. It is a persuasive argument, and it is the right argument. So, keep studying, keep thinking, keep questioning, keep discerning, and keep teaching. Our advocacy only becomes richer and more effective because of you, and together at this crucial point in our nation's history, there just may be a chance to actually advance the Beloved Community that Martin Luther King Jr. spoke about so eloquently. Thank you again for all that you are and all that you do. We look forward to working with you in the future.

Epilogue

Catherine Punsalan-Manlimos,
Tracy Sayuki Tiemeier,
and Elisabeth T. Vasko

In planning this convention, Shawnee Daniels-Sykes (1961–2022) was one of the first names that came to mind in brainstorming a list of plenary speakers. In particular, her work on life ethics inspired a plenary session tentatively titled, "'I Can't Breathe': Racism and the Church," intended to touch on the intersection of racism, health, and community in view of police killings and the COVID pandemic. Yet even in our planning, Shawnee did what she does best: she expanded our imagination, calling us to deeper reflection on the meaning of life as it is deeply felt and complexly embodied. In pre-convention sessions together, she changed the title of the plenary to "From 'I Can't Breathe' to the Breath of Life: Racism and the Church, Past and Present." In doing so, she reminded us that the last word is not death but the Breath of Life, the Spirit of God in whose perpetual light we know she now rests in peace.

Shawnee Daniels-Sykes has gifted us and the greater church with the power of an ever-expansive embodied moral imagination. Throughout her life, she called the community to prophetic action in the world and exemplified doing theology with and for the community. As a nurse, she cared for her community. This led her to the work of theological ethics, where she courageously named the death-dealing harm that racism brings to Black and Brown communities. This was not just something she observed;

she lived it as she struggled with her illness over the years. But, as was always her way, she did this with grace and positivity. She consistently invited those around her to not just squarely see injustice but to embrace God's work of life and justice, the work we are called to join, in the midst of it.

Shawnee's community-based ethics exemplifies what we learned through the long process of planning the convention and annual volume. Early on, we reached out to the leadership of the Black Catholic Theological Symposium (BCTS) and the Academy of Catholic Hispanic Theologians of the United States (ACHTUS). Both organizations stressed the importance of centering people's experiences in the pews. Theological wisdom flows from attending to the voices and experiences of people of faith, and not from conforming to the expectations of the White-dominated academy as it exists. Shawnee's life and theology were embedded within the communities within which, about which, and for which she wrote.

Relationship with the communities we seek to serve, and with whom we desire to speak, is critical. It is not just a matter of centering marginalized voices but hearing them and allowing their lived wisdom to shape the doing and teaching of theology. It also requires a type of listening that is self-aware. It is necessary to be aware of how our assumptions and worldviews not only inform how we hear but will also likely obscure what is shared. It is not enough to listen once; we must return again and again to the communities we hope to center to ensure that what we think we have heard is what was intended. A posture of humility and tentativeness is not always welcomed in the dominant culture of the academy; even so, it is necessary for a true community-embedded and antiracist theology.

The process of organizing the 2022 CTS Annual Convention, attending the meeting, and preparing this volume provided unique opportunities for teaching and learning, for all involved, at each stage. Yet the most difficult part of the process has been observing and experiencing the ongoing consequences of the long, unexamined impact of racism—on even those most desirous of being part of the work of creating antiracist classrooms, contributing to antiracist scholarship, and constructing an antiracist society. The ways in which good will unintentionally manifests paternalism, "lowered" expectations, and condescending "advice" reveals how much work there is to do. There may be a commitment to inclusion, but it is not yet an inclusion that makes structural change. Real structural change requires decentering Whiteness and recentering BIPOC voices. It requires a new way of communal being in the classroom, the church, the academy, and the world.

The wounds of the sin of racism run deep. Indeed, healing these wounds requires the expansive moral imagination that Shawnee and many others have called us to. It requires commitment, a capacity to find joy, compassion, and time. Healing cannot be rushed or forced. Those who have been wounded by the sin of racism cannot be pressured or forced to move toward reconciliation before they are ready. Nor can those who have benefited from White systems and structures that have caused harm suddenly decide that they do not belong to the society and culture that has formed them. To do so would be to suggest that human beings can act outside the world of history; it is to deny the very ways socialization occurs. God's response to us and our response to God are revealed in concrete ways.[1] Yet the desire and hope for healing and reconciliation cannot be rejected either. Healing is not completed, and reconciliation is not yet possible. It is not just that the wounds are still fresh, but fresh wounds continue to be inflicted. We are beings in process with God and one another, living within an eschatological reality of already but not yet—working together in, with, and for the Breath of Life.

---

[1]M. Shawn Copeland, *Enfleshing Freedom: Body, Race and Being* (Minneapolis: Fortress Press, 2009), 85–100.

Contributors

SimonMary A. Aihiokhai is Associate Professor of Systematic Theology at the University of Portland. He is the recipient of the University of Portland Outstanding Scholar Award for 2021 and a Fellow at the Westar Institute. His research focuses on religion, race, and identity; African approaches to ethics; African philosophies, cultures, and theologies; religion and violence; comparative theology; systematic theology; and interfaith studies. His publications include *Fostering Interreligious Encounters in Pluralistic Societies: Hospitality and Friendship* (2019).

Christina Astorga is Professor and Chair of the Theology Department of the University of Portland. She teaches theological ethics (fundamental moral theology), bioethics, sexual ethics, and feminist ethics. She is a well-published scholar, with her book *Catholic Moral Theology and Social Ethics: A New Method* having been awarded the Best Book by the College Theology Society in 2014 and third place by the 2015 Catholic Press Association of America and Canada Book Award.

La Ronda D. Barnes is a PhD student in practical theology, concentrating in homiletics, at Boston University School of Theology. Her research interests include homiletics, including contemplative proclamation, spirituality studies, Womanist theology, and critical animal studies. Barnes is a graduate of Columbia Theological Seminary (MA, Practical Theology), Emory University's Candler School of Theology (ThM and MDiv), the University of Michigan (MA, Journalism), Yale Law School (JD), and the University of Akron (BA, English).

Rachel E. Bauer is Coordinator of Academic Theatre Arts and Assistant Professor in Theatre Arts at Sacred Heart University. Her research examines representations of gender in theatre, especially in relation to science themes. Her work highlights the transferable nature of theatre pedagogy and theatre education, focusing on the skills gained through theatre training that are useful both on the stage and across many disciplines. Rachel received a PhD in Theatre and Performance Studies from the University of Missouri.

Emily Bryan is Assistant Professor of Languages and Literatures at Sacred Heart University. Dr. Bryan, who holds a PhD in English from Northwestern University, also teaches in Catholic studies and theatre arts. She is the director of the foundational English core class, Experiencing Literature, and the director of the health humanities minor. She holds degrees from Harvard, Brown, and the University of Birmingham in England, where she was a Fulbright scholar at the Shakespeare Institute. She previously taught at West Point and Dominican College.

Daniel Cosacchi is Vice President for Mission and Ministry at the University of Scranton. Previously, he taught in the religious studies departments at Marywood University and Fairfield University. He is co-editor of *The Berrigan Letters: Personal Correspondence between Daniel and Philip Berrigan* (2016) and author of *Great American Prophets: Pope Francis's Models of Christian Life* (2022). He received a doctorate in ethics and theology from Loyola University, Chicago in 2016.

Shawnee Daniels-Sykes (1961–2022) was Professor of Theology and Ethics at Mount Mary University, Milwaukee, Wisconsin. A noted expert on ethics, morality and Black Catholic studies, her research interests were in beginning, middle, and end of life issues, especially as these relate to institutionalized race, class, and gender oppressions. She received numerous awards, including a Black Excellence Award from the *Milwaukee Times* in 2020. A registered nurse by training, Daniels-Sykes was the only Black Catholic female bioethicist in the United States.

Karen B. Enriquez is Visiting Assistant Professor of Theological Studies at Loyola Marymount University. She teaches in the areas of Christian contemporary systematic theology and comparative theology. Her primary areas of interest include Buddhist-Christian comparative theology, with an emphasis on the diversity of voices from both traditions, the comparison of spiritual and social practices, and ways of learning from and working with each other; and Philippine/Philippine-American theology from an intersectional liberationist and feminist lens, with a focus on popular religiosity.

George Faithful is Associate Professor of Religion and Philosophy at Dominican University of California. His current book project analyzes ambiguities of race, gender, sexuality, ability, sanity, and species in the poetry and prose of Saint Juan de la Cruz. When he isn't wrestling with saints or working to defuse religious nationalism (a longer-standing project), he's running, swimming, hiking with his family, cooking, or (most likely) eating.

Charles A. Gillespie is Assistant Professor of Catholic Studies at Sacred Heart University. His research and teaching investigate religions, the arts, and culture focused on the Catholic Intellectual Tradition (especially Hans Urs von Balthasar), interpretation theory, systematic and fundamental theology, spirituality and ecology (especially the Irish mystic John Moriarty), and theatre and performance studies. He is currently working on his first book, *God on Broadway*.

Kim R. Harris is Assistant Professor of African American Religious Thought and Practice at Loyola Marymount University. Her research and teaching focus on Black liberation and Womanist theologies. She is also a liturgist, composer, and recording artist. She is composer of *Welcome Table: A Mass of Spirituals*, one of the complete Mass settings included in the *Lead Me, Guide Me: The African American Catholic Hymnal*, 2nd ed.

Vincent Lui is a student in the Master of Theological Studies program at Loyola University Maryland. He holds a Master of

Public Policy degree from the University of Maryland, College Park, specializing in social policy and nonprofit management and leadership. His particular interest is in Christian liberation theology and public policy, and he seeks a Christian theological perspective to questions that have arisen from his professional experiences in the government and nonprofit sectors.

Cecilia A. Moore is Associate Professor of Religious Studies at the University of Dayton. Her area of specialization is the history of African American Catholics. In addition to publishing in numerous scholarly journals, popular magazines, and books, Dr. Moore co-edited *Songs of Our Hearts and Meditations of Our Souls: Prayers for Black Catholics* (2006) with the late Father Paul Marshall, SM, and Dr. C. Vanessa White.

Joan F. Neal is the Deputy Executive Director and Chief Equity Officer at NETWORK Lobby for Catholic Social Justice. She holds a Master of Arts in Pastoral Studies from the Catholic Theological Union. She also is an associate member of the National Black Sisters Conference and serves on the boards of the Sister Thea Bowman Foundation, the Center for Migration Studies, the Mexican American Catholic College, and the Mission Committee of the Board of the University of the Incarnate Word.

Maureen H. O'Connell is Professor of Religion and Theology at La Salle University. She authored *Compassion: Loving Our Neighbor in an Age of Globalization* (2009), *If These Walls Could Talk: Community Muralism and the Beauty of Justice* (2012), and *Undoing the Knots: Five Generations of American Catholic Anti-Blackness* (2021). For the duration of the global Synod on Synodality, she directs Synod and Higher Education Engagement for Discerning Deacons, a movement to restore Catholic women to the diaconate.

Melissa Pagán is Assistant Professor and Graduate Program Director of Religious Studies at Mount Saint Mary's University. A decolonial feminist ethicist, her current research project provides a feminist decolonial and critical spatial appraisal of the tradition of Catholic Social Teaching to ascertain whether, and to what extent, the coloniality of knowledge, coloniality of being, and coloniality of gender undergird and therefore undermine its teachings on social justice. Dr. Pagán's areas of expertise and research include feminist social ethics, critical geographies, postcolonial and decolonial theories and theologies, and Latinx theologies.

Catherine Punsalan-Manlimos is Vice President for Mission Integration at Seattle University. She began her academic career at the Ateneo de Manila University (Philippines), where she received her Bachelor of Science degree in Physics and Master's in Theological Studies. She earned her PhD from the University of Notre Dame in Systematic Theology in the area of the intersection of religion, science, and the preferential option for the poor. Her current work examines the intersections of the Catholic Social Tradition, Catholic higher education, and the contribution of marginalized voices.

John N. Sheveland is Professor of Religious Studies at Gonzaga University where he is the current Flannery Chair in Catholic theology. He received his PhD in Systematic and Comparative Theology from Boston College. He serves on the USCCB National Review Board, is book review editor for *Horizons*, served on the College Theology Society board of directors, and has published *Piety and Responsibility* (2017) and a variety of journal articles and book chapters.

Victoria Basug Slabinski is a PhD student in religious studies at the University of Virginia, in the interdisciplinary area of Modern and Contemporary Religious Thought. Her work focuses on the relationship of Christianity to its colonial legacies and possibilities for contemporary decolonization, particularly in relation to the Philippines and Filipino American communities. Her research interests include postcolonial and decolonial theories, Christian theologies, feminist and queer theories, and constructive readings of literature and the arts.

John Sniegocki is Professor of Religious Ethics and Director of the Peace and Justice Studies minor at Xavier University in Cincinnati, Ohio. He also serves as co-director of the theology graduate program. He is the author of *Catholic Social Teaching and Economic Globalization: The Quest for Alternatives*, as well as numerous journal articles and book chapters on Catholic social teaching, economic justice, food ethics, nonviolence, ecology, the Catholic Worker movement, and Buddhist-Christian dialogue.

Karen Teel is Professor of Theology and Religious Studies and an affiliated faculty member with the Department of Ethnic Studies at the University of San Diego. Her research and teaching endeavors emphasize theological engagement with the problems of racism and white supremacy, and she speaks and writes on various dimensions of Christian complicity and participation in racism and white supremacy in the United States. She is the author of *Racism and the Image of God* (2010).

Tracy Sayuki Tiemeier is Associate Professor of Theological Studies and Director of Peace and Justice Studies at Loyola Marymount University in Los Angeles, California. Her research focuses on Hindu-Christian studies, Asian and Asian American theology, comparative theology, feminist theology, and interreligious dialogue. She is co-editor with James L. Fredericks of *Interreligious Friendship After* Nostra Aetate (2015). She is also the Catholic co-chair of the Los Angeles Hindu-Catholic Dialogue.

Emilie M. Townes is Dean of Vanderbilt Divinity School as well as the University Distinguished Professor of Womanist Ethics and Society and Gender and Sexuality Studies at Vanderbilt Divinity School and the Vanderbilt College of Arts and Science. She is the author of *Womanist Justice, Womanist Hope* (1993), *In a Blaze of Glory: Womanist Spirituality as Social Witness* (1995), *Breaking the Fine Rain of Death: African American Health Issues and a Womanist Ethic of Care* (1998), and her ground-breaking book, *Womanist Ethics and the Cultural Production of Evil* (2006).

Héctor M. Varela Rios is Assistant Professor of Theology at Villanova University where he teaches and researches Latinx theology, popular religion, and material culture. He has published on personal religious objects as inscriptions of belief, on political theology and "thing," and on the decolonial/theological valences of sancocho and Francisco Oller's "El Velorio." Dr. Varela Rios is currently working on a book proposal about the personhood and devotedness of religious artifacts.

Elisabeth T. Vasko is Associate Professor of Theology at Duquesne University. She teaches and researches in the areas of theological anthropology, Christian ethics, and liberation theologies. She prioritizes collaborative, interdisciplinary, and community-based methods in her work because she believes they are building blocks for expanding the moral imagination and creating a more just society. She is the author of *Beyond Apathy: A Theology for Bystanders* (2015) and co-author with Lyndsie Ferrara of *True Crime and the Justice of God: Ethics, Media, and Forensic Science* (2022).